Italian Locations

Reinhabiting the Past in Postwar Cinema

Noa Steimatsky

University of Minnesota Press

Minneapolis • London

This book was published with the assistance of the Frederick W. Hilles Publication Fund of Yale University.

The University of Minnesota Press gratefully acknowledges the work of Edward Dimendberg, editorial consultant, on this project.

Publication information for previously published material in this book appears on page 217. Every effort was made to obtain permission to reproduce material; if any proper acknowledgment has not been included here, we encourage copyright holders to notify the publisher.

Published by the University of Minnesota Press
111 Third Avenue South, Suite 290
Minneapolis, MN 55401-2520
http://www.upress.umn.edu

Library of Congress Cataloging-in-Publication Data

Steimatsky, Noa.
    Italian locations : reinhabiting the past in postwar cinema / Noa Steimatsky.
        p.   cm.
    Includes bibliographical references and index.
    ISBN: 978-0-8166-5087-3 (hc : alk. paper)
    ISBN-10: 0-8166-5087-X (hc : alk. paper)
    ISBN: 978-0-8166-5088-0 (pb : alk. paper)
    ISBN-10: 0-8166-5088-8 (pb : alk. paper)
    1. Motion pictures—Italy—History.   2. Italy—In motion pictures.
 I. Title.
    PN1993.5.I88S687 2008
    791.430945—dc22

                                                            2007039039

Printed in the United States of America on acid-free paper

The University of Minnesota is an equal-opportunity educator and employer.

15 14 13 12 11 10 09 08   10 9 8 7 6 5 4 3 2 1

Italian Locations

Introductions

Contents

INTRODUCTION Italy as Seen from the Moon   vii

ONE   Aerial: Antonioni's Modernism   I

TWO   Ruinous: Rossellini's Corpse-Cities   41

THREE   Choral: Visconti's Dramaturgy of Nature   79

FOUR   Archaic: Pasolini on the Face of the Earth   117

AFTERWORD The Ends of the Land   167

Acknowledgments   173

Notes   175

Publication History   217

Index   219

Figure I.1. Pier Paolo Pasolini, *La terra vista dalla luna* (The Earth as Seen from the Moon), 1966. Centro Studi / Archivio Pier Paolo Pasolini—Cineteca di Bologna.

Figure I.2. *La terra vista dalla luna.*

Italy as Seen from the Moon

A dilapidated, humble Italy and a Technicolor fantasyland are boldly joined in these images (Figures I.1–I.2) from *La terra vista dalla luna* (The Earth as Seen from the Moon), Pier Paolo Pasolini's contribution to the 1966 compilation film *Le streghe* (The Witches). We are at the Fiumara di Fiumicino, a subproletarian neighborhood at the mouth of the Tiber—just outside the Italian capital but as alien to it as a lunar terrain. Tourists might speed heedlessly past on their way to the airport, having consumed charming Mediterranean vistas, splendid antiquities, luxury fashion and design items—packaged together in advertising images by such forces as Alitalia and the Italian ministry of tourism, or by Emilio Pucci and Salvatore Ferragamo. Here children play in heaps of trash among hovels—would-be villas, or *villette,* to match the meager means of their inhabitants and most likely illegally erected—painted in bold colors, perhaps retouched for the film. This peripheral landscape Pasolini will juxtapose with the spectacular center of Rome, the Coliseum. But even as he makes light of that imperial emblem as an object of tourist littering and ready-made stage for the protagonists' cash-raising exploits, Pasolini's work reconsecrates the ramshackle, marginal world, seeing its humility as grandeur, its muteness as eloquence, its tragic-comedic resourcefulness as a "desperate vitality."[1] A mock-fantasy of widowed father and son—played, respectively, by Totò and Ninetto Davoli clownishly garbed and coiffed in exaggerated versions of what each must deem the fashion adequate to his station—the film flies in the face of the glossy, urbane cynicism that reflects the new standards of the Italian economic miracle.[2]

To this place they bring the perfect bride: a deaf-mute Silvana Mangano, whom we have seen earlier in *Le streghe* as the impenetrable, alienated, high-fashion movie star in the ski lodge of Luchino Visconti's episode.[3] Mangano is now dressed in a pea-green dress tied with yellow string, in turquoise stockings and red slippers, all dangling off her like the quaint garb of a rag doll. As much a creature of Technicolor as of the painted slum, she arrives at her new home. What Totò dubs their "nest" in fact looks just like one: partly roofed with straw, it is improbably assembled with found objects and discards (Figure I.3). Ruins and remnants of war meet here with fond memories of an earlier popular culture, but also with postwar vestiges of consumerism. Mangano sorts out the heaps: she tosses away a live hand-grenade that we hear explode off-screen but that cannot hurt her in her deafness. Then fabric bits, plastic toys, a transistor radio (playing military marches), a framed Charlie Chaplin poster suggest a useless abundance that cannot conceal the destitution of this pathetic habitat. In an instant, and as if by magic, Mangano rearranges the shack in a colorful bricolage (Figure I.4).

Set in the desolate landscape, the pastiche décor is only partly a nostalgic allusion to the black and white lyricism of iconic postwar films: the shanties of De Sica's *Miracle in Milan*

Figure I.3. *La terra vista dalla luna.*

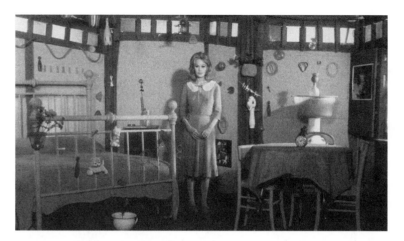

Figure I.4. *La terra vista dalla luna.*

(*Miracolo a Milano,* 1951) and *The Roof* (*Il tetto,* 1956), or of Fellini's *Nights of Cabiria* (*Notti di Cabiria,* 1957). In all of these, peripheral and makeshift, ramshackle housing is both the setting and the point of pride, even a fantasy object, for the disinherited. A bit further back and more gravely, one recalls Rossellini's ruinous heaps—the domain of postwar childhood games at their most desperate in *Open City* (*Roma città aperta,* 1945), *Paisà* (1946), and *Germany Year Zero* (*Germania anno zero,* 1948). Even earlier and imported allusions surface: alongside Chaplin's tramp, we locate a Fred Astaire top hat, the *clochard* utopia of René Clair's *À Nous la liberté* (1931), or Jean Vigo's image of a wedding procession among decrepit village corners, puddles, and children in rags.[4] But this nostalgic vision is revised as we consider that the plastic wares filling the scene—and to which the film's garish color scheme responds—are already in their second life.[5] Having made way for ever-updated gadgets, luxury furnishings of sleekly designed, export-quality kitchens, Pasolini's bold clutter of plastic discards may upset modernist good taste yet does not retreat to moralistic functionalism. But even if the modern is already aged or outmoded here, Pasolini playfully transfigures its ruins, projecting them as a heterogeneous, flexible set. Out of found and fabricated objects, fragments, ruins that reach back to pre-Fascist, even premodern lore, he conjures up an image of Italy as at once humble and parodic pastiche of contemporary excess. And just as Mangano's bricolage of discarded residues—drawing on an overabundant cycle of commodities that still cannot solve the economic or housing predicament of these characters—is raised to a phantasmic order akin to the filmmaker's craft, so Pasolini out of this landscape, with its refuse of modernity, assembles a precise, obverse vision of Italy's contemporary condition.

After a fatal fall from the Coliseum, having slipped, slapstick fashion, over a banana peel discarded by tourists, Mangano returns from the dead to the Fiumicino hovel. As she appears on the threshold before the terrified Totò and Ninetto, her cool ethereal beauty is modulated by her shy insistence, upon their questioning, on her ordinary self-sameness: in this forsaken terrain being alive or dead, as the film concludes, is really one and the same. Does this moral imply that this humble setting is still vital enough to give a second life to a decrepit modernity? Or, conversely, that to live in such a place is to be already dead—but perhaps to retain, like "a force from the past," magical, reconstructive power?[6] And where such frontiers can be crossed, other oxymorons proliferate: the plain and the lovely, the archaic and the belated, the everyday and the sacred reciprocate fluently. In quintessential form Pasolini's aesthetics, and his politics here, are predicated on a redemptive—even revolutionary—promise that in 1966 he still believed might be extracted on the periphery of the Italian economic miracle: a reservoir of archaic energy that feeds equally off the ephemeral wares of late-modern Italy as off revenant neorealist visions.

The act of filmmaking, according to the tradition mapped in this book, constitutes an imaginary reinhabiting of the landscape. Such assertive use of locations is posited as historical project and as cultural and aesthetic self-realization. In the

Italian postwar the reinhabiting of the landscape is bound up, moreover, with the predicament of reconstruction. It is figured in the act of magic or transformation—even with the humblest means—of the witch Mangano's redesigning the hovel: as a material, livable place, *and* as image. Pasolini's metaphor of *putting one's house in order* thus imbues filmmaking with a sense of function, of necessity; but the physical setting also implicates an imaginary order, a cultural, social, and a psychic one. Guided by a broad chronology spanning from 1939 to the mid-1960s, I distinguish in this tradition exemplary films whose figuring of space—as of its cultural parameters and affective resonances—coalesces in four tropes, intimated by my chapter headings. My synoptic readings of cinematic locations as privileged sites, images, texts, imbue the specifics of natural or urban settings with the charge of longer traditions, as indeed of contemporaneity. Other, polysemic terms enter this binding of past and present, local and national, material and symbolic constitution of locations. Pasolini's use of the marginal setting—even from the relatively late perspective of *La terra vista dalla luna*—already raised some of these. For Pasolini engages forcefully with an earlier tradition that, traversing postwar culture, we recognize as "neorealism." One of its primary discourses comprised the reappropriation of Italy's landscapes—often in a minor, regionalist key, but sometimes in a major, *monumental* one—to serve as an anti-Fascist national image. In this way the emphatic contemporaneity, even urgency of the neorealist enterprise itself had to confront diverse pasts, both recent and distant, inscribed in the location as cultural strata and as ruinous fragments—some, as Pasolini intimates, still explosive.

With a view toward an understanding at once broader and more nuanced than is often granted this sometimes rusty term, I will revisit the central concept of "neorealism" and a variety of "realisms" whose paths it crosses. What should promptly defamiliarize "neorealism" for many readers may be my emphasis on an oppositional modernist consciousness that dynamizes the prefix of the composite term. For a displacing and revisioning of terms, fraught with historical and theoretical ambiguities, is symptomatic of the neorealist enterprise. This introduction attends to the principal semantic clusters, though terms will continue to be qualified in the course of the book. The notion of modernism—we will soon acknowledge its accompanying antimodernist shadows—will itself need to be revisited for the national and historical concerns at hand. What was neorealism's dispute with Fascist modernization, or with Fascism's absorption of modernist aesthetic practices?[7] How does the cinematic location situate the question of neorealism at particular intersections of realist *and* modernist discourses? How was postwar cinema to tackle the flexibility of these terms, their difficulties, their abuses, their need for renewal? Since one of the purposes of this book is to open and animate such terms in light of particular cultures of landscape *and* of cinema, no shorthand definitions, no unitary style or single linear progression, will do: I have not come to simplify neorealism but to expand it, to mobilize, not to dissolve its equivocations. What follows, then, is a preliminary opening of the principal prospects, and of some obscure corners, in view of and sometimes against established limits.

Neorealism yielded exemplary encounters with the altered spaces of the Italian postwar. In this arena, national and regional cultures, distant and recent pasts, continuity and rupture overlapped in light of what has come to pass. Arguably after architecture, which had to tackle and rebuild physical spaces proper, cinema was the art form most rigorous in confronting the ruinous landscape, charting its provinces, figuring its dimensions, its rifts. Neorealism brought into play here a broad range of perceptions, some raised long before the recent crises of the Second World War and its aftermath. Yet that longer view, with which I am ultimately concerned, must be weighed against a more familiar, compactly circumscribed definition of neorealism as the film culture of the Resistance and Liberation.

This could be periodized most narrowly from Roberto Rossellini's 1945 *Open City* through the end of that decade, when production picked up again in Cinecittà, and the lessons of neorealism seemed to dissolve into pink.[8] Elsewhere, I have reconstructed the narrative of the Allied requisitioning of Cinecittà for use, first whole and then in part, as a refugee camp from early June 1944 through August 1950: this is one concrete way to date the high neorealist season.[9]

The lessons of the compact historical definition are crucial even as one goes on to project them beyond the immediate circumstances. This definition posits the use of location, alongside other inventive cinematic solutions, as largely a product of circumstances: the devastation of studios, the paucity of film stock, and generally impoverished and chaotic conditions across the country infused the neorealist turn to new postwar spaces opened up by the ruins of the old. The use of actual locations also corresponded, certainly, with cinema's new-found commitment to reportage, to chronicle, to documentation of the devastated state of things in a period of transition. At the same time, the rejection of studio conventions was not iconoclastic: Italy's ambiguous position as a vanquished nation whose defeat was cast as liberation entailed a moderate anti-Fascist agenda. Major strands in neorealism responded to the prevailing need to mediate tensions under the heroic myth of the Resistance and were ideologically geared to deflect a confrontational, revolutionary break feared by the emerging Christian Democratic force and its Allied support. Even as it claimed and internationally attained reputation as a revolutionary film culture, even as it aspired to break with institutional cinema as with the perceptual habits and blind spots of the Fascist era, the efforts of neorealism were geared toward national rebuilding and were *restorative* at that. Many films, and even aspects of the boldest neorealist interventions, interiorized this ideology in their systems of representation, as in their molding of the location. They took upon themselves to forge for post-Fascist Italy a myth of origins, to support its expedient emergence out of the ruins, to project and reconstruct a world not too heavily burdened with the crimes of the old: this world, with all its insecurities, was an often sentimental place, allegorically populated with children. Vittorio De Sica's *Bicycle Thieves* (*Ladri di biciclette,* 1948) thus supports its bittersweet resolution of tensions with what is, by and large, traditional continuity editing that circumscribes a coherent, secure, narrative space.[10] That earlier icon of neorealism, Rossellini's *Open City,* despite its adventurous circumstances of production and its dynamic urban consciousness, took it upon itself to bridge classes and ideologies, to displace conflicts from Italy, and from Italians, to the occupying Nazis. It has come to fulfill in this way an important conciliatory role in the national and international public consciousness.

The ways in which neorealism forged symbolic coherence and unity out of a deeply conflicted moment have been addressed in the literature.[11] A humanist restorative impulse in neorealism was poised to avoid a deep questioning of institutions—of actual state and social apparatuses *and* of representational codes. At a time when anti-Fascist purges were cut back, when personnel in the film industry sooner or later regained their posts, when the surviving studios opted for bankable stars and safe genres—having to compete as well with the flooding of the market by American films—in this environment also some of the boldest works would employ heroic or melodramatic idioms even as they turned their back on the studio, harnessed new social contents, and unveiled facets of a hitherto unseen Italy.[12] The historical tensions that neorealism contained nonetheless showed through the seams—often the most compelling aspects of Rossellini's *Open City* itself, as of its exact contemporary *Giorni di gloria* (Days of Glory, 1945), a documentary compilation production collaborated on by Mario Serandrei, Luchino Visconti, and Giuseppe De Santis, among others. Intimations of brutality, Manichaean characters, violent shifts of style across sequences, juxtaposition of reportage material with expressionist devices, incoherent spatial or narrative transitions evidenced the fragile surfaces of neorealist cinema. These could also be traced on the margins of neorealism, further beyond heroic or optimistic scenarios: for instance Alberto Lattuada's *Il bandito* (The Bandit, 1946) and *Senza pietà* (Without Pity, 1948) enfolded in their noir or gangster frameworks—themselves deemed subversive after Fascism—an acute perception of peripheral urban locations. These films spoke eloquently to the contemporary scene—the ruins of war, the economic and social reality of crime and the black market, the Allied presence, the African American GIs—even as they drew on genre codes and dramatic manipulation, as on the aura of expressively lit settings and made-up stars.[13]

What emerge are the limitations of hermetic neorealist definitions once one looks beyond strictly thematic concerns or an abstracted median of "period style." One might emphasize instead the productive openness of neorealism to the tensions and pain of its time, its self-consciousness as to the stakes in reconstructing a community, remaking the culture, revisioning an Italian landscape-image: negotiating breaks and continuities—but not as if nothing happened. One might allow not only a broader range of films—central and marginal, features, shorts, and documentaries—in the neorealist season but acknowledge trails of influence and appropriation in the longer and deeper expanses of that era; acknowledge as well the eloquence of rifts, of traumatic images. It is also against the conciliatory institutional rhetoric and sometimes populistic humanism of neorealism that I discriminate in this book a handful of works by directors whose careers negotiated most consciously with the neorealist historical-ideological center. On the margins preceding the high neorealist period I distinguish the earliest, documentary work of Michelangelo Antonioni, whose sources and implications have been largely overlooked in studies of neorealism. At the end point of that era I trace Pasolini's first project of literary adaptation. Both works—one proleptic, the other belated—visited peripheral sites with questions of Italy's historical continuities and ruptures. Perhaps for their oblique position they manifest a self-consciousness quite distinct from that of the heroic neorealist core. From within the heart of the heroic period I single out Rossellini's projection of a broader European orbit in locating a neorealist project in Berlin, and Luchino Visconti's assertive appeal to a classical and ornately theatrical landscape, whose wrought, monumental grandeur was at once central and exceptional in the neorealist canon. Experiences of belatedness and displacement, anachronism and a thoroughly contemporary anxiety, animate all these works. Their oscillation, at every turn, between pastness and contemporaneity, grandeur and humbleness, center and periphery, entails a critical reflection on the stakes of neorealism. Each refigures cinema's role in the reconstruction of space, of cinematic perception, and of the cultural imaginary of Italy in a transitional time: its role in the reconstruction of Italian consciousness itself after Fascism.

A vexed, ambivalent modernism, laced with antimodernist impulses, troubles these works and itself deserves a more nuanced interrogation than has been granted in film histories. This modernist perplexity, we will see, is sometimes related to neorealism's forays into diverse realisms: to representational, epistemological claims in the mapping of hitherto neglected terrains; to Italian regionalism as expressed in the history of art and literature; to the local, the minor, the quotidian landscape as it must come to terms, yet again, with modernity. This ambivalent engagement, while in part a response to the immediate past of Fascism and the war, also developed concerns launched in the preceding decade. The earliest articulations of a neorealist project betray an engagement with both realist and modernist genealogies breathing into the emphatic contemporaneity of that project. It is perhaps this contemporaneity that propelled an initially literary ambition toward a cinematographic practice. Important, as well, was the way in which the local and historical specificity of neorealism in Italian culture appealed to wider European and international frameworks. Already in the early 1930s Umberto Barbaro—the art and literary critic who will turn film theorist, educator, and director—brought up the term "neorealism" in a literary context and as suggesting a direction for a new Italian avant-garde. It was not immediately elaborated or followed through at the time, but his formulation nonetheless betrayed a desire for aesthetic renewal that would live up to other European developments of the early twentieth century. In his 1932 preface to a translation of Vsevolod Pudovkin's writings, Barbaro raised a notion of neorealism in a chain of widely varied and far-reaching comparisons: "Certainly there are close ties between realism, neorealism, magic realism, Proust, Joyce, *Neue Sachlichkeit* and even surrealism that preoccupy the cultivated cineaste."[14] Gian Piero Brunetta considers that *Neue Sachlichkeit*—the "New Objectivity" of Weimar art that grew out of and defined itself against expressionism—was the prototype of "neorealism." Brunetta sees in Barbaro's formulation the summation of a first phase of neorealist poetics based in the association of literature and cinema and rendering neorealism, importantly, as an open term, marking a rupture with the linguistic, thematic, and ideological experience of Italian culture. By the mid-1930s, however, this early and undeveloped theoretical discourse expires, as do most of the avant-gardes in Barbaro's European examples.

Yet something of the bold joining of a modernist narration and a realist-everyday setting, of a meandering consciousness and a bare matter-of-factness invoked in Barbaro's motley list survives—with or without a neorealist epithet. Consider how Giuseppe Pagano's 1936 exhibition and book on Italian rural architecture was also a photographic feat—in serial, grid-clusters of images—seeking out "proto-modernist" elements in vernacular constructions across diverse Italian regions. The syncopated modernist narration and chorale of Sicilian voices in Elio Vittorini's 1938–39 novel *Conversazione in Sicilia (Conversation in Sicily)*—originally published in installments and later with photographic illustrations—unfolds within an accentuated regionalist itinerary. At the same time, it was possibly a worldly outlook in Vittorini's subsequent anthology of translated American literature in 1942, set against a provincial Fascist "italianità," that triggered censorship of Vittorini's original prefaces and notes. Alberto Lattuada's 1941 photographic pamphlet *Occhio quadrato* (Squared Eye) located isolated figures in landscapes of refuse and ruin that prefigured neorealism's preferred locations and its itinerant beholders. Bare social margins and regionally marked spaces emerge, in these among other instances, as ground over which a modernist consciousness is explored in a contemporary landscape—often one on the brink of disappearance, and photographically supported. This consciousness traces here, already in the late 1930s and early 1940s, a meandering, fracturing, leveling perception that traverses the universal and the local: a modernist predicament that nevertheless commits to social content, to representation.

The exemplary early experience of Luchino Visconti is of a piece with these literary and photographic precedents. The values and tensions they raise are perhaps resifted, along with political possibilities and impasses, and refocalized for the cinematic imagination nurtured during Visconti's French sojourn, under the mentorship of Jean Renoir, in the period of the Popular Front. This is also the period of the coming-to-consciousness of many Italian intellectuals after the mid-1930s, when the racist, imperialist, and militarist ambitions of Fascism could no longer be ignored. Visconti's conoisseurship of French cinematic realism widens the new internationalist vision of Italian cinema. On location with Renoir's *Day in the Country (Partie de campagne,* 1936/1946) Visconti might have contemplated, as well, the cinematic appropriation of earlier realist ground: how a local and national tradition could support a class-conscious modernity.[15] The social pathos of Maupassant that infuses the minor event with shattering realization, the peripheral, reduced, but beloved countryside of Impressionist painting—both sources for *Day in the Country*—could be considered in relation to the tragic contemporaneity of Renoir's *Toni* (1934). The harsh workaday reality of *Toni*'s quarry locations unfolding in depth-of-field cinematography that firmly places persons in their milieu; the accented French that amplifies the regionalist setting with no concessions to folklore niceties; the *faits divers,* local newspaper source of the tale; the social and economic pressures narrativized in Renoir's film make *Toni* the more obvious precedent to neorealism. Yet for its appeal to a longer modernity as to realist traditions across the arts, it is the lesson of *Day in the Country* that must have enriched Visconti's consciousness of cinema's unique negotiation of high and low, of pastness and contemporaneity. Between these two films he must have already discerned the trajectory of Renoir's studies of regions, classes, responses to social impasses: a trajectory that traverses different phases of modernity and juxtaposes local, traditional values with modern lacks and anxieties. These are not alien to the world of Giovanni Verga, nor to that of James M. Cain's *The Postman Always Rings Twice,* a copy of which Renoir was to give to Visconti on the eve of the war.

In Visconti's reading of Cain, as in so much of his later work, a bold joining of sources and modes of perception perhaps harked back in some sense to Barbaro's above-cited speculations on a multifarious neorealist modernism. Upon first encounter with the rushes of *Ossessione* in 1943, Visconti's editor Mario Serandrei recognized, with astonishment, the adequacy of a neorealist epithet in confronting the bold continuity *and* rupture embodied in this film.[16] Continuity, as in Barbaro's immediate insight in 1943 on the affinities between these cinematic images of the Po River landscapes and fifteenth-century painting of the Ferrara workshop described by his friend, the art historian Roberto Longhi. Continuity, as that of painting when it could still integrate regional realism with the sacred charge of biblical themes, or as in the plenitude of a longer, slower rural temporality, like that of the river's constant backdrop.[17] Rupture, because emerging from beneath the smooth horizontal surfaces of *Ossessione*'s river landscapes one sensed from the first shot a disruptively modern, urban anxiety—imported along with Cain's American hard-boiled sensibility—fracturing any empathetic or harmonious joining of protagonists and environment. The sordid tale of murderous passion inscribes pressures at once psychic, social, and formal in the rural locale, disturbing its placid hierarchies, refusing consolation at every turn. The narrative of interruptions, accidents, disturbed desires, failed resolutions itself figures as a looming contingency while in the deeper planes of the image the threshing of grain in the fertile plots between the levees of the river Po goes on, as it always has, without relief. Produced during the already unstable conditions of the war, *Ossessione*'s mournful appeal to an imagined regional and pictorial plenitude was itself a response to thoroughly contemporary pressures. The interference of contemporary lacks and desires with a continued past, the anxiety and nostalgia that mark the Italian landscape in these formative moments of neorealism, disclosed the cinematic location as a transitional terrain.

The neorealist turn to earlier realist traditions—cinematographic and more broadly art historical or literary, Italian and imported—was then undertaken in implicit critique of Fascist rhetoric and its rural ideology. But it might have been also a response to Fascist culture's attempts—in part successful—for the domestication of modernism and the taming of the avant-gardes. The tracing in neorealism—even against progressive commitments—of an antimodern nostalgia may have itself been in critique of Fascism's appropriation of an all too flexible modernism; yet the ideological connotations of antimodernism themselves risk regression.[18] The divided conscience—and consciousness—of neorealism is inscribed in the constitution of the term: I already proposed that the "neo" prefix betrays here the need to consider realism itself through a modernist lens yet embedded at another level a critique of modernism's availability to Fascist culture. This folding-over, restorative *and* revisionary mobilizing of terms is itself a symptom of midcentury modernism—and underlies the specific investigations of the following chapters. One might acknowledge the productively recurrent confrontation of modernist and realist discourses, in varying ideological shades and depths, in the tradition that I distinguish in *Italian Locations*. My analyses will suggest that neorealism consciously reflected on such cultural and aesthetic modes and developed tropes by which to negotiate and test them—on location and as pertaining to an Italian landscape-image.

Defining realism as an agent of modernity—one readily thinks of the nineteenth-century European novel, or of painting in the age of national unifications—Fredric Jameson describes modernism as the critical reinhabiting of the new space that realism has produced. He argues for imbricating formal or aesthetic considerations in the cultural logic of periodizing modes of labor, institutional organization, social relations, and exchange forms. Jameson dwells on the constructive role of realism in transitional historical moments of the coming to consciousness, self-definition, and cultural legitimacy of classes or groups through the appropriation of an oppositional language vis-à-vis an ancien régime: realist practices define themselves against older institutional orders, conventions, academicisms. In claiming not simply an authentic expressive idiom but an epistemological force that would produce the "real," or the "referent," of the new order, diverse realisms thus articulate the new identities of national, ethnic, or other minorities, in a new spatial order. A broad, "elaborate" coding of such realism, once it begins to earn legitimacy and claim universality, may be subsequently unmasked for its own conventions and fallacies. But another, minor order of "restricted" realisms can maintain an oppositional potentiality against the broader dominant codes. An oppositional realism might maintain the epistemological claim of a representational language, might resist abstracting itself from the "content" of the realist enterprise, might resist withdrawing into the autonomy and purity of modernism, or dissolving in the allusive cultural ransacking of the postmodern. Jameson notes film history's recapitulation of the three-act periodization—realism, modernism, postmodernism—in compressed and multiple forms: within diverse national cinemas, within diverse cultural subspheres and modes of production, or reenacted in view of media and technological developments, as in the history of silent film, or of color film, or of video. Such overlapping and *en-abyme* histories break a dominant linear or evolutionary interpretation of the three-act scenario, inviting degrees of repetition, digression, splitting, and even reversal.[19]

One appreciates the productiveness of a subtle, fluid reciprocity between Jameson's "oppositional realism" and the more acute self-consciousness of modernism.[20] I wish to consider it for the Italian postwar: to acknowledge the realist ethos as a natural ally in a national project of reconstruction but also to consider its modernist critical elements. This bifurcated model allows for more nuanced formal and cultural evaluation of materials that, in fact, do not easily cohere on the surface. The oppositional realism that I ascribe to Antonioni, Rossellini, Visconti, and Pasolini is representational, largely narrative, and plagued by ambivalences, as was the more easily assimilable or "elaborate" coding of the conciliatory neorealist mainstream that attended to similar landscapes. But it is an oppositional stance—an aesthetic far more complex, bold, and demanding than could be conceived by a mainstream realism—that opens doors through these works for the rethinking of modernism itself. For modernism—I already noted—was itself tainted by Fascism and the war. Its contents and uses bent and exploited, modernism thus became an inherited past, a "reality," as it were, or a ruin itself in need of neorealist reconstruction. How might neorealism reinhabit modernity, revise it without effacing its achievements, harness its energies for remaking a landscape-image, for remaking cinema? How might neorealism approach an aged, damaged modernism while also engaging a demiurgic potential that—as Pasolini's episode suggested—cinema can figure so well as setting, as image, as guide to life, even after death?

Another term might be adopted for the returns and revisions proposed above. I borrow T. J. Clark's notion of "contingency" from *Farewell to an Idea: Episodes from a History of Modernism,* where it describes modernity's turning "from past to future, the acceptance of risk, the omnipresence of change, the malleability of time and space."[21] Clark reminds us that contingency is a process that must be grappled with as it seeks compensation in cult figures, mass movements, and totalitarian regimes. The internal ambivalence and continued struggle of modernist contingency regathers representational substance in the Second World War and prompts Clark's startling excursus on Italian neorealism in the mournful conclusion to his book. No false certainties of an earlier modernity, no celebration of modernist flexibility, liberty, an all-leveling utopia, yet a longing survives in Clark's snapshots of neorealist moments from Rossellini's *Paisà* and Visconti's *Rocco and His Brothers* (*Rocco e i suoi fratelli,* 1960), or Antonioni's *L'avventura* of the same year—and still within Clark's trajectory. A sense of "teeming humanity and mercilessness and nature"—Clark cites Italo Calvino here—must not flatten our view of neorealism's engagement with a modernist past. We have seen the claim to modernist and avant-garde genealogies embedded in the earliest attempts to define neorealism, and of which Calvino would have been well aware. But this was now, after the war, an altered engagement with modernist contingency, tempered by atrocious experiences suffered by "communists, humanists, Resistance fighters, survivors of the camps."[22] It is the divided consciousness, the sense of return and projection of a past that must be revisited *and* altered that gives neorealism its exemplary role in Clark's history of modernism. A confrontation with the cinematic location afforded perceptions of loss, division, displacement, and thereby the overlapping of historical strata as theme and as aesthetic consciousness inescapable at that moment. Not withdrawn from history, postwar contingency is internalized in neorealism's arbitration of defeat, of the anguish, the rifts that tore through twentieth-century Europe.

Among critics contemporary with the neorealist core, it was already a broad European perspective that afforded nuanced evaluation of the potentialities and the exemplariness of the Italian experience. André Bazin was perhaps the first to analyze how a radicalization of contingency—without severing altogether the temporal bonds of cinematic representation—induced neorealism's break with the illusionist transparency of the classical style. Bazin's ontological realism, refined in his reading of Rossellini, suggested to subsequent critics and practitioners alike a link between neorealism and New Wave modernisms. His analysis of *Paisà* demonstrates how neorealist narrative recedes into the setting to expose, between the filmic inscription of "facts," rifts and ellipses that interfere with conventional verisimilitude.[23] In its place, a realism embedded in the movie camera's photographic indexicality, its imprinting of an integral, continuous surface, adjoins the opacity of persons, actions, places in the profilmic world. This "objective" reality also effects the temporal threads that make an existential ethic of the neorealist aesthetic, in that they implicate the projected past in the spectator's unfolding present.

Against the constancy of the horizontal terrain of the Po delta in the last segment of *Paisà*, eruptions of action punctuate the duration—itself erratically distributed—of minor or nonevents in the elliptical short-story format of this episode. One can envision Bazin's sense of awe in the face of the striking extension of duration and space that makes palpable the *real time* it takes for a battered old boat to traverse a stretch of swamp, be dragged over islets of mud and reeds, loaded with the corpse of a partisan whose dead weight is as plainly communicated as the sign

"Partigiano" tagged on to it. One juxtaposes this with the elliptical narration of the episode's ostensibly central event: the
Nazi massacre at Maddalena's house. Alluded to in a flash of
distant gunfire and a quick whisper, its aftermath unfolds in
a not-quite-coherent point-of-view tracking shot over the
underlit dock where only a child's cry draws attention to the
indistinct dark masses: the corpses scattered about. This out-
of-sync cry—experienced, thereby, as an isolated, concrete entity emerging, as it were, from the image as a whole, or from a
horrific *elsewhere*—multiplies the opacity, the intrusiveness, the
shock of the representation. An almost "primitivist" simplifica-
tion of shot/reverse shot, alternating in the film with obstruc-
tions of continuity editing, accompanies Rossellini's increasing
recourse in the late 1940s and early 1950s to quotidian actions,
nondramatic passages of walking, looking, waiting. Bazin saw
in *Paisà*'s confrontation with "facts," with the surfaces of an
otherwise unavailable reality, an ethic of perception consistent with the altered historical consciousness of the postwar.[24]
Internalized in the film's means of articulation, contingency
thus interferes with the conventional illusionism of the studio
style. An opaque material reality, amplified on location, exposes
the shot to contingency and thus epitomizes neorealism's appeal to cinema's photographic provenance, in which Bazin
grounds much of his critical project. There is a way in which
what is addressed in Bazin's ontological realism are the conditions and limitations of the medium, the reality of an opaque
inscription—be it of the Po River delta in *Paisà* or, elsewhere,
of the written page in Robert Bresson's literary adaptations—
endowed with a consciousness that we would call modernist.[25]

The linear, prosaic "facts" that nonetheless interfere, as Bazin
suggests, with narrative causality and flow effected an episodic
chronicle form in shorts and feature films, both fiction and
documentary, in this tradition. The significance of its attendant
tropes—metonymy, digression, spatiotemporal dilation, and
the disjointing of action from time—enters Gilles Deleuze's

valorization of neorealism's means of articulation as a response to the "dispersive and lacunary reality" of postwar Europe. Neorealism inaugurates an altered sense of space, the salient temporality of its unfolding, and of its perception: all elements seem pulled apart and amplified in isolation.[26] In Bazin's footsteps Deleuze identifies what is, in effect, an evolved modernist consciousness of temporality in neorealism's mediating of a historical passage from the events of the war and liberation to the prosaic concerns of the everyday. Deleuze's theoretical periodizing, his projection of a crisis in cinematic consciousness across the divide of the Second World War, supports a reading of neorealism, and of Rossellini in particular, as inspirations for the *Cahiers du cinéma* critics and filmmakers who brought about the French New Wave a decade later. Here, as in the Italian radicalization of neorealist perception—consider Antonioni's "interstitial" mode—the quotidian spaces gaping between events destabilized dramatic values and genre certainties in a critical revisitation of cinematic form and of the politics of representation, *tout court.*[27]

The closest Italian correlate to the radical implications of the French critical tradition might be found in the practice of Antonioni, but it is approached early on—and with the rhetorical conviction of a manifesto—in the writings of Cesare Zavattini. From the 1940s through the 1960s Zavattini employed "neorealism" to describe a range of practices, much wider than the urgent postwar thematic-historical scope of the neorealist core. He considered that the circumstances of the war and its aftermath shocked the viewer to attend to minute but revelatory detail in the fabric of the everyday. From within the formative core of neorealism he called, already in 1942, for "One Minute of Cinema" wherein the brief action, documented on film, would give rise to analytic elaboration. This fed Zavattini's later idea of the *film-lampo,* the "flash-" or "blitz-film" springing from a concrete fact, singled out and illumined in a process of reconstruction.[28] In this avant-garde vision the filmmaker penetrates and occupies, as it were, the fractured, leveled reality opened up by the war and confronting the camera. The most banal event—like buying a pair of shoes—fully set in its milieu, in its network of circumstances and consequences, is suited to cinema's intensity of vision and thereby to its epistemological mission and to its social charge. Like Bazin, Zavattini considered the "moral impulse" of the everyday event, defamiliarized in its "longest and truest duration": "give us whatever 'fact' you like, and we will disembowel it, make it something worth watching. . . . The [neorealist] question is: how to give human life its historical importance at every minute."[29] Here too contingency informs cinematic temporality, singling out the claim of every instance, dramatic or no, endowing "historical importance" and existential value to the banal, the ephemeral. The practical value of this ideology for cinematic practice is evident. In fact Zavattini posits techniques of interruption, repetition, and dilation against assembly-line capitalist modes of film production, thus harnessing a new cinematic temporality and an assertive, revolutionary appropriation of the site of action. Little of Zavattini's own practice as screenwriter—his contribution to De Sica's *Sciuscià* (*Shoe Shine,* 1946), *Bicycle Thieves,* or *Umberto D.* (1952)—applies these radical insights as rigorously as his manifesto-style writings propose. Giorgio De Vincenti observes how, in the course of the years, and with renewed vigor in his collaborative projects of the 1960s–70s, Zavattini went on to dub, in his picturesque language, this cinematic doubling of the presentness of an event a cinematic "being on the piazza"—as in a "happening." His neorealism thus evolved to urban ethnography, *cinéma vérité,* radical interrogations of contemporary sites of daily life via cinematic strategies inherited from neorealism.[30]

These aspects of Zavattini's social ethic and aesthetic, or of Rossellini's practice promoted by Bazin, do not seem ostensibly concerned—as is Visconti—with precedents in the longer lineage of realist and modernist traditions. Yet for its legitimation

as for its far-reaching ambition, the development of an oppositional, yet locally resonant, Italian idiom drew on broad cultural
capital, as much as it drew on a chronicle of the contingent, for
its compound self-definition. The work undertaken in this book
elaborates and intensifies, in a sense, the network of histories,
genealogies, and affective connotations of the Italian cinematic
landscape that I have cast above, attending to its formal departures, to its interference with the inherited traditions. My critical
approach to canonical and minor works is itself meant to enrich
and complicate the larger picture even as it opens up particular
texts to diverse discourses, affinities, uses. I negotiate cultural
histories and close readings in a trajectory of tropes, which in-
troduce another logic to bind the play of sources, traditions,
media, and cinematic forms. These tropes—"Aerial," "Ruinous,"
"Choral," "Archaic"—make salient historical and formal itiner-
aries, the perception of continuities and ruptures, distance and
proximity, figure and ground. They afford horizontal and vertical cross-cuts turned to past and to future, and even to our time.
While some might suggest auteurist motifs, these tropes do not
propose exclusive or airtight affinities but reach more broadly
through cultural and aesthetic paradigms that support my historiographic interventions.

While not offering a comprehensive history of the era, I
have found it edifying to maintain chronology along my principal films intimating, at points, a revisionary periodization
that defamiliarizes neorealist historiographies. My placing of
Michelangelo Antonioni first—which no critical account of
neorealism has undertaken—may already be seen as a polemi-
cal breaching of neorealist definitions. This is matched by a re-
mapping of Rossellini's neorealist coming-to-consciousness in
a delayed, and displaced, response to the trauma of war. Jointly,
while doing much of the work of historical setting, the first
two chapters foreground the flexibility of neorealism as a fruit-
fully open, polysemic term, symptomatic of the transitional
historical moment. Against the pressing and immediate past

addressed in the first half of the book, my work on Visconti and Pasolini evokes longer historical spans and archaic reservoirs in their uses of locations. This is effected in part by the redemptive charge of their cinematography—the beauty of images that connote high-pictorial values—even as it elicits revolutionary energy in their time-honored landscapes. The two-part division of *Italian Locations* in light of such temporal modes is evidently challenged, at the same time, by the central pairing of *Germany Year Zero* and *La terra trema*, both of 1948: high-neorealist expressions vis-à-vis the decidedly off-center, critical consciousness of Antonioni and Pasolini.

Antonioni's early writing, photography, and first documentary production will serve to reposit an as yet unnamed neorealism as a recasting of modernist aspirations in the "mold of his native landscape."[31] In mapping regionalist-modernist intersections under late-Fascist culture, I draw a hitherto unacknowledged genealogy for Antonioni's imaginary of the landscape. The "aerial" trope, which seems to remove a temporal, narrative principle in favor of a pure, abstracted image predicated on distance and withdrawal, nonetheless acquires historical and *local* definition. While figuring Antonioni's continued search for an "intelligence" of place, it comes to be irrevocably marked by the circumstances of production in a devastated setting, by loss, by contingency as the historical condition of midcentury modernism.

Across the divide of the war, the urban ruins evidencing atrocities, defeat, death inscribe the body of Rossellini's cinema and his problematic of reconstruction. I chart Rossellini's delayed interiorizing of contingency in his move from *Paisà* to *Germany Year Zero*. A displacement of the postwar predicament—from Italy to Germany, from the aftermath of Fascism to that of Nazism—must have been a necessary condition for Rossellini's realization of the pervasiveness of the ruin, the horror, the guilt manifest everywhere as a physical, moral, psychic condition, and infecting any articulation, any image. As both material evidence and as allegorical figure, Rossellini's ruinous landscape speaks eloquently to contemporary discourses on commemoration. It adjoins neorealism's attention to human habitation, which itself comes to reflect on the question of reconstruction and the monument after Fascism.

The family habitation, an age-old communal coherence, confronting a modern consciousness and a will to change, is refracted in the resonant, embracing landscape of Luchino Visconti's *La terra trema*. Cycles of labor and commerce, social exchange, habits and traditions are seen in *La terra trema* to be as old as the human glance upon nature and not inclined to change. The theatrical, choral spatiality of the Sicilian landscape evokes here an enclosed mythical space. Yet its drama of "man and nature" seems posited against modern temporality, with its leveling of spaces, its openness to the future. Archaic and contemporary domains are mediated in Visconti's turn to nineteenth-century Italian modernity—literary, pictorial, and photographic—in which to ground his project. When compared with the immediate pasts evoked in the first two chapters of this book, Visconti's project evidently departs toward a sweeping historical temporality. How to bring such a deep past into cinematic contemporaneity, into a modern political program? Visconti rehearses here the contradictions of his own *verista* sources, yet his command of voices joins them in a chorale of historical force. This chorale embodies—even in the final silence, or sound, of the sea—a force of nature, the landscape itself as participant in the revolutionary drama.

I launched this discussion by observing the ways in which Pasolini will have come to locate in the peripheral landscape of the 1960s remnants of an archaic order perched on the brink of loss, now exacerbated not by war but by the ravages of neocapitalist speculation and commodity culture. This posits the most severe break in the continuity of the Italian landscape as occurring not in the war and its immediate aftermath but with the economic miracle and Italy's accelerated modernization in

the 1950s and 1960s.[32] While all filmmakers studied here are engaged in reconstructive projects, Pasolini's figuring of his locations out of myths and ruins, ancient and modern, marginal
and monumental—and including neorealism itself—is perhaps the most conflicted. Can the reservoir of the archaic that
Pasolini locates in the urban subproletariat and the peasantry—
first on the periphery of Italian cities, then on the margins of
Europe, and finally as far as the Arabian peninsula, sub-Saharan
Africa, or Nepal—assuage the ravages of modernity? Can it deflect the tragic end that prevails everywhere in Pasolini's narratives when people act to improve their lot, or when they stand
up against power and its institutions? Can it temper the violent
rifts in the age-old continuity of the Italian landscape? On the
margins of modernity, where the archaic is a contemporary
condition, Pasolini's films open a temporal breach, giving rise
to deliberate anachronisms and displacements. His bold invo-
cation of an archaic past in the unrelenting present inflects, as
well, the constitution of his cinematic image. The deceptively
plain frontality, the luminous simplicity of Pasolini's images
project a demiurgic force of transformation.

This still-redemptive vision of the mid-1960s Pasolini himself will come to reject in his "abjuration" a decade later of
such enclaves of archaic potency as we will see orchestrated in
The Gospel according to Matthew (*Il Vangelo secondo Matteo*, 1964)
or as just glimpsed in *La terra vista dalla luna*. He will come to
lose faith in such promises, generated by neorealism, and develop the conviction that only violence, shock, or despair could
constitute a filmmaker's response to the vicious circle of power,
domination, and morbid consumption embedded in what he
diagnosed as the Fascist fabric of neocapitalism. Pasolini's mur-
der in 1975—in Ostia, in a spot nearby and very much like the
Fiumara di Fiumicino where we began—corroborated what is
surely the bleakest vision of this time. Pasolini's last projections
were of a vacuous Italy, homogenized by corporate mergers
and consumer culture that subjugates bodies, identities, the

nation as one, to the all-consuming morbid power of commodities and the media. Inevitably this admonishing vision was
largely ignored in the following decade when so many, even in
the Italian left and the intelligentsia along with the media at
large, were absorbed in the commercial spin of massive private
conglomeration championed by Silvio Berlusconi and company in the 1980s. Italy is living its results today.

Was it already lurking in Rossellini's 1954 *Journey to Italy*
(Viaggio in Italia) where "Motta" advertising boards litter the road
to the mythical plenitude of Naples, and where only a miracle
can replenish a vacuous, contemporary relationship? Conversely,
can a redemptive perception, like that of the Technicolor terrain
of *La terra vista dalla luna,* survive in more recent returns: as in
Antonioni's aerial visitation in the 1990s to various neorealist
and other regional locations, removed, vacated as if after a cata-
clysmic transfiguration? Are these empty tourist fantasies of picturesque retreats, or of endlessly gratifying Mediterranean isles
floating along with contemporary Europe toward a featureless
and dissipated future? To arrive at such questions we must first
return to earlier efforts, trace the cinematic transmutation of a
location through a formative time.

ONE

Aerial: Antonioni's Modernism

For a Film on the River Po

On April 25 of 1939—designated also as "anno XVII," the seventeenth year of the Italian Fascist regime—Michelangelo Antonioni, film critic, publishes in the magazine *Cinema* an article accompanied by photographic illustrations: "For a Film on the River Po."[1] Though he had previously written for the local *Corriere Padano* published in his native Ferrara, Antonioni's article in the prestigious Roman film magazine with national circulation can be seen to constitute a first statement of intentions regarding filmmaking. While it has lent itself to association with early writings on neorealism, the article binds a regionalist-documentary pretext with a modernist imperative. Modernist movements and styles, such as "Second Futurism," art deco, and rationalism, among others, persisted and circulated under Fascism. Neorealism will seek to avoid or revise a tainted modernism, turning instead to realist narrative fiction in its attention to the regional, the quotidian, to a postwar collectivity that would bridge workers and intellectuals, populist and advanced culture. Perhaps sensing the realist fallacies and sentimental pitfalls of what was just beginning to emerge in the late 1930s and early 1940s as a proto-neorealist agenda of the "real Italy"—not yet quite distinct from a mythologizing, reactionary Fascist regionalism—Antonioni, already at this moment, articulates his own neorealist vision in modernist terms.[2] This early exploration, we will see, was undertaken under the auspices of his chief editor at *Cinema,* Vittorio Mussolini—the Duce's son, military pilot, and promoter of Italian film culture. Antonioni's article in this way exhibits tensions that the populist-humanist

tenets of neorealism will, by and large, subdue in the immediate postwar period, situating Antonioni in an oblique relation
to the aspirations of his colleagues; it betrays the ambivalence
of a formative moment—historically emblematic—when diverse, indeed contradictory, trends in late-Fascist Italian culture
converged.

While apparently focused on limited subject matter—on specific problems of documentary filmmaking and the cinematic
rendering of the particular regional landscape—"For a Film on
the River Po" raises questions on the ways in which location
shooting complicates the relation of fiction to documentary.
It evokes even broader questions on the relation of profilmic
actuality to rhetoric and poetic functions, the relation of landscape and history, and the consciousness of place in the national
imagination. All of this may not have been immediately apparent in 1939. Even anthologized as it is today, the text of this article may not suffice to clarify Antonioni's oblique relation to a
yet unnamed neorealist aspiration. Its literary, searching, meandering style evolves in a series of negations: Antonioni dwells
on what filmmaking should *not* be and only begins to envision
in this way what it might become. Yet surrounding this convoluted text, the photographic illustrations—not reproduced or
discussed in subsequent reprints and translations—will make
salient a modernist consciousness seeking crystallization vis-à-
vis diverse modes of landscape representation.

The text opens with what may be an allusion to the "pathetic fallacy," as in Ruskin's celebrated formulation of the
Romantic grasp of landscape.

> It is not a pathetic affirmation to say that the people
> of the Po region are in love with the Po. . . . In what
> does this *feeling* concretize itself we know not; we do
> know that it is diffused in the air and that it is sensed
> as a subtle fascination. This is, actually, a phenomenon
> common to many places traversed by large waterways.

It seems that the destiny of these regions coalesces in
the river. (255)

Even as he is cautious about projecting a subjective mood upon
the landscape, Antonioni maintains here a notion of *genius
loci*—a spirit of place that would figure, by means of the river,
the "destiny" of the region as a whole. Yet Antonioni goes on
to describe this "destiny" via the material, economic, and social
terms dictated by the river, which thus lends itself to culture,
and to art. The river in this way becomes an agent and figure
for temporality and change in the consciousness of its people.
The yearly floods punctuate the life of the river, dramatizing the
continued confrontation of the forces and rhythms of nature
vis-à-vis human endeavor and its modern sense of time. For

> the years did not pass in vain [not for people and] not
> even for things. There came also for the Po the time to
> awaken. And then there came iron bridges on which
> long trains clanged day and night, there came six-story
> buildings spotted with enormous windows vomiting
> dust and noise, there came steam boats, docks, factories,
> fuming chimneys, even more canals with cemented le-
> vees; this was, in short, an altogether modern, mechani-
> cal, industrialized world that came to turn upside down
> the harmony of the old one.
>   And yet in the midst of this dissolution of their world,
> the population had no regrets. (257)

The grand historical movement from a preindustrial golden age
to modernity brings forth the river from a background function
toward active participation in the life of the present: in industry, technology, and communication. This revolution Antonioni
describes as no cause for nostalgia—perhaps because the past
was not so golden or harmonious after all. But one might be
cautious as well about sentimentalizing the vision of progress

that Antonioni lays out. His concern is how to adjust human imagination to modernity. What begins to emerge here is the conviction that recurs in Antonioni's later writings, namely, that cinema is instrumental in this process of adjustment—and that it is especially suited, as a medium, to a mediating role between the modern environment and human perception and consciousness in transition. In effect, neorealism was to position itself six years later in an analogous mediatory or, rather, conciliatory role between a devastated, fractured postwar reality and the recuperating consciousness, and *conscience,* of those who will have survived Fascism and the war. But even sooner, as we will see, Antonioni will want to reconcile, in neorealist terms, Fascist modernism with an emerging consciousness of its problematic bequest in a new cinema.

The text of the essay seems to suggest that cinema as a medium may intrinsically promote such mediation between the contemporary environment and its people's cultural consciousness. Antonioni's conception of the trajectory of modernity, which he aligns with the movement of the river itself, becomes vaguely synonymous with a notion of film as such, though the latter must still be crystallized for its medium specificity. "All this," Antonioni states, "can seem to be but is not literature. It is, or wants to be cinema. It remains to be seen how it can be translated into practice. First of all there arises a question: documentary or fiction film?" (257). Antonioni's suggestion of a special adequacy of the modern landscape to the cinematic medium may be vague at this point, but in questioning the *mode* by which cinema can articulate this landscape in transition; in going on to complicate, as he does, the notion of *documenting* as well as that of *narrating* the landscape, Antonioni in effect problematizes that which many of his colleagues on the pages of *Cinema* will take for granted. For the neorealist ethos will imply a privileged status exceeding traditional generic classifications, unproblematically colliding a "correct" aesthetic and ideology that appear to be *guaranteed* by shooting on location in hitherto neglected (and thereby realist) sites.

A documentary that would develop via juxtaposition of picturesque detail and images of rural culture past and present, Antonioni fears, might lend itself to rhetorical cliché. While praising Pare Lorentz's 1938 film of the Mississippi, *The River,* Antonioni is wary of "the trite formulas of 'as it was versus as it is,' 'before and after the cure,'" and "the eternal river" (257). The American example suggests to him, perhaps, a lack of historical interrogation in an abbreviated passage from nature to modernity. Overdetermined, celebratory narratives of progress and destiny, set in a mythified landscape, were certainly a reigning principle of Italian documentaries—not only of fiction films—of the period. In envisioning, perhaps, a modernist medium specificity to match the modernized landscape Antonioni rejects here, as well, a certain hybrid of narrative and documentary associated with Robert Flaherty's work that would obscure the rigorous command of form, the precision and clarity of purpose that Antonioni seeks in the cinematic medium. He rejects folklore and anecdote, as well as the projection of sentiment that documentary propaganda and narrative or dramatic rhetoric might impose. In the essay's closing phrases he begins to describe, albeit rather enigmatically, a notion of a film that bypasses generic classifications and approaches instead an identification of the spirit of place with a purer cinematic vision.

> It suffices to say that we would like a film having as protagonist the Po, and in which not folklore—that is, a heap of extraneous and decorative elements—draws attention, but the spirit—that is an ensemble of moral and psychological elements. A film in which not the commercial need prevails, but the intelligence.[3] (257)

Although he advocates precision and clarity as cinematic virtues, Antonioni's writing here is rather affected and often obscure. Testing and erasing, as it were, tentative accounts of the Po River as the subject for film, Antonioni may be seen to channel diverse neorealist inclinations into what is ultimately a more radical position. But he cannot yet formulate this position as a positive, material aesthetic. In paring down "extraneous"—decorative, folkloristic, propagandistic, narrative, sentimental—elements from his envisioned film of the Po, he still seeks an intrinsic "spirit" of the landscape. His implicit critique of the pitfalls of Fascist rhetoric—some of which elements survived in neorealism—remains a generalized negation, not offering yet a coherent alternative but resorting to vague notions of un-mediated, a-rhetorical, idealist "essence."[4] Could the camera's encounter with the profilmic yield a "moral and psychological" reflection quite independent of the "extraneous" surface of vi-sual reality—the everyday, material, economic, and social life of the river that Antonioni has cited earlier? And if this spirit of place is distilled, would it not carry remnants of the pathetic fallacy? A fantasy of reconciling visual reality, the profilmic world confronting the camera, with a poetics of "essence" and "spirit" emerges in these closing lines. Implicit here, as well, is Antonioni's identification of this "spirit" with an "intelligence" proper to film as such. But the text of the essay fails to confront the difficulties of this proposal. In practice, Antonioni's post-war documentaries and, most famously, his fiction film work launched in 1950 went on to explore imaginative resolutions to such problematic terms. His discovery of the possibility of abstraction in the object and his concretizing, even narrativ-izing, of the void—the "interstice" between objects, between representations, between temporalities—are widely discussed in the literature.[5] But the genealogy of this aesthetic, its pre-cise modernist makeup, and its cultural-historical provenance remain to be addressed. In fact, at this early stage the prospect of resolving a modernist consciousness and a neorealist land-scape can perhaps only be articulated in fragmentary, contra-dictory terms. But more coherently than the written text, the photographic illustrations surrounding it—taking up more than double its space—step in where language fails to confront that which "is not literature" but "is or wants to be cinema."

This visual essay, running alongside the verbal one, I will attribute to Antonioni himself not only for lack of other acknowledgment on the pages of *Cinema* but as it is, we will see, close to Antonioni's vision as we come to identify it in subsequent work.[6] It also makes salient those aspects of contemporary Italian culture that inform the inception of his thought, his visual sensibility, and his film practice.

Organized in groups, eight of the nine stills share a horizontal format approximating a cinematic aspect ratio. The first pair (Figure 1.1) jointly titled "Nets for fishing in the Po waters," might suggest the reframing of objects within a single film shot whereby a camera movement linked two views of these elaborate contraptions of bent reed, supporting a fishing net on the bank of the river. With the change of angle from the first to the second still, the principal lines of the net slice geometrical sections out of the landscape and intersect exactly with the line of the distant riverbank. The sense of distance and perspective is thus negated in favor of sheer graphic relations of triangles and quadrangles of landscape parts, further flattened and summoned forth toward the photographic surface by the screening function of the net, which diffuses the expansive view of the river extending to the high horizon.[7] If in the first still the net's graphics were figured *against* the landscape-as-ground, the second begins to disrupt the figure-and-ground dichotomy, locating its transformation in the opening up of possibilities of reframing and movement *between* the two images. Such implication of movement as a product of shifting graphic relations is repeated in the essay's other photographic groupings.

The three stills on the facing page where the text begins are jointly titled "The banks of the Po" (Figure 1.2). All three frame river and bank laterally, with the perpendicular shapes of trees and vegetation distinct against a lighter background. In the first the branches constitute the foreground, in the second the middle ground, and in the third still the river fills the foreground while a slim row of trees is synonymous with the

Bilancia per la pesca nelle acque del Po

Figure 1.1. Michelangelo Antonioni, "Per un film sul fiume Po" (For a Film on the River Po), *Cinema* (April 25, 1939).

PER UN FILM
SUL FIUME PO

NON è affermazione patetica dire che le genti padane sono innamorate del Po. Effettivamente un alone di simpatia, potremmo dire d'amore, circonda questo fiume che, in un certo senso, è come il despota della sua vallata. La gente padana *sente* il Po. In che cosa si concreti questo *sentire* non sappiamo; sappiamo che sta diffuso nell'aria e che vien subito come sottile malìa. E, del resto, fenomeno comune a molti luoghi solcati da grandi corsi d'acqua. Pare che il destino di quelle terre si raccolga nel fiume. La vita vi acquista particolari modi e particolari orientamenti; sorge una nuova economia circoscritta, che dal fiume tutti traggono ogni possibile profitto; i ragazzi lo eleggono a giuoco preferito e proibito. Si stabilisce, in altre parole, una intimità tutta speciale alimentata da diversi fattori, tra i quali la comunanza dei problemi e la stessa lotta delle popolazioni contro le acque che quasi ogni anno, sul cominciare dell'estate o dell'autunno, si accaniscono in alluvioni talvolta violentissime e sempre tragicamente superbe.

Ecco dunque un motivo fondamentale del nostro ipotetico film: la piena. Fondamentale per due ragioni: per lo spettacolo in sé e perché ci rivela la sostanza di cui è fatto quell'amore cui accennavamo poc'anzi. È singolare questo attaccamento, questa fedeltà che resiste ai collaudi delle piene. Perché se queste, oggi, lasciano gli abitanti discretamente tranquilli, per la saldezza degli argini nuovi e dei ripari facilmente apprestabili, non è a dire che un tempo passassero senza lasciar traccia profonda. Non di rado portavan seco vittime umane, provocando in ogni caso visioni penose di campagne e borghi impaludati, di cumuli di masserizie sulle strade, di acque al livello delle finestre, di ciuffi e canne e alberi divelti affioranti dai gorghi orlati di bava. Ma i figli del Po, malgrado tutto, dal Po non hanno saputo staccarsi. Hanno lottato, sofferto, ancora lottano e soffrono, ma possono evidente-

mente far rientrare la sofferenza nell'ordine naturale delle cose, rubandole anzi un incentivo alla lotta.

* * *

Altro punto interessante e significativo è dato da un particolare riflesso della civiltà sulle stesse genti del fiume. Il quale aveva, in altri tempi, aspetto ben più romantico e pacato. Vegetazione arruffata, capanne di pescatori, molini natanti (ancor oggi ne è rimasto qualche esemplare), traghetti rudimentali, ponti di barche: il tutto sommerso in un'aura smemorata ed estatica, in un senso di forza irresistibile che sembrava evaporare dalla gran massa d'acqua e avvilire ogni cosa. La popolazione — gente solida, dai gesti lenti e pesanti — conosceva i lunghi riposi sulle rive e i vagabondaggi per i boschi che la rivestono, gli specchi pescosi e i piccoli seni nascosti sotto i salici chini a lambire le acque, e lasciava che in questa lentezza scorresse la propria esistenza, tuttavia occupata nei trasporti di merci e di persone, nei molini e, sopra tutto, nella pesca.

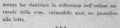

Le rive del Po

Figure 1.2. "Per un film sul fiume Po."

Figure 1.3. "Per un film sul fiume Po."

Ma nemmeno per le cose gli anni passano invano. Venne anche per il Po il tempo del risveglio. E allora furono ponti in ferro su cui lunghi tram sferragliano giorno e notte, furono edifici a sei piani chiazzati di enormi finestre vomitanti polvere e rumore, furono battelli a vapore, darsene, stabilimenti, ciminiere fumose, perfino altri canali dagli argini in cemento; fu insomma tutto un mondo moderno, meccanico, industrializzato che venne a mettere a soqquadro l'armonia di quello antico.

Eppure, in mezzo a questo sciuparsi del loro mondo, le popolazioni non hanno sentito rimpianti. Lo avrebbero voluto, forse, chè la loro natura scontrosa e contemplativa non si adattava ancora al nuovo stato di cose, ma non ci son riuscite. La evoluzione, a un certo punto, non soltanto non le disturbava ma in certo modo le accontentava. Cominciavano a considerare il fiume nel suo valore funzionale; sentivano che si era valorizzato e ne erano orgogliose; capivano ch'era diventato prezioso e la loro ambizione era soddisfatta.

* * *

Tutto ciò può sembrare, ma non è, letteratura. È, o vuol essere, cinematografo; resta a vedere come può tradursi in atto.

Prima di tutto s'impone una domanda: documentario o film a soggetto?

La prima forma è senza dubbio allettante. Materiale ricco, suggestivo, che va dai larghissimi tratti di fiume, vasti come laghi e talvolta interrotti da isolotti, alle stretture dove il Po scorre com'è da selvagge piante, assume aspetti di paesaggio africano; dalle casupole malandate addossate agli argini, con l'eterna pozzanghera nel cortiletto davanti all'uscio, alle villette novecento con lo chalet a fior d'acqua, che si anima certe sere di lievi musiche sincopate; dagli argini a picco alle grazione spiagge pretenziosamente mondane; dai molini natanti alle imponenti fabbriche; dalle barche ai motoscafi, agl'idroscivolanti della Pavia-Venezia; e via dicendo.

Materiale abbondante ma pericoloso, perchè si presta a facili inclinazioni rettoriche. Per cui, se ci alletta il ricordo di un magnifico documentario americano sul Missisipì: THE RIVER, ci lascia perplessi la trita formula del « com'era e com'è », del « prima e dopo la cura ». Nè ci tranquillizzerebbe l'intrusione di un esile filo narrativo. Diffidiamo degli ibridismi in genere, e di quelli dello schermo in particolare, dove non sarà mai troppo celebrata la forma che detta indirizzi precisi e non consente incertezze. O da una parte o dall'altra: l'essenziale è sapere esattamente quello che si vuole. Abbastanza recente è l'esempio offertoci da Flaherty, che pure è autore degno della massima stima. Nella sua DANZA DEGLI ELEFANTI, infatti, a causa del dissidio fra documento e racconto, il motivo lirico del lavoro, quella specie di religione panica della giungla, trova la sua più genuina espressione nelle sequenze documentarie, dov'è solo il tormento della scoperta poetica, altrove disturbata dalla narrazione.

* * *

Dovremo dunque accogliere l'idea di un film a soggetto? Detto tra noi, abbiamo molta simpatia per questo documento senza etichetta, ma non bisogna precipitare. Anche qui, naturalmente, non mancano gli ostacoli, primo fra tutti quello d'ideare una trama che risponda appieno ai motivi più sopra ventilati. Già gli americani,

ai quali nessun tema sfugge, ci si son provati. Due loro pellicole — vecchissima l'una; IL FIUME, di qualche anno fa l'altra: LA CANZONE DEL FIUME — ebbero buon successo, specie la prima, dal punto di vista contenutistico la migliore. Però ambedue erano molto lontane dal nostro pensiero e dalla nostra sensibilità.

Ma non vogliamo, qui, dar consigli a chicchessia

e tanto meno suggerire trame. Ci basti dire che vorremmo una pellicola avente a protagonista il Po e nella quale non il folclore, cioè un'accozzaglia d'elementi esteriori e decorativi, destasse l'interesse, ma lo spirito, cioè un insieme di elementi morali e psicologici; nella quale non le esigenze commerciali prevalessero, bensì l'intelligenza.

MICHELANGELO ANTONIONI

Barche e vapori alla riva di Pontelagoscuro

Veduta aerea di Pontelagoscuro e del ponte ferroviario per Padova

257

Figure 1.4. "Per un film sul fiume Po."

horizon line. In sequence, these images describe a movement of distancing of figures against the alternately stacked water-bank-sky elements, combined with the suggestion of lateral motion along the river. Following this exercise in figure and ground relations, the next page is divided between a pair of photographs jointly titled "Day and Night on the Po" (Figure 1.3) and contains the only human figures in the entire sequence, silhouetted and puny under the high horizon. Both stills are dominated by large expanses of water that approach the frame in magnitude, effecting an interplay of surface and depth, reflection and opacity: the water surface becomes comparable here to the surface of the photograph itself.

As the top photograph's caption on the last page of the essay (Figure 1.4) indicates, this is the bank of Pontelagoscuro, the small town on the south bank of the Po that will serve years later as the first stop in the protagonist's unhappy voyage in *Il grido* (1957). This is familiar landscape to Antonioni. Ferrara, his native city, is just a few miles from here. And as we are on the outskirts of an urban center, the built riverbank with its railroad bridge exhibits the first marks of industrial modernity in relation to what were thus far pure rural landscapes lacking clear contemporary orientation. Directly below this photograph, in the only vertical format of the series, is the last still—but it is one that, in fact, could be rotated and viewed in any angle. This "Aerial View of Pontelagoscuro and of the Railway Bridge to Padua" is centered on the same site but frames a much wider scope of the landscape, complete with factory buildings evidenced by massive chimney smoke and a network of what appear to be warehouses, canals, roads. Whatever marks of modernity we already noted are now heightened, for the camera work involved here is itself even more emphatically part of this modernity. And whatever human dimension, scale, and viewpoint may have marked the previous stills, whose modernism harked back to an Impressionist idiom, it now seems radically altered as we identify this photograph as part of a photogrammetric or else military project whose aim is objective, instrumental cartography or reconnaissance.[8]

Here Antonioni's visual essay ends. The striking terms of this conclusion to the photographic sequence may serve to crystallize what in effect remains obscure and mystifying in the written text. For the aerial photograph does suggest a correspondence between the modern landscape and its mode of representation—between modernity and modernism, concretely and historically placed. Is this the correspondence Antonioni was seeking? Of what does it consist? Does it suggest a new cinema that can exceed conventional compartmentalizing of landscape as graphic / geographic fact and as cinematic location, of technology and poesis, of documentary and fiction? Does *this* topographically and perceptually specific "intelligence" of the medium transcend circumstances, the weight of historical and political connotations? How can the Italian landscape, propelled into modernity during Fascism, be accommodated by an emerging neorealism while fulfilling a modernist program?

With the aerial image it is no longer a sheer formal correspondence between the landscape and its photographic conditions of representation, discerned in the first eight stills, that informs the modernist consciousness emerging in these pages. As the ninth, aerial photograph brings this correspondence to its limits, we acknowledge that it is not merely the graphically abstracted view or the industrial contents that are at work here, but the status and historical connotations of such an image that will embody for Antonioni an idea of a new cinema. The aerial photograph makes salient a modernist desire—suited, we will see, to Fascism's inclinations in the late 1930s—for a controlling, unifying perception poised to crystallize reality as an aesthetic object. But Antonioni's modernism will also be informed by a documentarist's conscience and by the lesson of photographic

contingency—the always specific, indexical image that testifies
to the tentative, the changing, and thus by the sense of movement and temporality that the sequence brings forth. How
might documentary cinema respond to the tensions between
the persistent and the changing, the tainted and the salvaged,
between traditional auratic fullness and its modern depletion
in the regional landscape, between an earlier modernist moment and its necessary revision in light of what has come to
pass? The marginal, unheroic regional sites of neorealism, its
vernacular expressions, its quotidian chronicles of works and
days often resorted therefore to pre-Fascist, to nineteenth-
century or even earlier models. For Italian modernism and
the avant-gardes, still perpetuated under Fascism, were now
deemed contaminated by its touch. In the late 1930s, the aerial
photograph is itself tainted thus. In the following pages I will
map its contexts and connotations in Italian culture, starting
from Antonioni's immediate circle and going on to chart the
difficulty but also the promise of Antonioni's aspiration at this
early phase. The lesson of the aerial photograph, so deeply im-
bricated in the historical moment, will project forth as a powerful paradigm in his work.

The Aerial and the Regional in Italian Fascist Culture

The aerial photograph emblematizes spatial perception in modernity. The aerial views of Nadar, who turned his lens on 1856
Paris from a balloon, foreshadowed developments in aeronau-
tic and short-exposure photography during the First World
War.[9] Military or cartographic applications of these distant,
compressed landscape photographs—decipherable by special-
ized scientific reading—appealed to a range of modernist and
avant-garde sensibilities.[10] For Le Corbusier the airplane is itself
a supreme example of the selective achievement of functional
comprehensive form, while the aerial view affords a modern

perception par excellence—one which unmasks the no longer viable traditional forms of landscape representation and urban planning. The camera's instrumental, automatic, indexical claim is amplified by the apparatus that bears it, the airplane, promoting the photograph's evidentiary, realist function—the iconic relation between image and landscape. Yet the anti-illusionistic effect of the aerial photograph has lent itself not only to "scientistic" but also spiritualistic conceptions of abstract art: in departing from ordinary perceptual notions of resemblance and the identification of figures that rely on upright and thereby anthropomorphic parameters, the sense of scale, depth, concave and convex, and figure and ground relations is also radically disrupted. Hitherto imperceptible forms—abstract patterns emerging to sight for the first time now—suggested the possibility of a hidden reality that awaited this lofty view of the whole, as if pertaining to some grander plan registered by the workings of the photograph's surface optics.[11] This was one way to conceive of abstraction as already inherent in the environment, to reconcile the difficulty of nonrepresentational art with the realist, testimonial value of photography.

The aerial view can be construed, then, as a limit case for photography. The ontology of the photograph as such had already intimated the absence of the human agent from the traditional role of the artist. More radically so, the human figure disappears from the position of both viewer *and* viewed in the aerial photograph. From a vertical axis the figure registers, if at all, as the most minute graphic mark: a speck, a trace of its former self and thereby, we might say, a sign of its own absence. The human figure no longer indicates scale and distance; it is no longer the measure of things. And as the landscape is thus vacated, becoming a cartographic notation, it becomes alien to itself. The ideological ambivalence underlying such a condition has been addressed in Siegfried Kracauer's writings on photography and on the "mass ornament" in the late 1920s.[12]

But one need not even go the short distance from Italy to Germany, and to these wider theoretical grounds, to trace the problematic connotations of the aerial photograph in Fascist Italy and in Antonioni's immediate milieu. Italy of the late 1930s, fresh from its colonial exploits in East Africa and the declaration of empire, glorified and romanticized aerial warfare, harnessing a range of cultural resources—both popular and elite-modernist—in its celebration. The authentic Italian invention of Fascism drew on such resources in its rendering of politics and of war itself as spectacles: such aesthetic conversions contribute to the very definition of Fascism. The encompassing, inspiring, abstract beauty of the aerial view in that historical moment cannot be quite detached from the aggressive, militarist, and imperialist uses of such images: the superior possession of vision and knowledge that aerial reconnaissance affords often prepared for the actual—not formal or metaphorical—controlling or leveling of the terrain by aerial bombardment. The aerial view has thus come to embody the perfect aestheticization of Fascist aggression.

All this could not have been far from view on the board of the magazine *Cinema* where a glaring exemplification of these cultural intersections may be located in the person of Vittorio Mussolini, the Duce's son. Mussolini the younger had just moved from aviation on the African colonial front to the forefront of Italian film culture, becoming involved in film production and, in 1938, becoming editor of *Cinema*. Just prior to this, capitalizing on the general excitement over the war in Abyssinia, he published in 1937 a popular account of his aerial exploits, illustrated by aerial photographs with such captions as "A pretty burst of bombs." These are matched by descriptions such as this:

I still remember the effect I produced on a small group
of Galla tribesmen massed around a man in black clothes.
I dropped an aerial torpedo right in the center, and the

group opened up just like a flowering rose. It was most entertaining.[13]

Back in Italy and into the movies, Vittorio Mussolini contributed to the production of Goffredo Alessandrini's vastly successful fiction film *Luciano Serra pilota* (1938) that celebrates Italian aviation. The film weds the persistence of Italian patriotism, heroic-paternal values, and nostalgia for one's native region to the ambition to expand the horizon through flight, itself synonymous here with imperialist expansion. The film allegedly received its title from Vittorio's father the Duce while, puzzlingly, Vittorio himself was credited as *auteur* in two enthusiastic reviews of the film by Michelangelo Antonioni.[14] The passion for aviation and for cinema were continuous for the young Mussolini. Applying the heroics of one to the other held a fascination even for the discerning film critic.

Vittorio Mussolini would have had access to such images as the aerial photograph of Pontelagoscuro, perhaps from military maneuvers in the Po Valley.[15] At least he may have inspired the idea of the aerial photograph that concludes Antonioni's vision of a film devoted to a regional landscape with such a departure from traditional imagery. My suggestion of shared "authorship" here bears, I believe, some metonymic potency; even figuratively it is at least as suggestive as Antonioni's ascribing of *Luciano Serra pilota* to his senior editor. What matter are the connotations and contexts made salient by these professional and personal ties. It takes a full-fledged Fascist sensibility like that of Vittorio Mussolini, or like F. T. Marinetti's, to explicitly glorify—always from a distance or from the air—the destructive, deathly perception of war.[16] But attenuated and, incredibly, still optimistic variants of this aesthetic were evidently still prevalent in the late 1930s despite the exposure of Fascism's worst faces in the colonial misadventure in Africa and the racism developed in its wake, culminating in the pact with Hitler. Now, Antonioni's hesitant text and its illustrations do not prescribe such Fascist visions, but they are not neutral, either. The rejection of nostalgic regional lore and decorative anecdotes of progress may be seen, in retrospect, to offer some resistance to folk mythologizing and heroic melodramatic aggrandizement—Fascist or otherwise. But does it confront that other, unifying and universalizing, possessive vision of the regional landscape manifest in Fascism's expansionist policy and in a cultural agenda that could convert such a modernist image of the terrain in its favor?

As an officially sponsored "Organo della Federazione Nazionale Fascista dello Spettacolo" (Publication of the National Fascist Federation of the Performing Arts), and under the auspices of one so intimately identified with the establishment, the magazine Cinema could offer considerable protection to its contributors, so many of whom were eventually to be aligned with dissident anti-Fascist culture. Did they need protection? Italian Fascist cultural policy—not monolithic and exclusionary, at least not when compared to its German counterpart—was confident in its power to mutate almost any text, any discourse in its favor, even if only by virtue of the absorbing proximity of the regime that would thereby perpetuate itself in the public eye.[17] It is thus that on the pages of Cinema—within the limits of its ephemeral newsprint surrounded with period deco graphics, advertisements for airline service to Addis Ababa, for Kodak film, for Coty face powder, for perfume, or toothpaste— one could find, in the late 1930s, articles attending to the marginal, the antimonumental, the unheroic neorealist vision of Italy.[18] Yet regionalist trends, which were to acquire distinct anti-Fascist connotations in postwar culture, in fact developed right out of Fascist glorification of rural life in keeping with folk mythologies of the late 1920s and 1930s.[19] So while proto-neorealist elements on the pages of Cinema were most likely read in light of Fascist regionalism, a dissident culture, as well as action, did eventually emerge from the midst of Cinema's contributors. Diverse positions and styles could suggest Fascist affinities on some level in the face of the regime, but many could also be seamlessly channeled to anti-Fascist ones in later years. *Cinema* in this way exemplified, to a point, the assimilative cultural policy of the regime: not a properly "pluralistic" outlook but rather one that sought to transform—if necessary by repressive measures—any and every material into self-serving cultural assets under the guise of apparent tolerance. Such was the insidious cultural make-up of Italian Fascism. Perhaps it is no wonder, in its light, that so *few* artists and intellectuals had to leave when they could continue working with relative freedom at home, right under its auspices.[20]

Certainly the Italian landscape image and its refashioning for modernity was a prime arena in which diverse trends competed for attention and support. As no uniform style or mode was officially endorsed by the regime, variants of modernism, regionalism, neoclassicism, and other historical revisitations competed—most furiously in the field of architecture, where the stakes and public consequences were greater in the remolding of Italy as an imperial center. In 1939, when Antonioni worked for the World's Fair planned for 1942 in celebration of the twentieth anniversary of the Fascist revolution, the "E-42" was already a vast arena of struggle between modernist-rationalist architecture and monumental classicism, often construed as Italy's "home style." Just outside of Rome, EUR, as the fair site is now called, still exhibits the tensions *and* compromises evinced in this struggle, where one style could be maneuvered to tame the other.[21] Regionalist elements could be used to domesticate the open, transnational rationalist aspiration of Italian modernist architecture. At the same time the potentially disruptive diversity of Italy's regional cultures could itself be contained under a unifying, progressive modernist outlook. Italian Fascism's assimilative power thus acquired great sophistication and was evidently still effective in the late 1930s when, even after the exposure of its worst face, a lively and, to a point, open debate on style in modernity continued under the regime.

Italy's earlier and most influential avant-garde, futurism, was itself revived in the thirties with the school of *aeropittura* (aerial painting) that registered the continued assimilation of universalist modernist aspirations within what was at times a nationalist and imperialist, at times a regionalist impulse, or all of those. Perhaps capitalizing on the imaginative force of the figure of Gabriele D'Annunzio as militant pilot-artist, *aeropittura* extended futurism's original engagement with the dynamism of modern life, with the new beauty of flying machines that revolutionize the human environment, or else destroy it—also cause for futurist celebration.[22] These ideas were articulated in a 1929 manifesto and an exhibition of forty-one *aeropittori* in Milan in 1931. Insofar as this "Second Futurism" rehearsed earlier concerns, it can be read as regressive when compared with the original, heroic first, whose militant connotations would have turned sour for many, if not by the mid-twenties then certainly a decade later.[23] It seems, however, that the aviational exploits in East Africa themselves reinvigorated the aerial imagination of Marinetti and his retinue. The manifestos, posters, murals, set and pavilion designs, architecture, sculpture, painting, and photography identified under the larger umbrella of *aeropittura* celebrated the conquering and liberating of space and perception from the forces of gravity and from a traditional, limited human viewpoint. E-42 itself, in both realized and unrealized projects, exhibited elements of this *aero*-culture: Adalberto Libera's Palazzo dei Congressi incorporated open metal trusswork shaped like airplane wings even as its hanging olive groves and rooftop theater harnessed regionalist and neoclassical elements. Libera's plans for an unrealized symbolic arch promised a soaring, gleaming gateway not simply to the sea and Empire beyond but also, by the suggestion of ascensional force, toward cosmic space upward from the horizon (Figure 1.5). The vast open spacing of buildings, the perspective views stretching to infinity, the celebration of progress and communications on a grand scale suggest a utopian

Figure 1.5. Adalberto Libera, "Project for a Symbolic Arch at E-42," as published in *Architettura* (December 1938). American Academy in Rome Library.

order whereby even from the earth the viewer is transported beyond human measure, beyond the terrestrial landscape.

Aeropittura could stress a spiritualistic sublimation of its potentially aggressive, militarist, and imperialist connotations in notions of auratic beauty and mystic power, the intoxicating embrace of a Fascist sublime. Gerardo Dottori's aerial landscapes perhaps epitomize this configuration. They are often dynamized by circular forms, drawn from landscape forms but also from the whirling, ascending experience of flight itself; this is matched by Dottori's rounded horizons that evoke the shape of the earth in a cosmic scale (Figure 1.6). Diverse perspectives, dimensions, and scales simultaneously dynamize the image in good futurist form. But what these works demonstrate as well is the interlacing of such modernist concerns with regionalist materials: Dottori's recognizable Umbrian landscapes, the roofs and bell towers of Perugia, and the gulf of La Spezia are matched with a cosmic suggestion of the bluish distance where entire towns, rivers, and gleaming lakes float upward on the surface of the canvas. Mario Molinari's 1938 *Gulf of Hammamet: Topographical Lyricism* lays out a "Futurist Mediterranean" in overlapping transparent surfaces where extension and layering invite an immersive, but at the same time cleansed, sublimated vision of the *mare nostrum*.[24] In these and numerous other examples we witness the confluence, through the aerial point of view, of regionalist specificity, nationalist/imperialist sentiments, and a universalist modernist engagement with the conditions of perception and representation at large. Critics have suggested that it is precisely due to this confluence that *aeropittura* served to disseminate modernist culture in 1930s Italy while cultivating decentered, heterogeneous, "local avant-gardes."[25]

Aeropittura aspires to capture the regional landscape from outside itself, from a dynamic, technological viewpoint that, finally, identifies the airplane with the camera. The futurist photography manifesto of 1930 promotes aerial vision as bound up with the photographic to supplant traditional pictorial, humanist notions of landscape.[26] *Aerofotografia* offers instead entire towns, vast terrains captured from above, independent of the human figure and unconcerned with its consequence. Familiar landscapes, rural and urban, are transfigured in oblique and vertical aerial viewpoints, or else in nearly abstract optical tracing achieved by long or repeated exposure in acrobatic flight— as performed by Filippo Masoero over the center of Milan (Figure 1.7).These images emphasized vertiginous height, the sensation of soaring or plunging at great velocity, radical shifts of scale and perspective that dynamize space, and bring a new consciousness even to familiar regional features or urban monuments.[27] Masoero, whose photography would suggest an avant-garde sensibility, was in fact a fiercely patriotic fighter pilot who had associated with D'Annunzio and Marinetti and, devoted to photography and cinema, was in 1930 appointed director of Istituto LUCE (L'Unione per la Cinematografia Educativa) in Rome: the newsreel and documentary propaganda wing of the regime.[28] Again, artistic explorations of innovative image technology appear inseparable from the Fascist cult of militarist and imperialist power. We might say that in

Figure 1.6. Gerardo Dottori, *Umbria,* 1934 (oil). Reproduced from *Dottori aeropittore futurista,* ed. Tancredi Loreti (Rome: Editalia, 1970).

aerial culture a modernist utopia of a futurist universe made local, and a vision of Italy made universal, lent themselves to Fascism's containment of oppositions and to its desire to command space in all its dimensions.

Italian fiction film of the period responded to these ideas, though its binding of the regional and the modern was often thematized through generic plot devices. Alessandrini's *Luciano Serra pilota,* a semi-autobiographical account of Masoero's experience, tells of a pilot (played by Amadeo Nazzari) and his son separated by the father's acrobatic flight work abroad; they are climactically reunited when the son, who has since become a pilot, is shot down and rescued by his own father on the Ethiopian front. The film surely suggested to its audience the persistence of Italian values—family ties, local patriotism, and

Figure 1.7. Filippo Masoero, *From the Airplane*, 1935 (aerial photograph). Reproduced from *Photographie futuriste italienne, 1911–1939*, ed. Giovanni Lista (Paris: Musée d'art modern de la ville de Paris, 1981).

the nostalgia for one's native, here distinctly northern Italian, home—alongside the ambition to expand the horizon through flight technology *and* imperialist expansion. Heightened melodramatic expression alternates in *Luciano Serra* with impressive location work involving masses of extras ("natives" and Italians) and the expertise of aerial cinematography. Inevitably, the conflation of these elements is subjugated to a propagandistic imperative that sentimentalizes the technology, positing imperialist warfare—epitomized by aerial exploits—as an emotionalized force of nature.

Other fiction films in the 1930s similarly narrativized in ways analogous to the paradigmatic engagement with aerial themes and forms, and even where these are not explicit, a smooth incorporation of modernity in traditional, regionalist values. Alessandro Blasetti directed some of the exemplary feature films in this vein: in *Terra madre* (Mother Earth, 1931) an urban culture of fast cars and jazz gives way to ultimately antimodern, nostalgic, and folkloristic ideals to allow the wedding of old wealth and agrarian labor in central Italy. The film appeals for its highly pictorial mise-en-scène to a range of traditional realisms—foreshadowing Visconti's frames of reference some years later—from Caravaggioesque interiors in peasant kitchens to the rural landscapes of the *Macchiaioli*.[29] Blasetti's *1860* (1934) historicizes the fusion of rural and modern by focusing on the participation of the Sicilian peasantry in the new myth of national unification forged in the Risorgimento. His *Vecchia guardia* (Old Guard, 1935) dwells on the "natural" continuity between the authentic vital elements of provincial life and the imperative of Mussolini's March on Rome. Also Roberto Rossellini's *La nave bianca* (The White Ship, 1941) and *Un pilota ritorna* (A Pilot Returns, 1942) exemplify an unproblematized assimilation of traditional values of family and romance in an aestheticized yet fierce Fascist technological culture. Something of an exception to this paradigm is perhaps Francesco De Robertis's *Uomini sul fondo* (Men on the Bottom, 1941), where the workings of a stranded submarine—its spaces, its dictating of perception, the distinct functions of its personnel—are rigorously explored with only the minimum sentimental punctuation. While harnessed by military propaganda, *Uomini sul fondo* is a film without stars, making use of actual seamen and largely authentic sets; its proto-neorealism is thus bound up with an engagement with functional form and the perceptual conditions of modernity. Yet tensions of human and technological, conservative and progressive values—not to mention ideologies—are neither interrogated nor historically contextualized here. Rather, they are neutralized in the service of complacency and submission—the sacrifice of the individual for the larger communal body, the immersion of the entire nation in the heroic story of the submarine.[30] The subversive force of Visconti's *Ossessione* (1943) truly stands out when juxtaposed with such films. *Ossessione*—as already suggested in the Introduction—sublimated no tensions and, in its melancholy regionalism, evidently swerved too sharply from the heroic mode, dwelling on outcasts and drifters reconciled neither to the community nor to the landscape that itself persists in refusing their accommodation. Despite the hope that, given his passion for American culture and an unprovincial cinema, Vittorio Mussolini would let *Ossessione* pass as he did the script proposal, the Duce's son apparently stormed out of the screening room proclaiming, "This is not Italy!" This reaction heralded the mutilation of Visconti's first feature. The image of the landscape was to evidence the land's plenty, the community's health, modernity's assimilation in a harmonious unified vision of progress, and thereby the regime's economic and social successes.

Documentary forms invited pronounced use of the regional landscape eliciting possible explorations, as Antonioni intimates in his article, of alternatives to sentimental and heroic rhetoric. The looser generic codes and conventions in the short-format documentary might have allowed for the pared-down modernist aesthetic that Antonioni promotes, even as a propagandistic imperative persists throughout this period. Films on Italian cities and towns, historical and contemporary sights, as well as documentaries devoted to the modernization of the rural countryside—the draining of swamps, the construction of new provincial towns, of monumental edifices, of dams, and other developments in industry and technology—abounded in the 1930s and must have attracted Antonioni's interest. In 1933 Raffaello Matarazzo directed several documentaries on grand Fascist projects: *Littoria* and *Sabaudia* focus on the new towns, *Mussolinia di Sardegna* on the building of a dam. Heightened formal, even geometrical compositions—rhythmic patterns of fields, canals, tracks, bricks, shovels, workers, often flattened in distinctly modernist high-angle shots—matched by the absence of voice-over commentary, make salient a quasi-abstract musical orchestration of engulfing development and heroic progress. Such strategies are familiar from Soviet and other European avant-gardes, as well as the poetic documentary of the 1920s and 1930s—perhaps brought to attention in Italy by Corrado D'Errico's *Stramilano* (Ultra-Milan, 1929), the Italian example of the city symphony on the eve of sound. As with *aeropittura,* the adaptation of earlier avant-gardes as a stylistic device was perhaps a way to assimilate no longer subversive modernist forms to the current inclinations of the regime. What might have held revolutionary force in the teens and twenties—the raising of modernity to consciousness and its dynamization in radical form—is echoed but diffused here in absorbing, satisfying rhythms that celebrate Fascist heroic unity and progress: the possession of the landscape, the mastery of space that leaves no room for question or doubt, for the interrogation of altered historical conditions, for the contingency of a heterogeneous, changing environment.

The Venetian poetic documentaries of Franceso Pasinetti appear free, in the first instance, from the burden of propaganda but are in fact strikingly lacking in any allusion to historical context, contemporaneity, and human consequence in the midst of the war when they were produced. *Venezia minore* (Minor Venice, 1941) and *I piccioni di Venezia* (The Pigeons of Venice, 1942) manifest Pasinetti's eye for the aesthetic promise of everyday gestures, the minor detail, the neglected corner that crystallizes a spirit of place. Unraveled in often surprising camera or object movements, or the deliberate patterning of background and foreground elements brought into new relations, these filmic images are not unrelated to Antonioni's vision in his article on the Po. However, Pasinetti's hermetic, *calligraphic*[31] bent is perhaps just what Antonioni rejects as the "decorative" pitfalls of cinematic landscapes divorced from modernity, change, a consciousness of historical process. If a formalist engagement comparable to Pasinetti's characterizes to some extent the photographic illustrations of the Po River

article, we have noted the startling sense of changing conditions of the environment itself, as of the means of perceiving
it, surfacing in the last page. In disclosing the problematic connotations of a utopic, universalizing modernism under late
Fascism, the aerial image departed, we have seen, from sheer
formal pictorialism—perhaps also by virtue of its position and
its participation in the movement and temporality of the photographic sequence as such.

One finds little in the cinema of the period that correlates
to such an oscillating position as Antonioni's article suggests.
Curiously, it is in the midst of documentary shorts—filmed
reports produced, ostensibly, in direct service of the regime—
that one locates echoes of such a consciousness.[32] The shorts
produced by the Istituto LUCE in this period often celebrate
Fascism's technological accomplishments in the spaces of daily
life: in regional, rural, or urban, industrial, military, and colonial landscapes in transition. While produced in govern-
ment service under a propagandistic imperative, it is perhaps
their hastier production circumstances—as well as the application of a looser chronicle structure—that allowed at times
for tentative, explorative forms to surface. In the documentaries produced by the Institute's East African arm, the movie
camera's proclivity for military feats, including aviation accomplishments, as vivid visual material is harnessed, certainly,
to the promotion of virile imperialist ambitions. But this is
somewhat modified in instances that, alternately, dwell on
the antidramatic, mundane elements of military life and actions in surprisingly digressive chronicle form by depicting the
labor, the mechanics, and the everyday chores surrounding the
maintenance of forces, the repetitive, marginal phenomena
contingent to their practices and feats. These contextualize
and modify the sheer force effected by the sweeping aerial
shots of desert landscapes, the large movements of troops,
the spectacular fall and explosion of bombs. In the midst of
heroic action small but significant spaces of hesitation open up

in such LUCE documentaries as *La battaglia dell'Amba Aradam* (The Battle of Amba Aradam, 1936) or *Conquista della Somalia Inglese* (Conquest of British Somalia, 1940), in place of the total-izing form and graphic technological and rhetorical sweep of the majority of documentary production of the period. And in these spaces, occasionally made salient by the withdrawal of heroic music and commentary, altered relations emerge in the contingent detail of this warfare in a foreign land whose condi-tions are so patently at odds with the imperialist war machine (Figure 1.8).[33] These occasional glimpses, formally elaborate and implicitly dissonant with the reigning ideology that spon-sored this institutional production, might be seen to betray an interrogative outlook that stands out against the more con-tained *auteur* documentaries of the period.[34] While it is hard to assess just how deliberate these scattered instances might be, it is quite possible that Antonioni would identify in such models

Figure 1.8. Istituto LUCE documentary, *Ore di guerra nel cielo africano* (Hours of War in the African Sky), 1941.

the modernist possibilities of the chronicle form wherein the minor, the dissonant, the contingent trace persists against the gripping embrace of Fascist instrumental filmmaking.

There is a way in which, matched by such scattered instances in the LUCE documentaries, Antonioni's photographic sequence with its aerial conclusion constitutes a lesson on the possibility of a neorealist documentary in open, contingent form by which to sort out what remains of cinematic modernism after the war. How to convert this lesson to a new order of filmmaking, free of heroism and sentimental ornamentation, of the imposition and closure of both traditional narrative and propagandistic documentary rhetoric? How to maintain an oscillation between the modern promise of the cinematic image with its now-tainted rational order, and the residual, contingent spaces of the regional landscape without quite subjugating or containing them? These would be the kinds of questions that a post-Fascist cinema would need to confront in working through cinematic modernism vis-à-vis a changing, discordant, depleted landscape—as the Po Valley itself was to become in a few short years. Looking at the way in which the queries of his prewar article survive in his film practice, one might consider that Antonioni was willing to risk the linking of pre- and postwar Italian modernisms for all its discomforts.

An Altered Terrain

Antonioni's essay was written four years prior to initial production and eight years prior to completion of his first documentary. In the course of this period, which included the war, the lesson of the Po River article was to be developed and refined. For while Antonioni's filmic images of the Po will on some level be strikingly reminiscent of the 1939 photographic illustrations with which we have been concerned, their new cinematic syntax, editing, and temporality offer important departures from that early exposé. In the winter of 1942–43, across the riverbank from where Visconti was working on *Ossessione*, far from centers of power, from the monumental and mythic connotations of Rome and the south, and from the softer contours of Tuscany that make up the ideal image of Italy in the touristic imagination, Antonioni shot *Gente del Po* (People of the Po, 1942/1947). The fate of this documentary—the negatives of which were stored in Venice during the particularly violent period following its shoot—could not be reversed, as was *Ossessione*'s upon its restoration. In 1947—a year after Roberto Rossellini also explored this same landscape in the final episode of his *Paisà*[35]—Antonioni could only put together the remains of the footage into some nine minutes of stirring filmmaking, about half of the projected length. Whether the lost footage—largely shots of the flooding in the Po delta—was deliberately destroyed under the puppet Republic of Salò or simply perished by neglect in humid conditions comparable to those depicted in the rushes themselves remains unclear. Either way a confluence of circumstances—the difficult conditions and interrupted history of the production, the violent shifts in political climate and prolonged struggles in the north of Italy from fall 1943 through the end of the war—have all left their scars on Antonioni's first film. Perhaps the loss both of footage and of prewar illusions that marks this production was *itself* important.[36] The experience of fragmentation and loss now altered the way in which Antonioni's neorealist modernism might be realized. It is a matter for speculation whether Antonioni was no longer comfortable with the controlling, unifying thrust of aerial perception implicitly promoted by the Po River essay—a perception that brings to its formal and historical-political limits, we have seen, earlier modernist visions. Revising this modernism, a principle of contingency now emerges to the fore, inflecting tensions of alienation and identification, abstraction and referentiality, modernism and realism in ways that modify the issues I have been discussing.[37]

Between quotidian detail and a movement of emptying-out

of the landscape, fragments of river life, less-than-episodes, and unpursued plot clues traverse, as it were, the documentary body of *Gente del Po*. These narrative elements are suspended, time and again, in descriptive passages or altogether inert compositions that refuse to lend themselves to classical representational disclosure and containment. Though the voice-over commentary—delivered by a female voice, so rare in documentary work of that era—points out potential neorealist story elements—"a man, a woman, a child"—these are allowed no development or resolution. Their lyricism is modified by their sparsity; their dramatic or sentimental potential is halted, *dissolved* in the image of the river itself: in shots of barge movement and the water expanses filling the frame. Following the fragmentary exposition, in the briefest visual account over which verbal commentary is suspended, other elements surface but hardly serve to organize the plot except insofar as they suggest a subtle interplay of figure and ground, surface and depth elements in the mise-en-scène: a sick child lies belowdecks, the parents' movements make salient the different levels and planes, the distribution of light in this domesticated interior space that moves through the river, just under the surface daylit world of machinery and routine labor and actions scanned by Antonioni's camera.[38]

Other narrative fragments intersect such early threads as described above only to be suspended again in stark, inert compositions. A bicycle rider crosses the frame: we might have noticed him earlier as part of the background of the riverside town. The commentary now calls attention to his presence as he crosses the barge-woman's path to the pharmacy and rides up and over the levee. Then, for the duration of a single startling shot, the bicycle rider pulses with narrative possibility, summoned from the descriptive-documentary plane of the film; for a few seconds he is a figure sharply drawn, only to be withdrawn again as the ground reemerges to the fore. A girl is sitting on the bank looking at the river, her back to the camera in medium shot; the bicycle enters the frame and is placed in between girl and camera. Several planes—bank, river, girl, bike—all compete for space in this dense and suddenly dramatic framing as the rider now settles down, partly concealing the girl as she turns to cast upon him an unfathomable look. His sports shirt with the logo "DEI"—a contemporary, solid make of bicycles—looms large on the screen, its flat modern graphics a striking intrusion upon what one had envisioned as a romantic-lyrical instance in the timeless embrace of the river. Then the camera pans away to the empty expanse of bank, river, opaque sky beyond—suspended landscape elements, signifying nothing in particular, opening, emptying up the little narrative all in the duration of a single shot (Figures 1.9–1.10). The narration is thus in constant withdrawal under an emerging principle of dissolution, recession, abstraction that inflects this short documentary at every level. From narrative promise to the graphic inscription of the sports shirt that blocks preceding connotations, and from the intrusive pause over the upright graphics to the opaque landscape that even refuses the consolation of a receding distance, we witness what is surely the earliest and paradigmatic instance of Antonioni's cinematic modernism.

In its look upon the regional, neorealist subject matter, *Gente del Po* maps a space of oscillating, fractured textuality and visuality that approaches a modernist perception on all things private and public, quite distinct to Antonioni's cinema as it will become more persistently recognizable in the years to come. The film's realist claims—the regional elements of everyday life that it documents—are repeatedly suspended, like its narrative, in motions of externalization and dissolution, symptoms of a modernist consciousness that identifies the landscape with the space of cinematic representation as such. The gray expanse of the river—"flat as asphalt," the voice-over observes—that fills the frame repeatedly, opaquely; the graphic division of light and shade on a wall under the opening credits; the "metaphysical"[39]

Figure 1.9. Michelangelo Antonioni, *Gente del Po* (People of the Po), 1942/1947.

Figure 1.10. *Gente del Po.*

premonition of the empty provincial piazza whose perspectival values are blotted by the expansive surfaces as by the sharp contrasts of long shadows and arcades; the high-angle shots of the barge filling the frame bottom to top, with depth and vision itself effaced by smoke as the camera tilts up—these turn attention to the grasp of the landscape *as* cinematic image *in process of being drained* (Figures 1.11–1.12). These are not neorealism's consoling, reconstructive gestures. The linear movement of the river toward the Adriatic and the final view of the marine horizon themselves seem fashioned as cinematographic entities to correspond to the modernist sensibility confronting them, reciprocating this movement of dissolution, draining, emptying-out. Like the aerial photograph of Antonioni's early essay that finally emptied the landscape of narrative anecdote and traditional connotations, so in the closing images of *Gente del Po* the landscape, like the film itself, is vacated (Figure 1.13). Yet the cinematic location is not subjugated here to an encompassing figure except under the sign of mutability, change. Might we witness in it the contingent perception of a postwar consciousness working through the provisional spaces that open up between realist representational conventions and the dispersive, fragmented chronicle of a modernist everyday?

In describing this particular position vis-à-vis neorealist cinema, we might now recall that of all the major filmmakers to emerge in this period leading to the great flowering of Italy's postwar film culture, Antonioni is the only one to dwell so rigorously on the documentary. Rather than simply appealing to quasi-documentary means of articulation (actual locations, nonprofessional actors, etc.) *in the service of* neorealist narrative or historical reconstruction, we find him preoccupied with distilling cinematic form from the profilmic subject at hand.[40] It may be that a documentary consciousness sharpened his sense of taking nothing for granted: nothing as settled and coded, realist or otherwise, in the face of postwar contingency that was so amplified by the violent shifts in power and ideology, the

Figure 1.11. *Gente del Po.*

Figure 1.12. *Gente del Po.*

Figure 1.13. *Gente del Po.*

disappearance of people, and the transformation of the landscape itself over the course of the war. The neorealist agenda—
harnessed as it was after the war to the urgent rebuilding and
restoration of Italy's image to itself—would avoid, at least for
a while, a rigorous exploration of cinematic modes that might
disrupt its consoling sense of humanist certainty and continuity: it would forgo documentary experimentation as well as a
full-fledged confrontation with a modernist consciousness as
such. Antonioni, instead, succeeded in casting his neorealism in
modernist terms via just such a confrontation with fundamental questions of cinematic representation and in light of the
obverse lessons of aesthetics and politics under Fascism. The
uncertain terrain that he had begun to explore so early perhaps
could not be quite accommodated in a film culture that identified its project of postwar commemoration and reconstruction
with narrative consolation and could not always afford to be in-

terrogatory or reflective. Thus, at the height of neorealism and through the end of the 1940s, Antonioni remained occupied with documentary production on the margins of neorealist practices. While his documentary choices invite some comparisons with the work of Visconti and Rossellini, Antonioni's radical concerns—informed by a prewar modernist promise that could not be taken to its conclusions during Fascism—had to wait before they resurfaced in the following decade as stunning cinematic disclosures in feature productions.

Antonioni's grasp of the landscape as a distanced, alienated terrain recurs as a critical, transformative principle much wider in its potential than the aerial view we have initially located as paradigm. The view from the iron bridge in *Cronaca di un amore* (*Chronicle of a Love Affair,* 1950) and from the tower of *Il grido* were already striking instances, although *L'avventura*'s (1960) island views came to be the most celebrated, and the finale of *L'eclisse* (1962) perhaps the most radical of Antonioni's elaboration on this perceptual paradigm. The island where a character has disappeared without a trace, the deserted towns and vacant hotel corridors, the crossroads in the EUR Roman suburb to which the camera, but not the protagonists, returns—these crystallize an "intelligence" of place stripped of "extraneous and decorative elements" as of overcoded rhetorical devices that would mediate human presence, and pastness. The analytic clarity of such filmmaking, like Antonioni's writing of that later period, exceeds that of the Po River essay, but he evidently drew from concerns already in place in that early, illustrated article.[41] His repeated movements of crystallization through the palpable withdrawal of narrative and dramatic figures and codes draw on a documentarist's sense of the unfolding of the profilmic place in the duration of a shot, the unraveling of relationships in time and space consciously differentiated from the suggestion of cause and effect, from narrative and expository remnants. The crystallizing of a sense of place—a regional specificity that still carries realist values—is bound up

with its apparent opposite: the withdrawal of definite figuration, a fragmented modernist interrogation of the conditions
of perception and of narrative, often accomplished through
the syntactic, temporal modality of cinema. Antonioni's work
was, from the start, thus based in a fracturing of the figure so
as to test the ground and see how ground emerges *as* figure,
capturing the movement by which one evolves into the other,
dwelling on the narrative digressions and graphic disturbances
that arise in this process.[42]

The oscillation between cinematic registers we have noted in
Gente del Po already projected an ambivalent perception of late
modernity in the wake of the Second World War. The forms of
contingency responsive to a lacunary landscape wherein some
of modernity's most solid edifices have been destabilized, the
shifts between a realist representational order and the dissolution of its secure devices, the discovery of abstraction at the
heart of the figure and the figurative potential of the void—these
persist as defining features of Antonioni's cinematic modernism. Antonioni located his first arena for such an interrogation
in his native landscape, bringing into play there the profound
tensions of Italian culture between the world wars. But it was
following the camera's recording of hitherto unseen atrocities,
following the panorama of European and other landscapes leveled by more than just a camera's vertical outlook, that one
came to realize how altered must be the look upon the terrain,
brought in all its devastation to its surviving beholders.

TWO

Ruinous: Rossellini's Corpse-Cities

> In terms of monumentality, neorealism
> speaks hitherto unknown etymons.
>
> —Manfredo Tafuri, *Storia dell'architettura
> italiana, 1944–1985*, 1986

In the concluding images of *Paisà*'s (1946) Neapolitan episode
we find Roberto Rossellini's early reflection on the eloquence
of ruins in the postwar landscape. The short story format of
the episodes begets here a terse, elliptical mode wherein what
remains unsaid, and only briefly seen, emerges as a resonant articulation strongly charged in the film's imaginary. Rossellini's
study of war and its aftermath is traced in the Neapolitan episode first as child's play, then as theatrical spectacle: recall the
emblematic scene when the African American MP intrudes
upon a puppet-show duel of crusader and Moor, wherein traditional roles and controlled identifications break down.[1] It is
further complicated, finally, in the MP's drunken fantasy re-
enactment of airborne and other feats as he sits on a mound of
rubble alongside the Neapolitan orphan who had attempted
to "sell" him earlier on the black market. Surpassing mimetic
realism or naive documentation, surpassing as well the awk-
wardness of performance and shifts of register in a dissonant composition whose rationale we will explore later on,
Rossellini's move from the child's and adult's playacting sequences, within and without theatrical settings, by means of extended traveling shots through the streets of war-torn Naples,
culminates in an extraordinary sight. The MP's story finally
lands him in a vast cave in which many children, among a host
of dispossessed poor, inhabit what one imagines is a temporary

but nonetheless appalling dwelling (Figure 2.1). We are in the Mergellina Caves, still on the outskirts of Naples at that time.[2] Part primeval habitation, part catacomb, part ruin, man-made and natural shelter meet here in a momentous space that seems to either precede or exceed the definition of civilized habitation. It is a place so wretched and elemental, bereft of anything but the most basic definition of "shelter," the pressing actuality of everyday life for so many, and at the same time a place so charged *as an image,* a limit vision of ruin and loss, that the MP—who has come there to retrieve his stolen boots and inform the parents of the urchin (who is orphaned) of their son's misdeeds—falls silent, drops the boots, and retreats in his jeep kicking up a cloud of dust.[3]

Ruin, monument, and habitation join in an instant in this location, at once exceptional and ordinary, and perhaps precisely *for* this reason. This yoking of terms is central, I will argue, to neorealism's project of reconstruction—which is both its con-

Figure 2.1. Roberto Rossellini, *Paisà,* 1946.

tribution to the larger material and civic historical effort and a prime attribute of its cinematic aesthetic. Rossellini's emissary observer is here, as so often in his films, an outsider under whose look material conditions and an altered consciousness coalesce in phenomenological realization. His look and his withdrawal impart to this consummate postwar image emblematic gravity. By the disclosure of his own deprived background, by his very silence and his turning away, the MP, and Rossellini's camera in turn—having offered only two very brief shots of the general view of the caves—enact in the face of this ruinous space a mode of seeing that is itself haunted, fragmented, traumatic.[4] Rossellini's ruins offer material evidence, proclaim the imperative of shelter, of housing; they constitute as well a symbolic commemoration. Yet they resist a solid, definitive articulation: they emerge as an arena wherein a monumental thrust is traversed by a force of contingency. The ruin is internalized, inscribed in the film's body that itself emerges as a ruinous edifice, redefining Rossellini's realism, and his modernism, in an exemplary intersection.

While the ruins of antiquity have been spectacularized since the early days of Italian cinema—consider *The Last Days of Pompeii* in its various versions (*Gli ultimi giorni di Pompei*, 1908, 1913, 1926), or the achievement of Giovanni Pastrone's *Cabiria* (1914)—they have surely responded, at the same time, to the documentary draw of actual sites, binding a (romanticized) archaeological fascination with the cinematic one. And even as the cinematic image of the ruins served a documentary function, it acquired, like the ruin itself, a commemorative and a figurative charge. We know that ruins from antiquity to modernity, the ones wrecked by men and those formed by natural disasters and the workings of time and neglect, have lent themselves to allegory and other manners of figuration. Perhaps because temporality inscribes itself so emphatically in the ruin, it acquires special resonance in cinema—the medium that itself, Erwin Panofsky observed, dynamizes—we will say temporalizes—space and spatializes time.[5] Recalling a lost whole, a time past, the duration of traces—of violence, suffering, death—in the intersection of presence and absence, of the visible and the invisible, the ruin embraces a resonant figurative poetic in its material gravity, famously articulated in Walter Benjamin's dictum: "allegories are, in the realm of thoughts, what ruins are in the realm of things." We will trace, later on, the transmutation of document to allegory in the ruinous terrain that extends the limits of neorealism in Rossellini's career.[6]

How is film history informed by the unprecedented scale and urgency of reconstruction out of the catastrophic ruins perpetrated by Fascist regimes and by the searing light of Hiroshima and Nagasaki? The ruinous landscape evolves as late-modern trope inflecting not only the space but the consciousness and the agency of postwar cinemas. Beyond the neorealist affinity that concerns us here, one may draw a genealogy that includes newsreel and documentaries evidencing the actual devastation in the 1940s on the one hand and, on the other, the contorted melodramas set therein, primarily in the German "rubble" genre: Gerhard Lamprecht's *Somewhere in Berlin* (*Ingendwo in Berlin,* 1946) and Wolfgang Staudte's *The Murderers Are among Us* (*Die Mörder sind unter uns,* 1946) being notable examples. We should also cite their almost forgotten Italian counterpart, Claudio Gora's *Il cielo è rosso* (The Sky Is Red, 1949). In the 1950s and 1960s we still find the ruins of Europe as a haunting figure in films as diverse as Jean Cocteau's *Orpheus* (*Orphée,* 1950), Chris Marker's *La Jetée* (1962), Jean-Marie Straub's *Not Reconciled* (*Nicht versöhnt,* 1965). More recently, in Wim Wenders's *Wings of Desire* (*Der Himmel Über Berlin,* 1987) and Jean-Luc Godard's *Germany Year 90 Nine Zero* (*Allemagne 90 neuf zéro,* 1991), the presence of the past, the ethic of history, the forces of change deeply inform cinematic space and temporality as still saturated with the ruins of World War II.

But in the initial postwar moment, the ruinous landscape

was *itself* an arena of confrontation between the imperatives of evidence and memory and the project of reconstruction, itself caught between material and symbolic fronts. While inextricably bound, these fronts often commanded distinct, even conflicting solutions to the problem of preserving the ruin as evidence and commemoration, to the problem of restoring some measure of national identity and community, and finally to the grave housing problem. The need to clear up a space often outweighed the conservation of ruins as monuments and compromised their restoration. At the same time the urgency of habitation—often without sufficient base in sound urban planning, spurred as it was by speculation as well as by the need to occupy and contain the masses—did not always fulfill the potential for housing to *itself* acquire, through communal, symbolic, and aesthetic functions, an alternative monumental value. How, then, to preserve, to restore, to reconstruct, to rebuild, or to build anew; how exactly to define such categories in the fractured, contingent postwar landscape? The ruin that bears the traces of recent events commands, on the one hand, the status of untouchable evidence, or is else retouched toward specific political, ideological, monumental uses. On the other hand, there loomed the urgent physical rebuilding of habitable space, the opportunity for physical and social reconstruction of everyday life in human measure. The radical reinvention of a future out of the rifts of war perhaps begged for an altered monumental principle. All these concerns emerge right out of the ruinous postwar landscape and describe its deepest tensions.

The flowering of realist modes in postwar Italy may be understood, in its finest instances, as keen inquiry into what preservation and reconstruction—the remaking of reality itself—might involve in the space of everyday life and in its cinematic rendering. In a landscape of ruins neorealism *was* reconstruction. We gloss its "realism" here as an intervention rather than a passive moment in modern culture, for neorealist cinema was certainly a lively participant in the "production" of postwar Italy.[7] On this terrain neorealism articulates its political and historiographic mission: its enactment of the Resistance myth as operative negotiation between cultures, classes, workers, and intellectuals. Neorealist cinema confronted here, finally, its own representational crux: its claim to knowledge, its evidentiary charge in documentation and chronicling functions, and, even more deeply as Bazin had sensed, its testifying to a temporal binding of past and present and the spectator's implication therein. How does the cinema, like the ruin, bear on our relation to the past? What is the historical and memorial value of a neorealist image? Or does neorealism supersede the past in the project of reconstruction, actual and cinematic? Might reconstruction efface memory and smooth over its rifts? Or might the preservation of the ruin as commemorative value and sight, or spectacle, promote a static, morbid position, unlivable but perhaps negotiable *as cinema* that can repeat death— "every afternoon," Bazin thought[8]--inscribing it in the fabric of contemporary life? How do cinema's own commemorative functions inflect the concern with the quotidian landscape? I will propose that neorealism's valorization of human habitation responds to such questions. While ostensibly set up as an antimonumental, even "antirhetorical," rhetoric—committed to the local, the minor, the vernacular—Italian neorealism did in fact fulfill, and heroically so, a cohesive symbolic and civic role in anti-Fascist cultural discourses of which film was one constituent, alongside literature and architecture.[9] And while ostensibly antimodernist in its regionalism and populism, neorealism's vernacular idiom has given rise—we have already noted—to modernist uses that after Bazin's inspiration the *Cahiers* critics promoted and radicalized in New Wave production. Neorealism's destablizing of the classical cinematic edifice, its episodic, digressive mode by which narrative recedes into the setting to expose rifts and ellipses, may itself be understood, in the strongest work, to *mimic* and then remake a landscape marked by loss. We have witnessed one model for such operations in Antonioni's earliest film practice. Rossellini's lesson of the postwar landscape, too, may be understood in light of the reconstruction of modernism itself—out of *its* ruins.

Location shooting in a new spatial order was key to neorealism's production of a postwar landscape. It evidenced aesthetic, industrial, and ideological principles that refracted Italy's image in the wake of war and the war's transformation of space. While Italy's state of ruin was not comparable to that of Germany, a complex of material and institutional transformations after what was nevertheless a momentous collapse brought on an early engagement with the ideology of reconstruction, an acute consciousness that only surfaced in Germany some time later. After the summer of 1943, increasing identification with the Allies helped to purge Italians of their full implication in Fascism, displacing complicity and guilt onto Nazi Germany. And, as has often been observed, Italy—in its ambiguous position as defeated nation, yet one so quickly identified with the Allies that its defeat was cast as liberation from an external occupier—emerged morally stronger from the war than it had entered it. This state of things engendered the complex fabric of anti-Fascist culture that would mediate a range of ideologies under the heroic myth of the Resistance, avoiding at the same time a proper, revolutionary remaking of the state. Neorealist culture subscribed by and large to this restorative, conciliatory stance. Symptomatically, it avoided a radical aesthetic: we have noted earlier the logic of its refusal of avant-garde strategies despite its reputation as a revolutionary cinema. It aspired instead to the status of socially conscious work that responded to the populist and humanist needs of the moment.

Certainly, Rossellini's participation in this restorationist project was, in some ways, emblematic of the about-face of many Italians upon the fall of Fascism. His neorealist work bypasses direct interrogation of Italy's vigorous contributions to Fascism and their grave consequences. It projects instead a largely benevolent vision of Italian fraternity across ideological differences, most emphatically in *Open City* (*Roma città aperta*, 1945), while *Paisà* cultivates the Italian affinity with the Allies, shifting emphasis further away from the primary contribution of the communist Resistance.[10] Critical periodization largely followed this logic, conforming the thematic logic of the films to historical groupings tout court: the Fascist wartime "trilogy"—*La nave bianca* (The White Ship, 1941), *Un pilota ritorna* (A Pilot Returns, 1942), and *L'uomo dalla croce* (The Man with the Cross, 1943)—is traditionally juxtaposed with the postwar neorealist "trilogy"—*Open City, Paisà, Germany Year Zero* (*Germania anno zero*, 1948).[11] But while *Open City* must remain, despite and perhaps *for* all its contradictions, a defining film in the neorealist canon, its heroic form and Manichaean dramatic mode reveal continuities, as Ruth Ben-Ghiat has shown, with the wartime films.[12] It is only with the episodic format of *Paisà* and more fully, we will see, with the fractured textuality of *Germany Year Zero* that a consciousness of loss, the interiorizing of the ruin, and the problematic of reconstruction inscribe themselves emphatically in Rossellini's work, bringing neorealism itself to a point of crisis that is at once its most idiosyncratic and its most revelatory moment.[13] The film's displacement of the Fascist presence-of-the-past to German soil gives rise to a realist confrontation unique in neorealism and at the same time places Rossellini's postwar work within the larger historical perspective.

Central to the concerns of *Germany Year Zero* is, then, Rossellini's direct reflection on the ruins of Europe and on the constellation ruin-monument-habitation in an era of reconstruction. I have drawn the wider outlines of these terms and will go on to develop their particulars in the film, situating them in relation to contemporary discourses and correlates. I will finally suggest their transmutation in Rossellini's later work, in a trajectory reaching into *Journey to Italy* (*Viaggio in Italia*, 1954). From the local war ruins of Italy where, precisely, the "open city" policy of immediate capitulation was rewarded with the relative safety of the precious urban monumental fabric, to Germany's absolute devastation where no such compromises were considered, on to *Journey to Italy*'s Pompeii—the supreme ruinous monument of the Italian peninsula—we witness the evolution of a trope from urgent material reality to the broader cultural perspective and aesthetic principle. On the one hand, the immediate evidence of ruins everywhere begged to be documented on film *before* reconstruction; on the other hand, here were the traces of the longer time-span—the slow-to-change natural and vernacular landscape *and* the older, surviving historical and artistic monuments that continue to define Italy's patrimony and identity. Rossellini will come to associate the contemporary ruins confronting him everywhere with the monuments of Italy's "established" past, among which his protagonists meander searching to reinhabit a present, to locate a future. If Rossellini's emerges as the exemplary work of its time, it is not perhaps for its heroic representation of the Resistance and the war of liberation, nor strictly for the documentary charge of the ruins that his camera captured, but for identifying in these ruins the predicament and the precise charge of contemporary history for cinema. It is this trope that binds quotidian and monumental values, that forges a collectivity out of these arenas of encounter between altering identities, diverse pasts. This figure of the landscape, traversing tradition and modernity, informs Rossellini's aesthetic in what I will come to call his ruinous cinematic edifice.

Corpse-Cities (Modern)

Observing the impenetrability of the close-ups in the last part of *Germany Year Zero,* which offer little psychological insight in the extended scenes of the child Edmund's meanderings through the ruins of Berlin or clearly accounting for the logic of his suicide, André Bazin has asked what it might mean that "the signs of play and the signs of death" are indistinguishable in the film.[14] Noting this particular ambiguity, which extends what he identified elsewhere as a hallmark of Rossellini's realism in *Paisà*,[15] Bazin draws attention to a fundamental disruption of categories in the apparently definitive finale of *Germany Year Zero*, which is set in a deserted ruin, the shell of a high-rise across the street from Edmund's home. The bareness of this final set—bereft, even, of the rubble that fills the streets—its gaping staircases, holes, missing walls and windows, initially seems to constitute for the child a realm of free and uninterrupted movement in opposition to the oppressive interiors of his home (Figure 2.2). In fact, a comparable use of Berlin's ruins as morbid playground where children hover on precarious structures in war games that conclude, more or less willfully, in actual death is also notable in Lamprecht's *Somewhere in Berlin*, a German production of the previous year that Rossellini must have seen. While the war games of children and their use of the ruins in war-torn zones is, alas, not unique to this time and place, Rossellini's attention to the opportunistic and morbid

Figure 2.2. Roberto Rossellini, *Germany Year Zero*, 1948.

underside of children's otherwise innocent actions in precarious spaces and his taking of these to the limits in Edmund's suicide leap, for which the spectator is never quite prepared, *is* unique. Certainly its bleakness is quite different from the redemptive finale of Lamprecht's film, or from the finale of any neorealist production, for that matter.

The final location of *Germany Year Zero*—the gutted building in which Edmund's suicide is enacted—swerves from the palpable opposition set up in the course of the film between the striking sequences shot on the actual streets of Berlin and the indoor scenes of Edmund's overcrowded home, shot in an Italian studio and markedly different in cinematographic style, blocking, and dramatic effect. We first note that the final ruin that Edmund enters and from which he leaps itself presents an interpenetration of interior and exterior spaces—an interpenetration that becomes, in effect, a condition for that seamless movement between play and death that Bazin has observed. Edmund climbs up through the different levels of the ruin, meanders through the open floors from which neighboring ruins are visible, looks through a blown-out window, slides down a beam to a lower level, and leaps to his death through what seems to be a missing wall. When we see his little lifeless body, prostrate, it appears in a semi-interior space, partly enclosed by a broken wall yet open to the street and to the ongoing movements of the city. Throughout this itinerary, views of Edmund's apartment building and the removal of his father's coffin that takes place in front of it are intercut with close-ups of the child looking, acting. Yet these appear dissociated, or merely synthetically joined and, as Bazin observed, fail to cohere in a unified subjective disclosure.

What does it mean, in the first place, to have entered such a ruinous space, a space that has no interiors, a house that provides no shelter but only a macabre skeletal form of indeterminate status whose functions seem exhausted by the range of the child's actions: play and death? Edmund is seen from the start as being "at home" in the ruins—he and his mates are intimately familiar with the ghastly topography, moving about freely, exploiting it in their dealings with the black market and with each other. But as the film progresses Edmund is rejected by these children of the ruins at that moment when he is no longer able to return home, having destroyed whatever foundation it might have had in the figure of the father he had killed. These German lives—Edmund's motherless family, other remains of family groupings, co-tenants in an overcrowded shared apartment—are all marked by those who are absent, who did not survive. Berlin, all of Europe, gapes with the palpable absence of individuals, of entire communities who have disappeared. This human absence—emblematized in Edmund's mind, confused by the teachings of his pederast schoolmaster, in the father deemed unfit to live—now figures an intolerable gap that cannot be filled. The shadow of the past falls heavily upon prospects of restoring life among the ruins of this urban landscape that testifies everywhere to the complicity and guilt of its inhabitants.

Yet another ambiguity animates the final sequence, stirring material and historical questions in its dense fabric. For in light of the actual urban process that hovers from the start in the world of the film—the clearing of Berlin's rubble, the housing problem, the conflicted sense of a future—one wonders if this shell of a building in which Edmund plays and dies is in fact a ruin or rather a construction site, or perhaps a ruin in process of restoration. In fact, the neat arrangements of bricks in some corners, the cleared-up passages between floors, the reenforcement beams, some visibly patched-up or freshly built walls, and the clear attic level all evidence work in progress here (Figure 2.3). Given that the location segments of the film were shot in August and September 1947, more than two years after the bombardments, this semi-restored condition of the high-rise is not surprising: already by the end of December 1945 Berlin had salvaged fifty million bricks—enough to put up 2,500 dwellings.[16] Citizens

Figure 2.3. *Germany Year Zero.*

hurried to remove rubble and rebuild right away, certainly out of urgent material need but one that we surely understand also as the need to clear up in a hurry a psychic space that would make the business, and the consciousness, of life itself bearable vis-à-vis the testimony of these ruins.[17] The inextricability of material and moral fronts—the physical reconstruction of homes and cities on the one hand, and the restoration of identity and community through monumental projects on the other—posited the most challenging questions for post-Nazi Germany. There was obviously an identity, a past that many were in a hurry to forget or to dismiss as a temporary aberration that now, in the process of reconstruction, may be neatly plastered over, along with these walls. Only a few intellectuals, as well as some bold architects, were immediately willing and capable of problematizing reconstruction as part of a profound critical, political debate.[18] For most, the need for healing, for coherence and continuity—even if fabricated and on some levels repressive—prevailed, betraying an inability to face up to the crimes of a regime that most of the population had supported until just recently. The entire enterprise of reconstruction and its representation emerge as the gravest issues in this climate, when pressing material needs or localized concerns were not always of a piece with the larger critical reflection on the saturated symbolic fabric of a city like Berlin.

The tense inextricability *and* lack of cohesion between material and moral imperatives is compounded when one considers that a notion of "dwelling" and "home" surely exceeds the bare necessity of "shelter" to encompass a broader domain of safety, retreat, and the positioning of self in a community. These difficulties, already suggested in *Paisà*'s Neapolitan episode, are raised from the start in the indoor sequences of *Germany Year Zero.* Yet one wonders, in view of the latter film, if a truly habitable space *can* really be cleared and if anything *should* be restored in this overbearing environment where even the most ordinary dwelling, the most banal building touched by war reflected back to Berliners an image of the past, of the ultimate cause of all this damage, and of their own culpability in it. The confusion of the signs of play and of death, and the disruption of interior and exterior spatial definition in the ruin, are extended in this reflection on the monumental function of ruins as evidence and commemoration vis-à-vis the imperative of reconstruction that they posit, their proclaiming of the urgent urban crisis: the housing of the dispossessed.[19] How to weigh the material against the critical and contemplative value of the ruin as monument? The broken emptiness of the final set, a playground-turned-grave for a young child, emerges as an emblematic site of utter devastation, but it also projects the foundation of a future—even though this future's habitability remains in doubt. This state of suspension may ultimately be the intolerable fact with which Edmund, and the viewer, are confronted. Rossellini brings this suspension to a critical point in the careful choice of final set, raising the ordinary residential building to monumental stature and begging for a reconsideration of the very notion of the monument, to which I now attend.

In March 1946, traveling through Germany, the English poet Stephen Spender commented on the condition of its "corpse-cities":

> One passes through street after street of houses whose windows look hollow and blackened—like the open mouth of a charred corpse. . . . The ruin of the city is reflected in the internal ruin of its inhabitants who, instead of being lives that can form a scar over the city's wounds, are parasites sucking at a dead carcass, digging among the ruins for hidden food, doing business at their black market near the cathedral—the commerce of destruction instead of production. . . . The great city looks like a corpse and stinks like one also. . . . The effect of these corpse-towns is a grave discouragement which influences everyone living and working in Germany, the Occupying Forces as much as the German. The destruction is *serious* in more senses than one. It is a climax of deliberate effort, an achievement of our civilization, the most striking result of co-operation between nations in the twentieth century. It is the shape created by our century as the Gothic cathedral is the shape created by the Middle Ages. Everything has stopped here, that fusion of the past within the present, integrated into architecture, which forms the organic life of a city, a life quite distinct from that of the inhabitants who are, after all, only using a city as a waiting-room on their journey through time: that long gigantic life of a city has been killed. . . . The destruction of the city itself, with all its past as well as its present, is like a reproach to the people who go on living there.
>
> . . . The Reichstag and the Chancellory are already sights for sightseers, as they might well be in another

five hundred years. They are the scenes of a collapse so complete that it already has the remoteness of all final disasters which make a dramatic and ghostly impression whilst at the same time withdrawing their secrets and leaving everything to the imagination. The last days of Berlin are as much matters for speculation as the last days of an empire in some remote epoch: and one goes to the ruins with the same sense of wonder, the same straining of the imagination, as one goes to the Colosseum at Rome.[20]

Though very much aware of the hectic activity of rubble clearance and rebuilding, Spender is impressed that very little has, in fact, been cleared away, that there are "landscapes of untouched ruin still left," and that Berlin's inhabitants were ultimately unable, in their "internal ruin," to "form a scar over the city's wounds."[21] Some architects and urban planners considered, in fact, that the monstrous corpse of Berlin should, thereby, be left alone, a monument to modern German history, while a new city might be erected from scratch in another place altogether.[22] Shy of such definitive statements, other thinkers understood that at least some ruins should not be reconstructed; that the destruction of certain edifices was as much part of German history and consciousness as their construction had been; that the profound inscription of the Nazi era upon the landscape must not be bypassed in the reconstruction of a hasty surface continuity with the grander and vaguely innocuous past that preceded Nazism. Yet the critical idea of rebuilding in a way that maintains a ruinous space, an idea that would mobilize a notion of "Year Zero" to construct the future through an interrogation of what has passed, rather than plaster over and continue as if nothing happened, was inconsistent with the strong drive for healing and the traditionalist need for continuity with an earlier, apparently secure past, for a fictive integrity that would surpass all rifts.[23] In their need, material and spiritual,

Germans ended up either removing most debris or else reno-
vating and reusing even the remains of Nazi buildings by removing surface traces of the regime in an effort to suppress
what was seen as a break in the historical landscape.[24] Across
the Alps, Italy's restorative impulse, though faced with a less severe predicament, betrayed similar symptoms. For even though
the crimes and the damages were not on the German scale, the
need to reestablish continuity dictated, of necessity, the fabrication of coherence in the postwar landscape. I have already cited
neorealism's general endorsement of this effort. But in departing from that general tendency toward a more critical reflection on the conflicted dimensions of reconstruction, *Germany
Year Zero* may beg for a redefinition of the neorealist trajectory.

Rossellini's contribution to the debate on ruin, reconstruction, and monument as the conflicted, emblematic question
of the postwar era emerges at its most precise and severe not
in his films produced on Italian soil but, in displaced form, in
Germany Year Zero. The most explicit articulation, approaching the syntax of an argument, is evidenced in the trajectory
that leads toward the ambiguity of final location but that
gains momentum in that central sequence of the film wherein
British officers on tour are seen to visit the ruin of the Reich
Chancellery. Accosted by Edmund and his black-market mates,
they enter one of its great halls, its floor strewn with rubble, to
have Edmund play for them a gramophone record of Hitler's
speeches. Against this voice-over we are offered a succession of
shots in diverse spaces, from the ground-floor hall to the vast
space of Hitler's office, where an anonymous elderly man accompanied by a child stop to look about (Figure 2.4). Then a
high-angle shot (from what is most likely a different building)
pans across a sea of ruins: we see here the debris of dwellings
that collapsed to the ground, having left behind only partial
shells and blown-out walls (Figure 2.5). The empty promise of a
thousand-year Reich reverberates in the hollowed-out center of
power. In this overdetermined sequence—itself monumental,

Figure 2.4. *Germany Year Zero.*

Figure 2.5. *Germany Year Zero.*

one might say, in that symbolic values are writ so large here—Rossellini makes didactically apparent how the dramatic fall of Berlin, a place so charged in the historical imagination, might lend itself to a monumental image of mythical defeat.

In the ruinous landscape that dominates the film, the Chancellory constitutes a distinct center, providing an explanation for an extraordinary historical situation. But it sends us back, changed, to the "ordinary" workaday rubble beyond this charged center, and to its implicated human plight—the punishing conditions, the scarcity of work, food, dwellings. In the activity of Edmund and his mates' lurking here to sell Nazi mementos to tourists are entangled historical-symbolic values as well as vital everyday needs of sustenance in the economic reality of the black market. This central sequence weighs the commemorative import of the monument and the pragmatic, quotidian circumstances that make up a neorealist landscape. For while the haunting voice of the Chancellory, reverberating across the ruins, as forbidding as it is mesmerizing, summons a monumental gaze and anchors it in the totality of the sight, multiple elements in the sequence interfere with that hermetic monumental function. Consider the British sightseers with their guide, observing, interjecting, pointing here and there toward areas where Rossellini's camera does not always follow: we are casually told of the white concrete structure of the bunker, of the spot where Hitler and Eva Braun's bodies were burnt. The mingling of curiosity and morbid prying, of casual observation and shattering realization in the touristic feat: *these* are the objects of Rossellini's camera. At last the visitors join to have their photograph taken by the guide, in a move that makes salient the ritualistic banality of the monument that this site is in danger of becoming (Figure 2.6). Consider as well the children hurrying in and out of the ground level, engaged—out of ignorance? cynicism? or out of pressing material need?—in the commerce of Nazi relics. Consider the hurriedly cranked gramophone that mechanically delivers Hitler's recorded voice

Figure 2.6. *Germany Year Zero.*

as itself a suspended relic. The speech acquires the quality of synthetic commentary in the overtly simple patching of image and sound, marked by its mechanical cinematic fabrication—as in so many didactic voice-over commentaries over newsreel footage. The elderly man and child who pause in the middle-ground of Hitler's office as if to listen are surely only looking about at the imposing space with its massive colonnade. Their step destabilized by debris, these Berliners, surrogates for Edmund and his father, are perhaps too old or too young to work in the rubble. Silent, they certainly appear more humbled and bewildered than the British tourists who, Rossellini emphasizes, can pay for their relics, chat and move about with the ease of occupiers commanding this space, consuming but never quite penetrating it. The inserted high-angle panning shot over the ruins, as if extending these humble visitors' look from the grandiose hall to the wrecks of ordinary buildings below, exposes even further the construction, the *tectonics* of the sequence. Based in stunning cinematographic documentation, the blunt syntax of roughly joined elements interferes with illusionist realism: the aesthetic of the sequence may be seen to mimic the ruinous, monumental cityscape confronting Rossellini's camera.

We know that, beyond the evidence of photographic and filmic documentation, of which Rossellini's film must be counted, the ruin of the Reich Chancellory did not survive as permanent reminder for the edification of citizens and tourists— and to test Spender's projection that it would bear a rarified air comparable to that of ancient monuments. More so than the Germans, foreigners—Churchill among them—initially visited the bunker underneath the Chancellory, already a tourist sight in 1946. Spender reports that for months there were still books of architecture to be found on shelves above Hitler's bed in the bunker: this would have offered a certain insight on the particular dictatorial imagination while projecting perhaps, as we do here, the high stakes of reconstruction and of the monument, before and after the collapse. The sight was closed in 1948 and the Chancellory subsequently leveled by the Soviets to be completely destroyed, in secret, in the 1980s by the East Germans, its stones used in a nearby train depot and in two Soviet war memorials.[25] The original architectural ruin, monumental or minor, was in fact deemed a technical and ideological obstacle to reconstruction. As ruinous monument the Chancellory might have lent itself, as Rossellini's film intimates, to mythified consumption and cult practices (like the sacred or taboo site of ritual)—in a mode all too consistent with the original fantasy of its builders. That Albert Speer, Hitler's official architect, anticipated the ruin as promise of future mythical aggrandizement built into his heroic architecture rendered the postwar consideration of the ruin and the monument, as such, problematic. The architectural hypertrophy of Fascist monumental projects under both Nazi and Fascist regimes—projects that often involved the destruction of old neighborhoods and the displacement of populations, often the urban poor—now effected a suspicion of any monument, including the edifying ruins of war whose pedagogical value was not universally embraced.[26]

Debates on the monument and on monumentality thus took a critical turn in the wake of war, but perforce harnessed terms already raised in the preceding era—and perhaps posited already then against Fascist monumentality. Lewis Mumford's 1938 declaration of the "death of the monument" had already questioned the adequacy of the monument to modernity as such and called for the displacement of its commemorative "House of the Dead" by the modern dwelling, the "House of the Living."[27] Yet after the war, when architecture had to focus on the pressing problems of housing and the resuscitation of the vital channels of everyday life in and between cities, many still maintained that the restoration of earlier monuments damaged by war, the construction of new ones, and the commemorative use of the ruins themselves should all play a role in organizing the community's material and symbolic cohesion in what was still deemed a valid monumental function.[28] It became a challenge, however, to dissociate large-scale symbolic edifices from the oppressive regimes that exploited them so massively in recent years. Already in 1943 in Italy, envisioning the problem of reconstruction in a postwar that he will not survive to witness, Giuseppe Pagano, architect, founding editor of the influential journal *Casabella,* photographer, and critic, revealed a heightened awareness of the stakes at a time when some proto-neorealist filmmakers, Rossellini for one, could not yet dissociate themselves from the reigning discourses. Having rejected earlier the waste of resources in the monumental zone E-42, the World's Fair planned in celebration of the twentieth anniversary of Fascism, Pagano addressed the historical and social responsibility in the postwar rebuilding of homes for those most in need, pitting that task, precisely, against the "luxury" of overrestoration and monument-obsession.

> [Monuments should not be reconstructed] for artistic reasons not foreign to . . . the fascination with the ruinous, with the incomplete, the unfinished; for artistic

reasons that partake in the true life of a monument
and prefer to see it ruined thus, but still saturated with
genuine suggestiveness when a cautious, caring hand
has treated it in its gravest wounds, rendering it a pure
symbol of "memory," an absolute sign of "document"
free of rhetorical function and transformed into "pure
beauty," beyond the utilitarian and practical interests of
our contemporaries.[29]

Pagano estimates that Italy's war ruins in their projected totality would still fall short of the damage perpetrated by the regime's mania of the "sventramenti"—the disembowelment of
old residential neighborhoods, especially in the imperial capital, to make way for monumental zones in Fascism's projects
of urban renewal. Rather than "reactionary" and "infantile"
attachment to the overrestoration of monuments, liable to result in a distortion of historical reality, Pagano promotes—in
his writing as in his photography (Figure 2.7)—the ruined fragment, the unrestored remnant for its authentic value as document, as art, and as symbolic commemoration.

Let us be satisfied with resolving at least the problem
of human habitation in an order of taste and of technology suited to a coherent and mature society. And, who
knows, but that by this honest path we shall prepare for
the coming generations the elements, and the stimuli,
and the conclusions and the experiences that will enable
them to confront one fine day also the problem of the
monument.[30]

What is perceived as the grave destruction of war to the cultural heritage may offer a unique occasion for radical renewal
in urban planning. Pagano suggests that focused attention on
the problem of habitation and urban planning might be a wel-
come side-effect of the bombardments: it might offer a lesson

Figure 2.7. Giuseppe Pagano, *Corfù*, 1943. Archivio fotografico Giuseppe Pagano, Napoli.

in the vernacular arena to enlighten, one day, the luxurious realm of the monument. The hierarchy of center and periphery, representative and quotidian, major and minor, for all its physical-topographical and symbolic-ideological values, is reversed in what may be posited as a manifesto on postwar rebuilding. According to Pagano's proto-neorealist position the supreme achievement of the present should be articulated and honored in the spaces of human habitation: might this quotidian arena displace the monstrous "shape of our century" that Spender identified in the ruins of the World War?

Pagano's ideal was only partially realized. Urgent rebuilding in Italy's immediate postwar period often followed a makeshift course rather than sound planning. First, several monumental plans, launched while still under Fascism, were brought to completion in Rome between 1947 and 1950, some with little or no adjustment.[31] Pagano's priorities also were unheeded in that, before resolving housing problems, attention turned indeed to monuments, albeit new ones. We will consider the Mausoleum of the Fosse Ardeatine (1944–49), the first postwar monumental project in Italy, that commemorates the March 24, 1944, Nazi massacre of 335 Romans—alluded to in *Open City* and, perhaps, haunting the image of the cave I have described in *Paisà*.[32] Heated debate also focused public attention on the 1946 Monument to the Dead in the German Concentration Camps in the Cimitero Monumentale in Milan. Invested planning of proletariat neighborhoods that would respond to Pagano's concerns—and to his interest in vernacular and regional forms as consistent with an innovative modernism—arrived a bit later, with the INA-Casa national housing plan that became law in 1949 and the vast scale of building projects in the following decades, such as the Viale Etiopia residential towers (1948–54) and the Tiburtino quarter (1949–54) in Rome.[33] Evidently the need for monuments preceded and was perhaps experienced as preparing the ground for material and social solutions to the housing problem. Symbolic commemoration, like funerary architecture, partakes of that primal imperative to bury the dead, without which the past cannot be laid to rest and time cannot take its proper course.

Indeed, the new Italian monuments, considered together even as we differentiate their forms and connotations, may be said to prefigure Rossellini's conception of location, displacement, and the ambiguity of spaces in the ruin / monument as described earlier. The Mausoleum of the Fosse Ardeatine by Mario

Fiorentino and others is, in Manfredo Tafuri's words, "an impenetrable mass in suspension, a mute testimony facing the site of the massacre." Namely, it is a monument *on location*. Its momentous, earthy weight hangs upon the lined-up graves below, so that a complex of visceral devices and allusions figure processes of projection and identification for the observer, or the survivor (Figure 2.8). Conversely the Milan Monument to the Dead in the German Concentration Camps, by the BBPR group, is symbolic not only for its removal from its referent but for its abstract, cubic-skeletal transparency. A metal lattice on a stone base, an urn filled with earth from German camps at its center, the geometric BBPR monument is not corporeal or identificatory in the experience of its materials, masses, and form (Figure 2.9). Humble in size, despite or perhaps against the immensity of the event it commemorates, it transpires as more intellectual, and more lyrical, than the Fosse Ardeatine

Figure 2.8. Mario Fiorentino et al., Mausoleum of the Fosse Ardeatine, Rome, 1944–49. Photograph by Sean S. Anderson.

monument. In fact it can hardly be envisioned in a city like Rome but only, perhaps, in that singular modern Italian city, Milan. The conclusive sense of commemoration in the funerary tradition that one finds in the Fosse Ardeatine may be juxtaposed with the BBPR monument's abstract reflection on continuities with prewar Italian modernism, specifically the rationalist tradition in architecture, thus critically poised against the heavy neoclassicism of the surrounding cemetery. Its lyricism that, Tafuri suggests, "makes us look backward, that does not let us forget, is, however, accompanied by a commitment to search for specific tools that could contribute to the problem of reconstruction: this culture intent on the new immediately appeared to be tied to discursive practices in use since the twenties and thirties."[34] These distinct yet complementary postwar projects disturbed traditional monumental "habits" while bringing into that symbolic arena the functional, industrial constructions

Figure 2.9. BBPR, Monument to the Dead in the German Concentration Camps, Cimitero Monumentale, Milan, 1946. Photograph by Norberto Lenzi.

of workaday modernity. The tensions between an "antirhetorical" stance and heroic residues in these monuments—most clearly the Roman one with its appended figurative sculpture perhaps poised to embrace both intellectual and collective, modernist and realist sensibilities—reproduces the neorealist disposition.[35] In just these contradictory ways did the two seminal postwar monuments—*and* the debates surrounding them— succeed in fulfilling symbolic, purgative functions, and in ways that echo Rossellini's ruins: his gaping voids that are never light, his oppressive spaces that barely shelter the dispossessed. They disclose, with Rossellini, a reflection—or is it a conclusive judgment?—on the past in projecting a contingent potentiality, a doubt, an opening. In the obstructive gravity of Rossellini's rough joining of elements, in his deliberately simple shot/ reverse shots, location and gaze, material evidence and consciousness are laid out. They do not quite coalesce in a totality but open up passages through irrevocable loss, projecting onto the everyday.

Within sight of the monument, the contingency of daily life persists, and itself wavers between modernist revisions of the housing problem and a longing for earlier states of being. Tafuri suggests how on the margins of Rome, in the Tiburtino housing complex, traditional, local, even rural building motifs perhaps assuaged the anxiety and nostalgia of intellectuals seeking immersion in an organic collectivity via neorealism's antirhetorical, antiformalist aspirations; or how the INA-Casa high-rise quarter on Viale Etiopia negotiated between grand scale and the minor detail, between "volumetric imperiousness" and nostalgic populism. This negotiation of tensions is perhaps already inscribed in Ernesto Nathan Rogers's "House for Everyone," first articulated on the pages of Vittorini's journal *Il Politecnico* in 1945, and subsequently his notion of "the House of Man." These articles proposed not only a material solution to the most urgent problem of the postwar period but the symbolic union of "a style, a technique, a morality as terms

of a single function . . . [and] a matter of building a society."
This vision of a material, social, and symbolic reconstruction
in an aesthetic-cum-ethic of daily life evoked, consistently with
neorealism, not the private bourgeois dwelling but the emer-
gency shelter and the elemental, communal dwelling of the
proletariat and the poor.[36]

These aspirations of contemporary architecture, and the
circumstances and material reality it had to confront, are consistent with neorealist cinema's valorization of the local, representational, and in effect lyrical everydayness of postwar
reconstruction, *even when* channeled to monumental functions.
Indeed, one finds in the neorealist imagination a negotiation of
epic monumentality and local, piecemeal practice, of aesthetic
consciousness and collective, indeed popular, representation. A
reciprocity, or inversion, of monument and collective dwelling
was echoed in German reconstruction as well when, after the
war, the imperative of housing was elevated to the status of
symbol, assuming the representational, ideological, and didactic functions of the monument.[37] It is consistent with the trajectory of *Germany Year Zero* from the central, overdetermined
monument of the Chancellory sequence to the residential
ruin / construction site of the film's closing movement: a closing that, we will see, opens onto the surge of the everyday. The
architectural example finally suggests how neorealism could
define itself not as mimetically representational, or restorative
and backward looking, but as participating in a continued rebuilding of reality, wherein its "realism" gains an "oppositional"
consciousness. If what came to be called neorealist architecture turned to a vernacular aesthetic and ideology, heroicized
the marginal, the quotidian, in the attempt to forge a collective out of disparate social forces, it did so also to differentiate itself from neoclassical historicism on the one hand and,
on the other, from the grids of rationalist abstraction and *Neue
Sachlichkeit*. Similarly, Rossellini's neorealist breakthrough—
which I have now redefined in the displaced production of

Germany Year Zero—is differentiated from both the classical-representational studio molds as from the iconoclasm of the first cinematic avant-gardes.

In the interlacing of positions, perspectives, lacunary views, we discern built already into the ruins of the Chancellory sequence not the static, sublimating dimension of the monument that lends itself whole to tourist consumption but intimations of a fractured, malleable, contingent vision that modifies what the monument and its relics, actual and cinematographic, involve in a minor, vernacular, neorealist key. If, as Roland Barthes postulated, the ephemeral, *mortal* photograph has already usurped and undone the role of the monument in modernity, is it not possible that Rossellini's cinematography reanimates—but as a lacunary, contingent perception—the ruinous edifice, disturbing it with human consequence, with a multiplicity of views and uses, the pressures and the transactions of the everyday?[38] While the ruinous, grandiose monument may no longer epitomize the "shape" of the twentieth century, its inscription in film, itself now marked as ruinous edifice, might fulfill this function. Rossellini projects the momentous questions raised in the Chancellory onto a mundane contingent terrain, no less devastating, of the life that we see lived out—and ended, annihilated—in the ruins. Suspended, the ruin of the Chancellory gives way to the ordinary, anonymous, part ruin, part communal high-rise in process of rebuilding. The gravity of this final site displaces that of the official monument and, we have seen, in its own ambiguous spaces and disruptive cinematic vision inscribes Rossellini's leap to a more comprehensive, more severe consciousness of the postwar condition.

Corpse-Cities (Ancient)

There is a way in which the disruption of categories in the devastating ending of *Germany Year Zero* is synonymous with the crumbling of the solid cinematic edifice—conventionalized, polished, academicized in the preceding decades in Hollywood, in UFA, in Cinecittà. Rossellini's deliberate paring down or dissociation of shot and reverse shot, of close-ups—themselves inexpressive—and insert views, the dissociation of cause and effect in the interpenetration of play and death, of interiors and exteriors, ruin and reconstruction, effect a disruption that is itself part and parcel of the mute, stunning impact of the film. Its contingency is not the film's conclusion in ambiguity (which one doubts, as Rossellini's judgment of Germany is stern), but in the use of the opaque, suspended fragment, the incorporation of loss and failure in the ruinous architectonics of the film. If cinema, a tool of ordinary Fascist propaganda even in Roberto Rossellini's hands just a few years earlier,[39] was complicit in Fascist monumentality—namely, in heroic mass commemoration turned to the past in static, unambiguous mythification—then how will it now approach the postwar memorializing and reconstructive project? How to rebuild out of these ruins? Rather than going on to refine his cinematic language toward a classical modality after the war—the move that American investors expected from him following *Open City*—Rossellini manifests, violently, even if with something of a delay, a break with the transparent monumental structures of classical cinema. In his ruinous vision there emerges, rather, a set of tropes that depart from classical narration, as well as from prewar modernisms. Rossellini's look is defined not by a metaphoric juxtaposition of fragments as practiced by the first cinematic avant-gardes—one thinks of Eisensteinian montage or surrealist poetics—but by the crumbling of dramatic expression, the draining of signs in a severe and didactic linearity, supported by digression, metonymy, and, subsequently, taking a self-alienating turn to allegory. These are Rossellini's figures of the ruin, figures of failure adopted when expression is traumatized and cannot be sustained in integrated structures but remains suspended, contingent. Starting from *Paisà,* Rossellini's bypassing of the secure classical edifice, his sense of the cinematic image and narrative as fallible and contingent, his mute, apparently inarticulate confrontation, on location, with limit situations that—as Deleuze has noted—are at the same time banal now opened a door to failure.[40]

Rossellini works under the sign of loss and failure throughout this period. For contingency carries with it a threat to stability in a moment when stability is most wanting, a disruption of the initial neorealist impulse to heal, to bury the dead, to go on unhindered. Encompassing continuities and discontinuities, spatial and temporal, contingency makes for a difficult relation to the past, now undone by the refusal of settled memory and of its illusions in secure monuments. It makes, in fact, for a dispersive, even explosive form in the present, promoting a disturbance that is critical to the always-unfinished business of history.[41] Rossellini must have sensed that a cinema made out of ruin and loss, and at the same time a cinema that participates in reconstruction, a cinema in need of renewing its own modalities, cannot be confined to petrifying the past—not even in the monumental image of the ruin. Neither the Chancellory as tourist sight, contained and consumed, neither the residential building, a ruin in process of restoration, nor its conversion to a monumental grave for a young child—none of these adds up to a conclusive image. *Germany Year Zero* is suspended in an upward tilt of the camera from the little corpse with the lamenting figure of an unknown girl beside it, up to a passing streetcar: no impression is stabilized between the ruin and the gaping construction site, between the iconic image and the surging street, between living in the grave that is Berlin, and dying in it.

In retrospect, it is hard not to associate the ruinous views of *Germany Year Zero,* historically specific as they are, with Rossellini's turn some five years later to what one might call Berlin's phantasmic sister-city: Pompeii as it emerges into view in *Journey to Italy* (Figures 2.10–2.11). In both films Rossellini's

Figure 2.10. *Germany Year Zero.*

Figure 2.11. Roberto Rossellini, *Journey to Italy,* 1954.

protagonists meander through ruinous cityscapes—the former perpetrated by recent war, the latter by distant natural disaster and by time—that embrace them in a vision of the past as an immense catastrophe, its debris extending as far as the eye can see.[42] The ruins of modernity in *Germany Year Zero* and the archaic remnants in *Journey to Italy* are distinct, yet Rossellini's cinematic excavation compares them under the glance of his emphatically contemporary, itinerant observers. Thus both films work to bring their monumental images of the past to a crisis wherein the limit vision, disclosed by the ruinous landscape, is released in a final surge of the ordinary street, crowds, traffic, offering no definitive answers except in the indication that things go on despite what one has seen. We have launched this discussion in attending to a proleptic instance of such crisis of seeing in *Paisà*'s Neapolitan episode. In the move from the contemporary ruins of *Germany Year Zero* to the classical, epic but also natural realms of *Journey to Italy*, we pass from realist milieu—itself partaking in the pressing contemporary debates that I have mapped out—to allegorical circumlocution. For while the earlier film still had to confront the urgent reconstruction of life out of its ruins, the latter work, already removed from the vital postwar issues of survival and rebuilding, gathers force as a glaring figure.[43]

The loose narrative dwells on an English couple on a visit to Naples. Their marital crisis and reconciliation provides the ostensible plot of *Journey to Italy*, yet this does not proceed by character development and dramatic exchanges but is, rather, diffused in a series of excursions (largely on the part of the Ingrid Bergman character) to tourist sights that span the architectural and artistic remains and the volcanic phenomena of Naples and its environs. Their disruptive impressions echo elements we identified in the final sequence of *Germany Year Zero*: a "porous" interpenetration of unfinished and of ruinous fragments, of regeneration and decay, but also of the sacred and the vernacular, of monument and street, interiors and exteriors, private and public, observer and participant in the remarkable spectacle of the Neapolitan streets. In the lively city nestled in the shadow of an active volcano, alongside stunning sites of devastation in the ghost cities of Pompeii and Herculaneum, such porosity of categories is effected by the proximity of life and death that make up this landscape, adding a sense of fatality to its flux, a mournful poignancy to its exuberant beauty.[44]

In Rossellini's obverse melodrama, the interpenetration of categories is joined with the fracturing of the protagonists' bourgeois, circumscribed selves; it reaches a crisis among the spectacular ruins of Pompeii. The film's "limit vision" is achieved here, in the couple's witnessing of the exhumation of human remains at the archaeological dig. Like the negative image of the living streets of Naples where the business of life is seen in continuous flux, the Pompeiian landscape—ruined houses in different states of excavation and restoration, empty streets, scaffoldings, digs—evokes an apocalyptic vision of an entire city and its inhabitants having been swallowed and regurgitated by the earth. In preparation for the climactic moment of the film, Rossellini gives special attention, in didactic manner, to the unearthing of human remains: when hollow ground is identified, plaster is injected to fill the empty spaces left by corpses that have disintegrated. The surrounding volcanic ash is then removed so that a mold of the entire body's outward form and gesture, often incorporating skeleton remnants, engulfed in the moment of asphyxiation, emerges into light.

These are relics of the past, an extraordinary kind of ruin, distinct from archaeological monuments and artifacts. These bodily indices of the catastrophe caught in distressingly vivid gestures are as expressive as statues in a museum but bound, like mummies, to their origins as imprinted guarantees of authenticity—in excess of artistic representations—that renders them so poignant. As she looks down at the traces of a man and a woman, whose lives were interrupted on August 24, AD 79—a couple suspended as a solid imprint and brought to light before

Rossellini's camera—the woman cries out. The archaic terrain and the modern look, documentary footage and fictional, acted elements are confronted here. The synthetic matching of these disparate domains in simple shot/reverse shot configurations infuses this limit situation—akin to ones we identified earlier in *Paisà* and *Germany Year Zero*—with uncanny effect. For an excruciating moment the plaster casts appear as mirror images of the protagonists who, gazing down as if at their own reflections in an open grave, encounter the fearful, static symmetry of death that, as the framing and editing suggest, returns their look (Figures 2.12–2.13).[45] Confronted by this mirroring—or as in a photographic negative where distinct features are not immediately discernible—one recognizes in this instant the allegorical figure of death hovering in the optical surface. Indeed, the photographic image itself finds in the unearthed Pompeiian couple its ancient forebear: a positive replica of a negative imprint that has arrested living motion and is brought to light in an elaborate process, unfolding in time.[46] The pared-down, tectonic simplicity of the shot/reverse shot, in further draining illusionistic realism, amplifies the mournful allegorical trajectory of the film as a whole.

This morbid embrace of the earth recalls the closing images of the child's corpse among the ruins in *Germany Year Zero*. There, no distinct barrier separated the life that sustained itself in these ruins and the death predicated therein. So too, in *Journey to Italy*, viewer and viewed, original living body and its vacated image, figure and ruinous landscape are bound. At this limit vision of the ancient corpse-city, Rossellini's observer also confronts *herself* as an emptied shell, a shadow of her former self cast in the image of death. The landscape of ruins is condensed here as allegorical filmic figure. It reflects in turn an image of the body itself—one's own body—as ruin. It is proper that at such a limit situation, where figures are drained by the workings of allegory, the ruin's bodies and the body's ruin join in a landscape that emerges, in its totality, as a funerary

Figure 2.12. *Journey to Italy.*

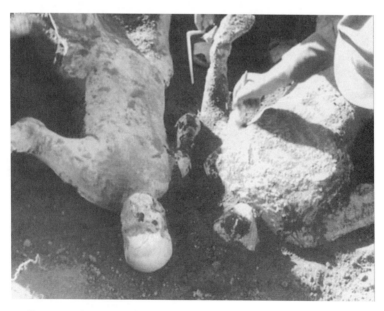

Figure 2.13. *Journey to Italy.*

monument. Yet, again, its deadly grip is released in the final instances of *Journey to Italy*, in a return from the land of the dead to the surging street where the miracles of daily life—of its recognitions, reconciliations—persist. Such is this cinema's monumental mode, not petrified at the limit vision but joining it with the banal as modernist emblem. Here Rossellini's post-war can conclude.

THREE

Choral: Visconti's Dramaturgy of Nature

> Cinema being of its essence a dramaturgy
> of Nature, there can be no cinema without
> the setting up of an open space in place of
> the universe rather than as part of it.
>
> —André Bazin, "Theater and Cinema," 1951

Verismo; Photography

When Luchino Visconti undertook in 1947 the production of his second feature film, he was ostensibly committed, under the auspices of the Italian Communist Party, to a documentary rendering of the labors and hardship of Sicilian fishermen. This was to be the first in a projected trilogy on Sicilian workers that, following the *Episodio del mare*—the "Episode of the Sea," a subtitle that survives in the opening credits of *La terra trema*—would treat the strike in a sulfur mine and, finally, the peasantry's occupation of the land whereupon, with all three orders of labor united, the revolutionary struggle would be resolved.[1] Francesco Rosi, assistant on the production, attests to Visconti's commitment to the documentary project, but he also asserts that it was above all Giovanni Verga's *I Malavoglia*—the uncredited source text for the project—that Visconti always had in mind for a film set in the specifically designated location of the novel, the fishing village of Aci Trezza, on the shore of the Ionian Sea.[2] An avid reader of the European novel, versed in French, German, and Russian literature and in the nineteenth-century Lombard novelist Alessandro Manzoni, Visconti sought to redefine for postwar Italian cinema a realist aesthetic drawing on regionalist sources in literary and pictorial traditions. Although regionalist strands persisted, as we have already observed, under Fascism, these were largely geared toward rural folk mythology that would forge a heroic union with the Italian soil rather than expose gaps and conflicts between national and regional orders.[3] In privileging pre-Fascist models such as Verga, Visconti sought to reconstruct a cultural genealogy that would bypass this immediate, tainted past while maintaining historical and social awareness.

Verga's practice and theory of verismo in the late nineteenth century are a touchstone of Italian literary realism. Its sources were markedly naturalist, after the French tradition. Possibly in France a broader and more nuanced realist tradition, which Italy did not match, made the distinct methods of naturalism stand out. Some of these do inform, however, the Italian variant: a scientific (or *scientistic*) sociological ambition inflected by a deterministic, even positivist outlook on narrative causality, namely, the relation of character to heredity and milieu. In the exemplary work of Émile Zola such aspects, expounded in rigorous descriptive method of systematic observation, would be interpreted as more markedly modern, indeed progressivist, vis-à-vis earlier realist projects—it is in such terms that Erich Auerbach compares Zola to the Goncourts and to Flaubert. Verga too employed sociological and linguistic research and cataloging methods. But one might also note that, broadly compared, verismo did not apply an equally minute, deep investigation of motives and circumstances, privileging instead the bare impact of a fabric of "facts" imprinted whole, as it were, and seemingly unprocessed in descriptive narration or analysis.[4]

Visconti and his neorealist colleagues were drawn by Verga's seemingly unadorned yet artistically potent confrontation—by no means, as we will see, simple or conflict free—with a contemporary regionalist reality of hitherto neglected milieus, on the margin of Italy's slow entry into European modernization. Verismo, in this way, came to be a paradigm for what could be understood as an analogous historical response to Fascist modernization, to which a proto-neorealist consciousness began to apply itself already in the 1930s. But it was also the epic bent of Verga's work—its tragic-heroic pathos, its poetic layering of voices—that appealed to Visconti when he traveled along the eastern coast of Sicily still during Fascism, years before *La terra trema*'s production, in the footsteps of Verga's narratives.[5] This was the period of Visconti's encounter with the group of early theorists and practitioners of what became neorealism, associated with the magazine *Cinema* and including Giuseppe De Santis, Mario Alicata, and Gianni Puccini among others who came to constitute Visconti's professional and intellectual milieu in Rome from around 1940. Their collaboration in fact resulted in several treatments of Verga's writings toward possible adaptation as well as critical reflections on verismo as model. Visconti's first script of a Verga narrative in that period, "L'amante di Gramigna" ("Gramigna's Mistress") was flatly rejected by the Fascist minister of popular culture who had written on it with a red pencil: "Enough with those bandits!"[6] Tales of bandits and their mistresses unfolding in a scorched, primal Sicilian landscape seemed hardly adequate to the desired image of a centralized, imperially ambitious Fascist Italy as it was entering the war: an Italy that denied the voice of indigenous cultures that might corrupt the standard language, question the Europeanized progress of the north, critique—as Antonio Gramsci had already done—the virtual colonization of the south, and mar the workings of a Fascist rural ideology as well as the "White Telephone" genre production of Cinecittà. What was it, in the complexity of the Verghian model as read by Visconti, that offered such a departure from Fascist regionalism and its mythologizing functions? One answer is offered by the fortunes of Visconti's first realized project, for following the rejection of "Gramigna," he went on to adapt Cain's *The Postman Always Rings Twice*, following the suggestion of his mentor Jean Renoir. This imported text may have initially seemed to the authorities less threatening than Verga's though the result, *Ossessione* of 1942, was notoriously censored following its production and first screening. Once again the Fascist establishment, this time in the person of Vittorio Mussolini, the Duce's son, whom we have already encountered as general editor of the magazine *Cinema,* sought to suppress the future of the film, angrily pronouncing, "This is not Italy!" In light of such verdicts it is clear that Visconti's regionalist practice was deemed threatening to Fascist rural ideology. Its image of the Italian landscape is inscribed by unsublimated tensions traversing at every level the body of *Ossessione,* whose illicit and murderous passions evidently interfered with official visions of national character and the health of the countryside.

Dwelling on the critical fortunes of Verga, the literary critic Romano Luperini observes how a revival of interest in his work after the Second World War rehearsed an earlier revival in the wake of the social and political upheavals of the First World War and how this interest surges again in the 1960s. Luperini credits this attention on the part of advanced critics in periods of crisis to Verga's exceptional joining of an investigative approach to material data with an avant-garde opening to formal rupture.[7] He goes on to list a string of fruitful contradictions that animate the language of neorealist critics regarding *I Malavoglia* : regionalist specificity laced with Homeric classicism, faithfulness to the conditions of the place yet traversed by the fantastical connotations of the Sicilian landscape. The oxymoron "verità e poesia"—"truth and poetry"—is emblematic in the bifurcated commitment implied in the title of an influential article by Mario Alicata and Giuseppe De Santis, published in *Cinema* in 1941. In this early neorealist credo, Alicata and De Santis define the cinema as driven in principle by a documentary impulse, but also as an inherently narrative form, bound to the novel and to realism as the novel's most powerful mode. Verga's work is taken as a prime model for a properly Italian, yet unprovincial, realist cinema:

Instead of the more habitual use of back doors to realism, there is a main entrance. . . . Giovanni Verga. Not
only did he create a great body of poetry, but he created
a country as well, an epoch, a society. Since we believe
in an art which above all creates truth, the Homeric,
legendary Sicily of *I Malavoglia, Mastro Don Gesualdo,
L'amante di Gramigna,* and *Jeli il pastore* offers us both
the human experience and a concrete atmosphere.
Miraculously stark and real, it could give inspiration to
the imagination of our cinema which looks for things
in the space-time of reality to redeem itself from the easy
suggestions of a moribund bourgeois state.[8]

And in the second installment of the article:

We too, want to take our movie camera into the streets,
into the fields, into the ports, into the factories of our
country; we too are persuaded that one day we shall make
our finest cinema by following the slow and weary pace
of the laborer as he returns home, narrating the essential
poetry of a new and pure life, that contains within itself
the secret of its aristocratic beauty.[9]

Such romantic glorification of the humble worker in the
heroics of the everyday is the most salient feature shared by
neorealist ideologies ranging from Marxist to Christian and
humanist varieties, and verismo's epic grandeur invested, even
within the confines of a short story, in marginal, hitherto neglected subjects. However, the ambition to reconcile a social
and political agenda, informed by documentary sources, with a
so-called poetry of truth inevitably rehearsed some of the productive contradictions already embedded in verismo. In later
neorealist positions a shift to a more outspoken social and realist commitment often resulted, paradoxically, not in a more
rigorous practice but in what is often noted as the school's

sometimes naive, self-defeating notion of capturing "life as it really is." In this way, soon after the "truth and poetry" articles, Alicata himself comes to condemn the digressive, "lyricizing" elements—"the sound of the waves . . . the sublime narrative rhythm"—in an adaptation of Verga, recommending instead a linear, progressive structure advanced by the emblematic conflict of types and wills in the social drama, in place of the mythical temporality of the original novel.[10] But Visconti is frankly explicit in his fascination with, precisely, the archaic rhythm and pathos of *I Malavoglia*. In a 1941 article for *Cinema* titled "Tradizione e invenzione," he notes:

> It occurred to me that . . . the key to a cinematographic realization of *I Malavoglia* is perhaps all here, that is, in the attempt to resound and to grasp the magic of that rhythm, of that "vague desire for the unknown, for that realization that one is not well off or that one might improve one's lot," which is the poetic substance of that play of destinies that cross each other without ever meeting. . . . A rhythm that gives the religious and fatal tone of an ancient tragedy to those humble facts unfolding in everyday life, to that story apparently consisting of scraps, of refuse, of matters of no importance, to that shred of a peasant "chronicle," enframed by the monotonous sound of the waves that break on the Faraglioni.[11]

Neorealism appears in these early articulations on the pages of *Cinema* as neither unconscious of nor denying the aesthetic drive or auratic resonance that would inflect its ideological program and epistemological claims. The chronicle, "consisting of scraps, of refuse" of "everyday life" but infused with high poetic grandeur, will inform Visconti's realist project whose synthetic complexity was quite conscious. It will keep its hold on Visconti's imagination even after the war, as he will commit himself to a documentary project sponsored by a political party on the eve of elections. His was not an artistic sensibility to shy away from the charge of cultural and affective connotations that would inform even the most radically committed work of the era.[12]

Gianni Puccini, Visconti's colleague in the *Cinema* group, tells of an evening—just before Italy's entry into the war—spent in conversation on the subject of Giovanni Verga between the aspiring filmmaker and Gianni's father, Mario Puccini, himself a writer who had known Verga personally. Puccini the elder gave Visconti an old picture postcard of the landscape of Aci Trezza, which Visconti hung in his study. Though dating some fifty years before Visconti's film, this image—with its prospect of the marine horizon enclosed between the volcanic rocks that punctuate the shoreline—might have appeared to him like an inherently cinematic panorama waiting to unfold, for he would later say that it was "of the landscape in that postcard that was later born the desire for *La terra trema*" (Figure 3.1).[13] And it was

Figure 3.1. The old postcard. Written in Visconti's hand on top: "Aci Trezza, where Giovanni Verga's *I Malavoglia* takes place." Fondo Luchino Visconti of the Fondazione Istituto Gramsci.

this image that first drew him to explore the eastern shores of Sicily and visit Aci Trezza. Upon his return he asked the painter Renato Guttuso to prepare a series of drawings of Sicilian fishermen, with Verga's characters in mind. In "Tradizione e invenzione" Visconti affirms the value of a "visual and plastic reality" available to a cinematic adaptation of the *verista* project; he raises more broadly a conception of cinema as capable of dismantling the symbolic mediation of language in favor of the sensory concreteness of cinematographic realism.[14] Interestingly, Verga himself had promoted an increasingly visual approach to verismo: an acute linguistic consciousness led him to reflect on the gap between language and action, verbal description and visual evidence. This visual sensibility, already signaled in the literary text, peaks in that short story that Visconti approached first, "L'amante di Gramigna." Herein we might describe verismo's impasse, its modernist perception, and locate its deeper promise for neorealism.

Verga was reluctant to burden much of his writing, especially in such a short story as "L'amante di Gramigna," with extensive descriptive detail. What distinguishes his vivid prose is, rather, the interweaving of Sicilian dialect expressions. The *verista* ambition to let the material "speak for itself" is thus distinct from the "realistic effect" of the seemingly "unsignifying notation" described by Roland Barthes as effecting an illusion of a raw and concrete reality imprinting itself in the work of sheer description, *as if* independent from the commands of signification.[15] In Verga, linguistic data—assembled as in an anthropological survey or catalog—suggests an evidential, documentary aspiration, as if to give voice to the object itself, but not before it is translated into high literary Italian. Close to *I Malavoglia*'s adapted language of gossip, superstition, proverbs, and epithets, "L'amante di Gramigna" is marked by a synthetic, layered style—engaging the voices of the place even as it affords a deliberate distance, a remarkable pathos. The heroic dimension of primal passions in the rough, humble milieu is punctuated

by the laconic irony of understatement as narration is stripped
to bare outline. Curiously, almost a third of Verga's story of
1880 is taken up by an expository prologue, a *verista* credo of
sorts addressed to his contemporary and colleague Salvatore
Farina. For its subtle evocation of all the terms that were to animate the cinematic sensibility of Visconti and his colleagues, it
is worth considering the "Gramigna" prologue in some detail,
knowing how closely Visconti must have contemplated its implications for cinema.

> Dear Farina, here is not a story but the sketch of a
> story. It will at least have the merit of being very short
> and of being very factual—a human document, as they
> say nowadays—interesting perhaps for you, and for all
> those who study the great book of the human heart. I
> shall repeat it to you just as I picked it up along the paths
> in the countryside, with nearly the same simple and
> picturesque words that characterize popular narration,
> and you will certainly prefer to find yourself face to face
> with the naked and unadulterated fact, without having
> to look for it between the lines of the book, through the
> lens of the writer.
>
> The simple human fact will always make one think;
> it will always have the force of what *has really been.* . . .
>
> We renew the artistic process to which we owe so
> many glorious monuments, with a different method,
> more attentive to details and more intimate. We will-
> ingly sacrifice the effect of the denouement to the logi-
> cal, necessary development of passions and facts leading
> to the denouement, which is thus rendered less unfore-
> seen, less dramatic perhaps, but not less fatal. We are
> more modest, if not more humble; but the demonstra-
> tion of this obscure tie between causes and effects will
> certainly not be less useful to the art of the future. Shall
> we ever reach such perfection in the study of passions

that it will become useless to continue in this study of
the inner man? Will the science of the human heart,
which will be the fruit of the new art, develop so much
and so generally all the powers of the imagination that
in the future the only novels written will be *faits divers?*

When in the novel the affinity and cohesion of its
every part will be so complete that the creative process
will remain a mystery, like the development of human
passions, and the harmony of its elements will be so
perfect, the sincerity of its reality so evident, its manner
of and its reason for existing so necessary, that the hand
of the artist will remain absolutely invisible, then it will
have the imprint of an actual happening; the work of art
will seem *to have made itself,* to have matured and come
into being spontaneously, like a fact of nature, without
retaining any point of contact with its author, any stain
of the original sin.[16]

A native of those same eastern Sicilian parts in which
"L'amante di Gramigna" and *I Malavoglia* are located, Verga
in fact composed the major part of his Sicilian writings in the
northern city of Milan. Having accumulated lists of dialect expressions and studies of Sicilian folklore, he cut short a career
of composing romantic novels on society life to write his *verista*
work about the people of his native region from the distance of
the Europeanized metropolis. This biographical fact suggests a
nostalgic outlook and betrays as well the modern anxiety that
spurs the regionalist imagination. Indeed, the removed, alienated scene of writing may have facilitated the wide embrace of
varied materials, Verga's grafting of the literary fiction's epic
grandeur upon linguistic and sociological documentation. The
modern "scientific" ambition articulated in the "Gramigna" prologue is partly fulfilled in that Verga's texts contain specific and
accurate geographical descriptions complete with place-names,
and veritable catalogs of Sicilian habit and idiom. Verga's em-

ployment of the term "picturesque" *(pittoresche)* may suggest his sense of that removed, nineteenth-century vision that locates an aesthetically satisfying visual coherence in the eclipse of an archaic world and its idealized poor in the face of modernity. Luperini notes that, nonetheless, Verga's portrayal in *I Malavoglia* of the overlapping of archaic modes of life alongside the advent of modernity is itself historically informed: a sense of stasis and cosmic circularity intersects in the novel with the emerging social and spatial mobility of the town's inhabitants. But in the linguistic texture of Verga's work, particularly in the use of free indirect discourse, Luperini locates an inherent yet fruitful ambiguity that informs our understanding of verismo.[17] For Verga does not simply transcribe or "repeat," as his credo would have it, the popular language of the countryside but rather, out of the particular Sicilian dialect incomprehensible to most Italians, and the narrator's high-literary language, he establishes a synthetic construct all his own, one that departs both from sources in actual speech *and* from Italian poetic convention. Verga's masterful interlacing of voices yields a fusion of speech and reflection, vernacular idiom and ironic commentary or poetic turn. Critics have noted Visconti's adaptation of this aspect of Verga's linguistic chorale.[18]

Certainly, the realism of this chorale cannot be transparent: even as Verga's translation renders Sicilian idiom comprehensible, he infuses his literary Italian with the vivid concreteness of distinctive regional voices—but the result is intricate artifice. Verga's hope that "the hand of the artist will remain absolutely invisible" in the process of literary synthesis is surely frustrated thus. The desired authenticity of linguistic sources, data, and sentiment undergoes a poetic transfiguration, effecting fruitful contradictions that are echoed on all levels of the text. For example, Luperini notes, Verga's precise geographical indications are countered by elusive descriptions of the inner spaces of the village: these remain indistinct, idealized in an effort to have them conform to a mythical image of an archaic, serene world

where persons and their environment merge harmoniously—
this in nostalgic contrast to the modern, urban Milanese environment from which Verga was actually writing. Similarly, a
linear realist narration that would conform to the quotidian,
horizontal world of Aci Trezza—a mode that would be adaptable to Visconti's prospects for a Marxist trilogy of an impending revolution—is disrupted already in Verga by an enclosed,
cyclical, rhythmic sense of time, a mythical order of fate. In
this "vertical" order Aci Trezza appears unchanging and un-
changeable, obeying the cycles of nature, itself mythicized to
include the constellations above, the volcano behind, and the
repetitive rhythm of the sea opposite. In fact, the year following "Gramigna," Verga's prologue to *I Malavoglia* intimates that
it is only a removed and encompassing vision—but not of a scientific sort—that could achieve an aesthetically satisfying grandeur in tracing the transition from premodern to a modern life,
the eclipse of an archaic world in the face of progress.

> The fateful, endless and often wearisome and agitated
> path trod by humanity to achieve progress *is majestic in
> its end result, seen as a whole and from afar.* In the glorious
> light which clothes it, striving, greed and egoism fade
> away, as do all the weaknesses which go into the huge
> work, all the contradictions from whose friction the
> light of truth emerges.[19]

Another, earlier short story set in Aci Trezza, "Fantasticheria," reveals Verga's awareness of the pitfalls in the outsider's aestheticizing vision. The story is designed as a letter to
a noblewoman passing through on a tour of Sicily. The narrator's didactic, ironic yet gentle voice implores the aristocratic
traveler to see beyond the picturesque appeal of the place and
into the difficult lower depths of the south, yet it gives meticulous attention to landscape.[20] Verga's implicit call here for a realist correction to conventional images with which the tourist

is armed suggests competing perceptions, tensions too rich to fit the theoretical mold of the *verista* ideal. Written language as such begins to appear unsatisfactory, as the "Gramigna" prologue already intimates, in Verga's declared search for the "work of art of the future." Could the novel reveal *directly*— without the mediation of the artist's hand or voice—the determinant causes for the dénouement, as if those were already imprinted upon the face of the earth, waiting to be simply "picked up along the paths in the countryside"? Searching to resolve this difficulty, Luperini cites Verga's notion of "intellectual reconstruction" performed from an objectifying distance and informing the written work. But what we also find here is an opening to an altogether different practice, perhaps more radical in its implications than what Luperini acknowledges. Planning to revisit his chosen location of Aci Trezza after having worked on *I Malavoglia* in Milan, Verga writes to his *verista* colleague Luigi Capuana:

> Don't you think that, for us, the aspect of certain things cannot be dealt with unless *seen from a specific visual angle*? And that we never succeed in being genuinely and effectively true *[veri]* unless we do a work of intellectual reconstruction *not with our mind but with our eyes*?[21]

"Intellectual reconstruction" here is no abstract conceptual process but, interestingly, a labor for the eyes, pertaining to vision as a specific, concrete, even if subjective practice: vision grasped moreover as an already intellectual processing of the optical imprint of phenomena "from a specific visual angle." This conception is of a piece with Visconti's subsequent search for a "visual and plastic reality" in the cinematic adaptation of *verista* practice.[22]

The substitution of verbal conceptualization by a visual intellect is in other writings qualified as approaching the "perfect impersonality of the work of art," positivistically confirmed by scientific or technological means.[23] In this turn to the visual so as to achieve what remains frustrated by language, it is perhaps the example of contemporary painters that Verga may have initially had in mind. The school of the Macchiaioli forms with Verga and his colleagues the broader gamut of the Italian nineteenth-century culture of realism.[24] For beyond the choice of subjects, the aesthetic of this quasi-Impressionist movement betrays, as well, the desire for a spontaneous artistic creation whose imprint of reality is understood as self-manifesting through the effects of light in the painting. These optical impressions the Macchiaioli professed to capture *all'aperto* and express in brushstrokes, patches, and spots—*macchie*—that have given the movement its name. The effect of the painting upon the eye was understood to repeat the perceptual imprint of reality itself. Verga's thinking and formulations are very much in tune with such a definition of the *macchia* as appeared in an 1852 dictionary:

> Painters use this word to express the quality of certain drawings and sometimes paintings done with extraordinary facility and with such harmony and freshness, without much finish or color, and in such a way as to seem not made by the artist's hand but *to have appeared by itself* on the sheet of paper or canvas.[25]

Verga's trust in a manifest, objective truth of the visible has come to respond to his search for an art of the future that will fulfill the realist aspiration. What must now enter this search is a consideration of photography. The photographic effects that punctuate the work of the Macchiaioli and their occasional use of actual photographs in the work process evidences the increasing influence of photography on conceptions of realism and of the image as such. The appeal of the photograph as unmediated impression upon the plate by nature itself via a causal, indexical imprint now sheds a different light on the "Gramigna" prologue.[26]

You will certainly prefer to find yourself face to face
with the naked and unadulterated fact. . . . The simple
human fact . . . will always have the force of what *has
really been.* . . . [When] the hand of the artist will remain
absolutely invisible, then [the work] will have the imprint of an actual happening; the work of art will seem
to have made itself, to have matured and come into being
spontaneously, like a fact of nature.[27]

Verga comes to grasp the determinant causes of action as physically manifest, optically inscribed as a total, continuous visual
reality and thus available to representation. It would surpass in
revelatory power, so Verga suggests, the novel's speculations on
"the inner man." Verga's utopian notion of realist art points
outside literary discourse, toward a spontaneous indexical tracing of the premises—or shall we say *referents*—of literature
"from a specific visual angle," in a nonverbal, nonsymbolic
form of representation. The impasse of the *verista* ambition,
which the novel could not overcome (and remain literature), is
what, one speculates, contributed to Verga's eventual suspension of literary writing altogether. For his biography is sharply
marked by a retirement from literary fiction, roughly coinciding with the return to his native Sicily.

It was then that he discovered photography. After the publication of *Mastro Don Gesualdo* in 1889, followed in 1891 by a
volume of short stories, Verga began writing the third novel in
his "I Vinti" (The Vanquished) cycle, launched by *I Malavoglia,*
but never completed it. The coinciding of his retirement from
writing and his growing engagement with photography raises
several hypotheses—not mutually exclusive. It may suggest, as
already intimated, that Verga perceived photography as a self-
sufficient fulfillment of that which literature could not achieve,
and hence altogether a substitute for the written text. It is also
possible that specific difficulties with the third novel in the cycle
led him to photography as an aide, an artist's tool. The photographic project might now replace the lists of linguistic and

sociological data and the precise topographical detail assembled in preparation for writing. But yet another ambition may have driven Verga's photographic project. For Verga's camera yielded a visual reinterrogation, an *adaptation* as it were, of the objects and modes that engaged him earlier as a writer. The letter to Capuana concerning the fulfillment of the *verista* project from "a specific visual angle" might itself suggest a *photographic* return to the scene of literature by way of optical verification, which is equated with intellectual reconstruction.

Verga's turn to photography links him with other Italian advocates of verismo such as Capuana[28] and Federico De Roberto but also, clearly, with his naturalist contemporaries, most famously Émile Zola in France. Zola, too, devoted himself to photography *following* the writing of his major work and often as a return to its objects and locations. Yet while Zola's general interest in photography, amplified by his friendship with Nadar, might have been triggered early, Verga's photographic *practice* precedes that of Zola by some fourteen years. Verga's photographs—some four hundred of them were identified by his archivist in 1970—date from 1878 to 1911.[29] He was most prolific in the 1880s and early 1890s, that is, contemporary with but mostly following his late literary production. Among Verga's photographs there are, alas, none of Aci Trezza, the designated location of *I Malavoglia* and the theater of its adaptation in *La terra trema*. Nor can we draw a direct link between Visconti's cinematographic return to Aci Trezza and this part of Verga's *verista* project, which was not available in the 1940s. But this body of work nonetheless claims our attention, for it sheds a direct *photographic* light on verismo and reflects thereby on the neorealist interest in the *verista* aspiration.

More specifically, Verga's photographic engagement with places and persons, settings and expressions, rehearses the methods and tensions that have animated his writings. One witnesses in the photographs the grouping by classes, occupations, types: men, women, and children are examined in relation to their habitat or workplace by contiguity with domestic objects or tools of labor, animals, and other props. Here are workers and farmhands, in work clothes and Sunday clothes, posing against hilltown views, fields, houses, alleys, or simply walls. The frontal poses suggest an interest in the typical and the evident, the documentable physiognomies and expressions of people in their native habitat—enclosed courtyards are a favorite setting—with no suggestion of shadow or mystery enfolding them. Rather these are fully illuminated human features, with no touch-ups, often contorted under the strong sunlight, confronting the camera among everyday objects: a chair carved out of a tree trunk, a bowl of beans waiting to be sorted, complement a family portrait, set up against the stone walls enclosing a courtyard (Figure 3.2). In several portraits a piece of cloth stretched clumsily behind a posing figure determines the flat

Figure 3.2. Giovanni Verga, Tébidi, 1892. Collezione G. Garra Agosta. From *Verga fotografo* (Catania, Italy: Giuseppe Maimone Editore, 1991).

and functional simplicity of the composition, supporting a clear outlining of the human figure as its proper object. Such compositions suggest that the photograph was intended as record of an "interrogated" object, set up to eliminate distraction, narrativizing links, or the complexity of spatial depth, striving instead for a standardized likeness, almost like that of an identity card whose "discursive space" is that of the sociological, anthropological, or topographic survey. Verga's captions and notes to the photographs often specify not only dates, names, and general locations but nicknames, street names, and particular camera positions.[30]

We witness this inclination matched in Verga's landscape photography. Even where the views are panoramic, they are usually not of the sweetest or touristic sights of Sicily, nor are they, by and large, aesthetically elaborate images. Towns and villages are often registered in their vernacular, unmonumental aspect, through specifically named streets, houses, or courtyards. Two 1892 views of the hilltown of Vizzini register from different angles the town's nested position within the landscape, the particular angularity of its roofs and facades in relation to the hillside striving to enframe, it seems, the most complete and advantageous views (Figures 3.3, 3.4). In other photographs people are grouped or altogether distanced as they are inserted in deep, detailed, revealing surroundings, as if to register all possible ties— topographical, material, social—with the milieu, an integrity and continuity of persons and places, even as individual expression is thereby reduced. In a photograph of 1897 a crowd of people turn to face the photographer at a crossroads in the town of Mascalucia (Figure 3.5). The camera captures the townspeople at a distance, as if they had just paused and turned around for a moment in the public place in response to the photographer's prompting. Yet the grouping of posing figures against the surrounding buildings also suggests deliberate staging and blocking, as of a chorus upon the stage, as perhaps for a scene in Mascagni's opera of Verga's own *Cavalleria rusticana*.

Figure 3.3. Giovanni Verga, Vizzini, northeast side, 1892. Collezione
G. Garra Agosta. From *Verga fotografo*.

Figure 3.4. Giovanni Verga, Vizzini, southwest side, 1892. Collezione
G. Garra Agosta. From *Verga fotografo*.

Figure 3.5. Giovanni Verga, Mascalucia (?), 1897. Collezione G. Garra Agosta. From *Verga fotografo*.

And so we witness the tensions of literary verismo transpire in these images, reproducing—to borrow Roland Barthes's terms—the inherent denotational/connotational bind of photography itself.[31] The "factual," documentary, instrumental function of the photographs coupled by the impassive disposition of human figures is often modified by an expressivity that one might call dramatic, even theatrical in orientation. For instance, while Verga's organization of the frame and choice of angles often appear straightforward and simplified, sharp contrasts of light and shade, unsoftened by the lens or in processing, eloquently impart the subjugation of these Sicilians to the Mediterranean climate, the punishing sun, the arid earth, in expressive terms. The drama of the light and the textured contrasts become as much objects of the representation here—with grandiose mythical resonance—as they are the means *by* which we see and differentiate what the camera has enframed. Is Verga's work conscious of this warping of fact and expression, reference and *poesis,* denotation and connotation? Does it interrogate the interference of documentary photography's claim to knowledge and a dramatic resonance, or a modernist aesthetic perception? Is it aware of photography's amenability to myth? Under the violent sunlight and harsh shadows that mark their faces, three Sicilian farmers from Tébidi are frontally grouped, framed from the waist up in an 1897 photograph (Figure 3.6). Such an image clearly exceeds the neutralizing function of cataloging or the identity card. The subtle low angle of the camera just suffices to endow these figures with a heroic aspect that is rendered even more eloquent by the unsoftened light, enhancing the shiny, deeply marked foreheads, the hands looming large in the front, the depth of the three diverse glances confronting the lens in defiance of the sunlight, each from a different position, intersecting at the camera.

A late photograph (1911) of a little girl at the window in Novalucello (Figure 3.7) is reminiscent of some of Visconti's most memorable framing in *La terra trema*: the elegance of its composition seems dictated by the window's "natural" enframing of the

Figure 3.6. Giovanni Verga, Tébidi, 1897. Collezione G. Garra Agosta. From *Verga fotografo.*

Figure 3.7. Giovanni Verga, Catania, Novalucello, 1911. Collezione G. Garra Agosta. From *Verga fotografo*.

girl, just as the theatrical organization of other photographs appeared to be "naturally" offered by the given setting. Yet precise choices determine these graceful images of Sicily. For here, again, the slight angle and harsh contrasts do not simply impart as "facts" the texture of the surrounding wall but indeed amplify the expressive complexity of the image, its play of depth and surface, its aesthetic consciousness. The image of the girl, dramatically defined against the dark interior of the room behind her as she emerges into the sunlight, is evocative of "the woman at the window" as conventional pictorial trope—to which such *metteurs-en-scènes* as Visconti will frequently appeal. Yet even here the conscious interframing aspires to present actuality as itself already fully expressive, "naturally" poetic, enframed, and *as such* poised to lend itself to the photographer. These Sicilian images—like Verga's literary chorale of factual, documentary sources and poetic embellishment—aspire to render reality-as-art by sheer, spontaneous self-manifestation. The *verista* yearning for unmediated registration invariably results in an aesthetically satifying chorale, composed from "a specific visual angle."

The case of Verga as photographer serves to identify an impulse behind a nineteenth-century realist tradition as it aspires to and is taken up by photography and film. While he contemplated cinema in corresponding with several institutions concerning practical and economic possibilities for the adaptation of his work, Verga's thought on this front is not developed or embedded in an exploration of the medium as was his work with photography.[32] Nor can one form, as already acknowledged, a direct causal or biographical association between Visconti's cinematic adaptation of verismo and Verga's photographic application. Yet the neorealist turn to Verga may have responded *in the first place* not just to an available, indigenous realist model but also to Verga's specific confrontation of modern social and scientific methods with regionalist materials and archaic domains, of instrumental, documentary outlook with aesthetic reflection, without compromising any of these fronts in the process. Namely, even without knowledge or evidence of Verga's photographic practice, verismo already embedded a photographic modernity, which made it adaptable to the neorealist project. Writing from the modern urban center of Milan about the predicament of an archaic, backward, peripheral south as it is beginning to confront modernity, Verga evoked—and Visconti will go on to amplify—the presence, and presentness, of the past in terms at once documentary, critical, and mythical, even nostalgic. His photographic return to these sites translated this modernist ambivalence to the instrumental and honorific oscillation of the medium itself.[33] Visconti's compound allegiance to a functional, progressive documentary, a resonant archaic mode and a reflective aesthetic will echo this position. This is why Verga's photographs speak so eloquently as associative threads that lead from verismo to neorealism and to Visconti's cinematic return to the sites of I Malavoglia. For they themselves constitute an adaptation, a modern technological reinhabiting of verismo, affording insight into its fantasy of art as an "imprint of an actual happening." But while photography may have seemed to Giovanni Verga capable of superior perception and scientific verification, it inevitably repeats the tensions of the verista text that precedes it: the desire for objective truth invested in the medium is itself articulated as myth. Neorealism was to rehearse a similar, and comparably rich, play of allusions, aspirations, contradictions some half a century later.

The Staging of a Neorealist Landscape

Like the self-exiled Verga writing of Sicily from the northern Milan, the Lombard Visconti gone south acknowledges that an artist's necessary distance from the landscape affords a unifying visionary perspective. In the 1941 "Tradizione e invenzione" he notes the figurative suggestiveness of Sicily: an enclosed geographic form defined against the sea and the mainland, the Mediterranean island itself becomes an anthropomorphic embodiment of the past, both Homeric and Verghian. Indeed, rather than deny a mythicizing or pictorial outlook, Visconti acknowledges it fully, spelling out its sources. And it is in these

glowing terms that he contemplates the cinematic possibilities
of the novel:

> To me, a Lombard reader, accustomed by tradition to
> the limpid rigor of the Manzonian imagination, the
> primitive and gigantic world of the fishermen of Aci
> Trezza . . . always appeared exalted in the fantastic and
> violent tones of an epic: to my Lombard eyes content
> with the sky of my native land that is "so nobly fair
> in fair weather," Verga's Sicily appeared truly as the
> island of Ulysses, an island of adventures and ardent
> passions, lying immobile and proud opposite the waves
> of the Ionian Sea. That is how I thought of a film on
> I Malavoglia. From the moment I decided not to discard
> this thought as the improvised fruit of a solitary rapture
> but to seek in every way possible to realize it, the inti-
> mate doubts, the councils of prudence, the estimate of
> difficulties, always surrendered before the excitement
> of being able to give a visual and plastic reality to those
> heroic figures that have the allusive and enigmatic force
> of a symbol but not its abstract and austere frigidity.[34]

The northern aesthete's enchanted grasp of the south partakes of formulaic propensities in Italian regionalism. Sicily's geographical separateness, its unstable, intricate history, its shifting
status as the garden of the Mediterranean whose topographical
features have given rise to myth but also as a colonized, exploited, vanquished land—all these contribute to the rich imaginary fabric of the place. Ovid's Metamorphoses describes Etna,
which commands the eastern coast of Sicily, with which we are
concerned, as the one-eyed chief of the Cyclops who, in seeking to destroy Acis, transforms him into a stream. Several place-
names in this vicinity—Aci Reale, Aci Castello, Aci Trezza—thus
connote the mythic, metamorphic being. Homer's rendering of
Odysseus's encounter with the Cyclops is the most celebrated

narrative that animates this place: the pointed basaltic rocks scattered opposite these shores are the Scogli dei Ciclopi, colloquially named the Faraglioni, the rocks hurled after Odysseus by the raging, blinded giant. These mythical landscapes have informed ancient art and offered a pretext for some of the earliest regionalist landscape paintings. In the first-century BC Roman frescoes of the *Odyssey*, now in the Vatican Library, the adventures of the epic hero among the Laestrygonians are set on a grandiose rocky seashore, extending in deep perspective beyond trompe-l'oeil architectural pillars that organize narrative succession and composition, while the rocks rising from the sea further enframe the horizon, enhancing its depth *and* its containment (Figure 3.8).[35]

Visconti's awareness of such uses of the landscape intersects with the realist's social conscience in privileging neglected milieus. It is in this way that the humble Sicilian fishing village—an archaic enclave barred to modernity except as an object of exploitation—will somehow come to enfold the gigantic world

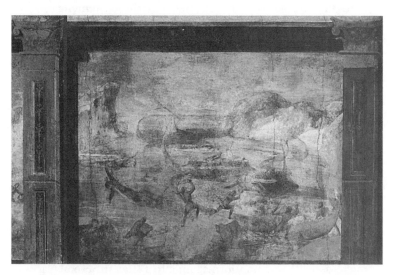

Figure 3.8. *The Laestrygonians Destroy Ships in Odysseus's Fleet,* from the Odyssey Landscape frescoes, ca. 50–55 BC. Photograph from Vatican Museums. Reproduced from *Odysseus: Mythos und Erinnerung,* ed. Bernard Andreae et al. (Haus der Kunst München and Mainz am Rhein: Philipp von Zabern, 1999).

of the *Odyssey,* where historical transformations evolve in mythic terms. While endorsing the developing consciousness of his fisherman-hero and his preliminary moves toward an open, dynamic, revolutionary order, Visconti endows the suffering of his characters with an aura of grace and grandeur that, in some sense, may seem to draw on an opposed impulse—to maintain an archaic state of being. In fact little here, in *La terra trema,* corresponds to the largely urban sensibility of neorealist settings, whose contingency is more closely aligned with the roadside locale where drifters converge in *Ossessione* than with this grandiose, dramatic, mythically coherent landscape. The rifts in the tranquil riverside surfaces of *Ossessione* are quite distinct from the resonant world of *La terra trema.* Class conflicts, desires to surpass one's lot, and ensuing personal tragedy may touch both worlds, yet in Visconti's Aci Trezza characters and actions reverberate with the archaic permanence of the setting to produce an embracing choral spatiality. This endows the protagonist's nascent consciousness with definition and depth, against which the film traces his awakening and will to participate in modern history. Visconti's appeal to a fully wrought, legible landscape in which "man and nature" are chorally bound mythifies, *monumentalizes* the progressive, linear narrative drive. Possibly it articulates on Visconti's part an impulse to legitimize cinema itself, to buttress it against the difficulties of contingency, as against one's own bifurcated identity: the threat of political modernism for even the driven Marxist aristocrat. The epic and theatrical connotations of the landscape itself already constitute a transfigured reality out of the humble village, making it amenable to human form and destiny, casting it as a set for impending action. Rather than profess to expose a definitive "reality behind the myth" of the place—as some, lesser documentarists might envision as their mission—Visconti boldly grafts diverse visions, scales, spaces, narrative and historical orders in a resonant chorale, embracing the traditions of which his film must partake and to which it now contributes.[36]

To achieve this, Visconti, Lombard aristocrat, reverses Verga's removal of the site of writing from the site of the fiction and comes to immerse himself for many months in the designated location of *I Malavoglia*. He imports to Aci Trezza a modern consciousness: that of an urbane cosmopolitan, a Marxist intellectual, out to inhabit the remote provincial place with cinema's own reconstructive perception: with neorealism's negotiation of continuity and rupture. His ostensibly documentary-driven choice—informed as well by a Gramscian awareness of "The Southern Question"[37] and of the intellectual's role in the world of labor, bridging regions and classes—opens up, however, to the imaginary and poetic charge of Aci Trezza. Accounts of the production of *La terra trema* betray the confluence of "truth and poetry": the photographic social-documentary aspiration and the elaborate literary, pictorial, and theatrical artifice constituting the work. Hence Visconti's use of authentic dialect, incomprehensible to most Italians—and a more radical move than any neorealist project ever undertaken—is only in part designed to serve the purposes of authentic reportage. Dialogues were based on what were initially improvised responses in local idiom of the participating townspeople of Aci Trezza. Yet, once satisfied with the selected expressions, Visconti would fix them in the script, to be as carefully rehearsed as a composed text in a controlled performance. Inseparable from the commitment to authentic sources is Visconti's fascination with the dialect's archaic auditory quality, whose incantatory rhythms might have connoted to him the Greek oral epic. Incomprehensibility may itself contribute to musicality as, transcending verbal communication, languages might thus acquire an operatic, acoustic spatiality. The use of standard Italian in the voice-over narration—which initially connotes documentary practice—itself enhances poetic and musical values, as well as irony, by way of rhythmic repetition and variation on the spoken/subtitled dialogue. Such layering is specific to the possibilities of cinema, multiplying the complexity of Verga's literary chorale.

The discipline Visconti demanded from his nonprofessional performers was reiterated in the degree of preparation and control that he exercised on all planes of the image. Exceeding the thematic and linguistic planes of adaptation, the reach of his layered realism extends to the meticulous workings of mise-en-scène, comparable to the spectacular construction of Visconti's theater and opera productions. While he insisted on the use of authentic interiors in *La terra trema,* sites had to be altered architecturally or by editorial conceit to simulate the contiguity of disparate spaces. We know that three houses were in fact combined to allow for Visconti's seemingly interlaced interiors, which always seem to project onto adjacent spaces. The built spaces were thus remolded to serve not so much a sense of spatial integrity but a deliberate and controlled theatrical order that would lend itself to the choreography of the actors' motions and blocking. Windows were added so as to extend the view, while interiors and exteriors across from windows—as with Mara's basil-plant window appearing to overlook the bricklayers' workplace—were matched in synthetic editing of what were in fact different parts of the town.[38] An intricate binding of planes via figure and camera movement across windows or thresholds is also afforded by depth-of-field cinematography, itself seemingly prompted by the location's conditions. At dawn, doors and windows of houses and courtyards at Aci Trezza are opened and remain open throughout the day: this, we gather, affords the most advantageous use of daylight. Without even the barrier function of glass panes the town's sounds and sights—the song of the bricklayers, the gaze of the police officer—are brought indoors while exposing to neighbors the goings-on in the home and yard.[39] Visconti's amplifying of such detail—when doors and windows do close in *La terra trema* it is in a moment of crisis, when the family is cut off from the community—inscribes the town's social and economic life in its conditions of perception. The vernacular Mediterranean architecture, the light and weather by which it

is seen, as well as the preindustrial economy and tightly interlaced community that goes along with it are all taken up by
Visconti's camera, as they were by Verga's own, and elevated to
an aesthetic principle.

The courtyard constitutes a pivotal space, mediating open
and closed, public and private spaces. Here, the episode of the
selling of the anchovies to the wholesalers unfolds: it is a paradigmatic instance of the deterministic theatricalization of spaces
in the film. The camera's position makes salient a centripetal enclosure[40] of the family group by the surrounding walls, formally
echoing the interframing of the women at the window earlier
in the sequence. Reframing, afforded by camera movement
and the shifting of the actors' positions, is designed to consummate dramatic situations, end sequences, and connect different
phases of emblematic tableaux in relation to the setting, to the
frame, and to each other. This is epitomized in the summary
image of the family's failure at the anchovy-sale negotiations at
the end of the season (Figure 3.9). Formal repetition of such enclosed compositions at different phases of the economic process
clearly reflects the prefigured fate and inevitable outcome of the
narrative. The elegant blocking of actors among the architectural elements follows a deterministic theatrical spatiality. As
well, these virtually static group compositions of the family in
its native habitat, against the bare walls of the courtyard, beg for
comparison with the photographic family portrait that punctuates key instances starting early on in the film. Standing for an
idealized, lost past that precedes the narrative time frame, and
set in a photographer's studio with fringed theatrical curtains
enframing a blackdrop of snow-tipped Etna, the studio portrait
offers a sentimental vision of harmonious continuity and integrity. It may be juxtaposed with Verga's photography *all'aperto,*
where the principle of grouping and choice of milieus partake
of the relatively functional, instrumental, even cataloging project of verismo. Visconti's static group shots oscillate between
the two photographic genres, seeing one (the documentary) in

Figure 3.9. Luchino Visconti, *La terra trema,* 1948.

terms of the other (the affective narrativizing of ties). In a sense
it serves to reconcile the *verista* outlook, with its impulse to return to an earlier state of things, with a Marxist conception of
the inevitable outcome of the economic process. Visconti's cinematographic orchestration of the décor suggests a reciprocity
of *both* photographic modes and complicates the connotations of both.

The *verista*-naturalist notion of determinant cause-and-effect
relations of milieu and character was akin, in Verga's thinking,
to the ontology of photographic reproduction, whereby documentation from "a specific visual angle" not only inscribes the
aspect by which we perceive phenomena but accounts for and
may even replace narrative dénouement. Visconti's sense of
the location as controlled and contained space correlates to this
conception of narrative and image. It is applied, we have seen,
to the architectural spaces of the town but it is also at work,

most daringly, in the use of exterior natural spaces. While interiors are rarely entirely closed in *La terra trema,* in that they so often incorporate adjacent spaces, exterior spaces are never quite open but always circumscribed within a range of enframing elements themselves emphatically enclosed by the film frame. Visconti's camera grasps both interiors and exteriors as homologous participants in the molding of a cinematic space. In the desire for the perfectly controlled mise-en-scène, Visconti thus defied the heterogeneity of the location and, as Francesco Rosi recounts, even the contingent moods of the sea. A month passed before shooting of the opening sequence—the fishermen returning from sea at dawn—was complete, as Visconti waited for perfect weather, light, and marine conditions, for the obedience of the sea itself to the exacting demands of the filmmaker. The process of filmmaking as such emerges, by this account, as a mythicized creative moment when, as under the touch of Prospero, the island and the sea are forced to yield their imaginative burden. Clearly, the *verista* aspiration to photographic imprinting of "what has really been" and the quasi-documentary film project are altogether permeated by Visconti's elaborate control of the landscape. This is not nature nor the illusion of nature caught in the raw but a landscape manifestly yielding to a dominating artistic will, a vision that grasps it as ready material for its own use in a theatrical chorale.

The accumulative effect of exterior panning and traveling shots delineates the topography's near and distant parts as interlocked spaces modeled, once again, on theatrical tableaux, with or without actors. And as with the interior tableaux's echoing of the demarcation, the containment of the film frame, so the theatricality of the natural landscape emerges as the setting up of a stage that bestows upon this world a sense of spatial determination and dramatic necessity. No differentiation here between nature—the forces of the sea, the storm—and the representation of landscape as image and discourse. The natural landscape of Aci Trezza participates in Visconti's choral spatiality: its forms, its proclivity, its prospects are made to appear as if they themselves direct the camera's framing and movement, its passages from one tableau to another. The town in its entirety and its natural environment thus emerge as one huge set, or soundstage, properly called in Italian *teatro di posa*.[41] The dialectic of exterior and interior, open and closed, of meandering camera movement that would seem to draw out multiple possibilities at every turn, vis-à-vis orchestrated control at every part of the shot—all these inform the cinematographic consciousness of *La terra trema*. And it is just this consciousness that confronts us with the material, formal condition of the landscape *as* theatrical space. In this confrontation we also locate Visconti's modernism.

A succession of slow, wide panoramic shots over the landscape in the gradually increasing light of early dawn opens the film, under the credits. The camera finally rests as it comes to enframe the approaching fishing boats returning with their nightly load between two of the monolithic Faraglioni (Figure 3.10), these Rocks of the Cyclops that punctuate the curved coastline, harbor Aci Trezza's small fishing port, and define its prospect as if in parenthetical enclosure. The horizontal row of boat-lanterns is surely the footlights in this theatrical setup of the overture, as the light rises on the view of the small Sicilian town. Embraced by the easternmost slopes of Etna, the town descends, directing the look toward the perpendicular basalt rocks scattered along this coast—rocks that themselves extend the volcanic embrace of the rough landscape. As one quickly acquires a sense of this place in the film, one learns that this is the camera's most emblematic grasp of the undulation of the coastline and the Faraglioni, which appear in the film repeatedly from a limited variety of angles but always referring back to this initial theatrical enframing. The Faraglioni may well have been perceived by a director immersed in the world of the theater as the *coulisses,* or the *paraskenia* of the classical

Figure 3.10. *La terra trema.*

open-air theater: the side scenery projecting frontally on both
sides of the stage, concealing its wings as they define the site
of dramatic action.[42] Only twice in the film are we offered
reverse shots (as it were) to this initial paradigmatic position
revealing, from the marine horizon, the coast as a distant background: first in the celebratory image of 'Ntoni and his brothers fishing for the first time as their own masters. In the film's
closing shot a similar position from the open sea is repeated,
now with the added pathos of 'Ntoni's gaining of consciousness, despite catastrophic failure. Extending the startling shift
in breaking open established narrative spaces is the film's last
cut on movement, which further dynamizes the sense of open
and ongoing action. But this impact is drawn against the dominant interiorizing of both the built and the natural landscape
throughout the film, which the camera follows and obeys.
Other than the two shots of the open sea, it does not leave the

defined spaces of social interaction in the town. The comings and goings of characters—the fishermen's brief detention, 'Ntoni's business in the Catania bank, the grandfather's move to the hospital, Lucia's disappearance as if to the nonspace of a backstage—punctuate the narrative but do not alter the dominant cinematographic-cum-topographic enclosure.

In response to the topography, as well, the camera simulates the position of a spectator in a vast theater, overlooking the stage below while backed by mountain slopes and the town itself.[43] The trajectory of the view descends with the angle and enclosure of the terraced alleys that section the town's concave, tiered layout, toward the orchestra below: the piazza overlooking the beach and the small fishing port. These are the sites of public action and exchange where the fishermen weave their nets and negotiate with the wholesalers. The town as a whole projects, then, toward this theatrical stage whose extension is the Ionian Sea, itself enframed by the *paraskenia* of the volcanic rocks. The natural landscape with the marine horizon is thus grasped *as part of* the town's theatrical layout, even as the architecture itself appears crystallized out of the materials and rhythms of the location. It appears that some Hellenistic cities were conceived as great theaters, with mountains pressing up behind while dramatic panoramas opened before them, projecting across the Mediterranean landscape toward the sea. And as we consider the landscape's unfolding in the film in reciprocity with persons and actions, we see it embodying, finally, the place of a chorus in this acoustic space. Framing and camera work consistently amplify this choral resonance that echoes and complements the landscape, bringing together culture and nature in dramatic reciprocity, as fully determined as a set. In this way the film embodies and articulates its location, figures it as an intelligible entity that thus subjugates consciousness to history, to revolution.

In opening its realist-*verista* sources to epic and theatrical connotations, the film's appeal to the archaic becomes inextricable from its self-conscious modernity whose ideological and aesthetic ambitions are perhaps the highest we could locate in Italy of the immediate postwar. We have seen how the theatricality of the landscape stages a dialectic of closed and open spaces, of the continuities and ruptures that inform Visconti's historical consciousness. It is bound, finally, with the inception of Visconti's work as director and designer for the stage at just this period. Following some unrealized plans to produce plays "off stage" by making use of garden vistas, courtyards, and *palazzi* windows as enframing devices, Visconti commissioned for a 1949 production of *Troilus and Cressida* a vast three-dimensional model of Troy for an outdoor staging of the Shakespeare play in the Boboli Gardens. This was a miniature city complete with walls, gates, towers, hanging bridges in rounded details, and shifting perspectives that allowed for this integral set to be seen from numerous points of view (Figure 3.11). The ambition of this experiment and its spectacular results (not to mention cost) constituted a bold intervention in an era of humble postwar production and defy any narrow conception of neorealist culture.[44] This "stretching" of the theatrical set toward the continuous, open, penetrable space available in principle for a film shot on location reflects, in reverse, *La terra trema*'s landscape grasped as a theater. The choral landscape of *La terra trema* is distinct; yet its theatricality prefigures Visconti's later film work, inflecting his continued exploration of cinema's realist heritage as of its modern historical consciousness.[45] Following an opening plunge into an opera stage, *Senso*'s shots of a resonant, nocturnal Venice will suggest, in 1954, a comparable identification of the workings of theatrical space in the actual location grasped as historical stage. *White Nights*'s Livorno, replicated within a studio as an integral environment complete with canals and bridges, will call attention in 1957 to theatrical machinery in panning shots that link disparate times and places in a simulated revolving stage, whose material reality is disclosed by camera movement.

Figure 3.11. Luchino Visconti, *Troilus and Cressida* set, 1949. Fondo Luchino Visconti of the Fondazione Istituto Gramsci.

La terra trema's cinematographic grasp of the location as an enframed chorale suggests a conception of nature as a contained, determinant, humanized stage—and a conception of reality as itself such a set. The movie camera, purporting in the *verista* tradition to register "as they are" human and social phenomena, the milieu's raw inscription of fate—as if these preceded consciousness, ideology, the act of representation—displays these conditions, this theatricality, as natural. It finds in Aci Trezza a particular susceptibility to such a vision: an immanent figuration of nature even in its wildest aspect seems possible here.[46] *La terra trema*'s choral theatricality appears thus as *already* scripted into the location. Still committed to the neo-realist faith in the integrity of an authentic profilmic reality, the film betrays, like Verga's photographs, a need to anchor the aesthetic and ideological coherence of the work in an enhanced sense of nature's own participation in the production of art.

It is not, we have observed, direct influence that describes the relation between Visconti's film and Verga's photographic project but rather an oblique analogy, a subterranean gene-alogy of cinematographic modernity. The seamless grafting of a poetic aspiration upon documentary photography inflects verismo's claim to knowledge but also amplifies its resonance, giving its humble subjects an eloquent voice. Visconti's graft-ing of what is perhaps the most radical neorealist scenario and the most complex aesthetic vision upon the humble provincial location is most astonishing in his choral molding of the land-scape. In this he adapts the *verista* trope of *verità e poesia* that had permeated his literary source and generated Verga's pho-tography. Returning to the sites of *I Malavoglia* with a docu-mentary crew and no proper script, settling in Aci Trezza for some eight months to transform the location into an elabo-rate set in which the large, slow motions of the novel will be rehearsed—Visconti produces a work that quite exceeds the concern with the present state of Sicily as well as the practical needs of the Italian Communist Party.[47] In the late 1940s, in the midst of a general effort of recovery from the devastations of Fascism and the war, in the revival of art's nostalgia for a re-stored, unfractured reality that survived it all, we find Visconti positing cinema as a dramaturgy of nature: nature as coher-ent and legible, amenable to the work of a camera. It is thus brought into reciprocity with modernity as with its postwar aesthetic and ideological recuperation. Even in the most humble location Visconti locates the forms that render the world as a winged, choral stage—a tableau not quite penetrable, but drawn to the measure of a screen.

FOUR

Archaic: Pasolini on the Face of the Earth

> What I tell you in darkness, that speak ye
> in Light.
>
> —Matthew 10:27

If, as it has often been suggested, the cinematic apparatus—
its optics, its forms, its subjects, its ideological effects—is de-
scended from Renaissance perspectival tradition, then is one
describing film against itself when seeking still further back,
when looking *through* cinema to identify an archaic mode for
the cinematic imagination? In isolating the aesthetic system
underlying the film work of Pier Paolo Pasolini, one is drawn
to consider just such an archaic domain. A deep ambivalence
about modernity and, therefore, about cinema's own historical provenance, its modern predicament, makes for the hybrid,
uneven, difficult texture of Pasolini's film practice and theory.[1]
Its appeal to the archaic may be read as a special instance of
an *impure* cinema: this is André Bazin's epithet for films that
adopt—or adapt—extraneous materials and devices from the
traditional arts—literature, theater, painting—*without* effacing their origins in distinct "ontologies," without attempting
a seamless integration in cinematic form. Bazin suggests that
an impure cinema, at its strongest, employs the "interference"
of the ulterior media to turn cinema inside out, as it were, in
a deliberate gesture of self-alienation and that, paradoxically,
cinema can achieve thereby a heightened self-consciousness
of "its own true aesthetic structure," of its "specificity." Such
mature consciousness, Bazin implies, is distinct from the first
flush of the medium's self-discovery in its early years, as in the
comedy of the teens or—this remains implicit in Bazin—in

the first avant-gardes. Succeeding the early manifestations of
"pure" cinema is a self-consciousness realized in bold encounters between heterogeneous modalities. It engages—as Bazin's
critical study of films as different as Laurence Olivier's *Henry
V* (1944) and Robert Bresson's *Diary of a Country Priest* (*Journal
d'un curé de campagne,* 1951) demonstrates—the yoking of diverse spaces, temporalities, modes of address, strategies of
interruption, displacement, and anachronism. It is a form of respect for artistic traditions even as it advances cinema's mature
exploration of its own "aesthetic reality."[2] Such terms, we will
see, may be identified as central tenets of Pasolini's aesthetic,
made salient in a practice of adaptation but defining, as well,
his very consciousness of the cinematic medium. In thinking itself through an archaic "other," Pasolini's work achieves, in this
roundabout way, a modernist consciousness after all, complete
with nostalgia for the premodern. Certainly his is not the secular modernism of an Antonioni. What compels in Pasolini's
work is the *impure*; Pasolini would say the "contaminated." *The
Gospel according to Matthew* (*Il Vangelo secondo Matteo,* 1964)[3] is in
this respect an exemplary work. Starting from the prehistory of
its production in the 1963 *Sopralluoghi in Palestina per il Vangelo
secondo Matteo* (Locations in Palestine for *The Gospel according
to Matthew*)—his documented search for the film's locations—
a distinct archaic space opens up in Pasolini's work to be set
against modernity and, more specifically, against a dreaded late-
capitalist emptying out of those reservoirs of revolutionary
energy that Pasolini envisioned he could locate not only—as
we have seen in the Introduction—in the urban periphery but
on the margins of Europe: in Palestine,[4] Anatolia, north Africa,
the Arabian peninsula, and beyond.

Winter 1960–61 marks the beginning of Pasolini's work as
a filmmaker; it is also the time in which he began to travel.[5]
Filmmaking and traveling were to become closely linked in the
following years, when the search for locations itself became a
key creative moment in his work, while film production in turn

served as a pretext for further exploration of remote places and foreign cultures. Even a superficial glance at the films reveals this mutual implication of the two activities—filmmaking and traveling—as fundamental to Pasolini's work. This ambition may appear dormant in such early works as *Accattone* (1961) and *Mamma Roma* (1962), based on original screenplays rather than adaptations, and located in a contemporary, emphatically urban Italy. But it can be identified even in these films' exploration of the Roman *borgate*—the city's peripheral neighborhoods—as sites of marginality: primal, vital, exotic landscapes external to hegemonic Italian culture. Here *borgate* inhabitants, often sub-proletarian southern immigrants or their descendants—who, in Pasolini's mythicizing view, still bear traces of premodern physiognomies and cultural forms—could enact hagiographic narratives of martyrdom in the conflicted intersection of the archaic and the modern.[6] Later in his career, in a complementary motion, classical and medieval texts will be "exported" outward, beyond Europe, adapted to historical and social processes at work in the Third World of the 1960s and early 1970s. The presence of the archaic within contemporary life complements in Pasolini's oeuvre a vision of the present in an allegorical projection of the past.

The Gospel according to Matthew is located at the crossroads of these two complementary modes: between the original scripts located by and large in contemporary Italy, and the works of adaptation, shot largely abroad. The latter were often preceded by elaborate *sopralluoghi*: "location-hunting" voyages of exploration documented in writings and diary-like films. In fact, Pasolini's documentary cinema consists almost entirely of such work done in preparation for his adaptations (some left unrealized). These relate the search for actors and locations, the faces and places that Pasolini lays out as proper materials for his work. Three of the travel documentaries can be seen to constitute in this respect a trilogy, launched by the *Sopralluoghi in Palestina*, followed by the *Appunti per un film sull'India* (Notes for a Film on India, 1968), and the *Appunti per un'Orestiade africana* (*Notes for an African Oresteia,* 1969–70). Rather than faithful historical reconstruction of his source texts, Pasolini's travels led him to experiment with bold geographical, contextual, and stylistic displacements and anachronisms. His exploration of an archaism of the present resulted thereby in a jarring, heterogeneous textuality. In the years following *The Gospel,* with the experience of the various *sopralluoghi,* and the production of *Oedipus Rex* (*Edipo Re,* 1967) and *Medea* (1969–70), notions of "analogy" and "contamination," elaborated in his theoretical work, were to further inform this practice of adaptation. In the location-hunting documentaries we find Pasolini's most forceful reflections on adaptation as a working principle in an *impure* cinema, whose modernism consists of an altered consciousness of the relation between the cinematic apparatus and the worlds it confronts, between image and material reality, between *representation* and *represented* on film. The passage from the *Sopralluoghi in Palestina* to *The Gospel according to Matthew* serves to clarify this relation: in the course of this passage we glimpse the evolution and crystallization of a willfully scandalous aesthetic, unique in the history of cinema.

Location as *Terra Sancta*

The story of the production is complex. In October 1962, as a guest in Assisi of the Pro Civitate Christiana, an institution attentive to left and liberal trends in the promotion of Catholic culture in contemporary Italy, Pasolini read the Gospel he found at his bedside there. In an exchange of letters with his producer Alfredo Bini and members of the Pro Civitate, Pasolini described his response to the text in glowing terms that connote a sense of religious possession, interchangeable in his mind with an aesthetic revelation. In view of such enthusiasm on the part of a famed, albeit notorious cultural figure, the directors of the cinema office of the Pro Civitate, upon consultation with priests, theologians, and Bible scholars—who revisited also Pasolini's preceding treatment of a crucifixion story in the short *La ricotta* (1962–63)[7]—agreed to support Pasolini's project. This was surely in the spirit of tolerance in the contemporary church under Pope John XXIII, to whom Pasolini later dedicated his adaptation: "To the dear, happy, familiar memory of John XXIII." The intimate style of this dedication on the part of a nonpracticing, anticlerical Catholic itself reflects upon the personality of its addressee. During his brief papacy (1958–63) John XXIII caused a stir in Italian and Church politics when he articulated in 1962 a sympathy for an opening to the left. As Paul Ginsborg observed, his encyclicals were the first to address not only Christian believers but "all men of good will," emphasizing the need for social justice and anticolonialist struggle in the Third World, for cooperation of different ideological positions across the barriers of the Cold War, and for the integration of the working classes, women, and the otherwise disinherited into the political order—all this as part of the social mission of the Church.[8] Also suggested by the dedication is Pasolini's submission of his adaptation to the Church—a gesture by which he in fact inserts his work into the tradition of commissioned and endorsed Christian art.

In preparation for the production, the Pro Civitate Christiana sponsored Pasolini's expedition to Palestine under the guidance of Don Andrea Carraro and one Dr. Caruso. A representative of Alfredo Bini's production company and a cameraman accompanied the tour to Israel and Jordan, which took place between June 27 and July 11, 1963. Under the scorching Middle Eastern sun the little group drove through what one recognizes in the location-hunting documentary as pre–Six-Day War Israel, from the vicinity of Mount Tabor to several Christian sights around the Sea of Galilee and along the Jordan River, up to Nazareth, then stopping in both a Druze village and in an Israeli kibbutz. Following this edifying juxtaposition of a rural subproletarian village and the progressive agricultural community, Pasolini

and his entourage made a detour through Beersheba, attending
to its Bedouin minority, and drove on to the Dead Sea and the
Judean desert before making their way to Jerusalem—then a divided city. Here they crossed the border to Jordan, concluding
their tour in nearby Bethlehem where, as Pasolini observes, the
story of Christ in fact begins (Figures 4.1–4.2). Apart from this
final stop, then, the *Sopralluoghi in Palestina* itself roughly follows, like the Gospel, the itinerary of the life of Jesus: from the
Galilee region and the Jordan River, through the desert, and on
to the sites of the Passion in Jerusalem. Discussions between
Pasolini and Don Andrea, and their reading of corresponding
Gospel passages on site, punctuate the fifty-five-minute travel-
ogue. Pasolini returned to Italy with six reels of film, which
he hastily spliced together in preparation for a meeting with
investors. The film remained technically primitive, raw, noisy,
laid out in the rough chronology of its shooting, largely edited
in camera with even the jarring motions at the ends of shots—
when the cameraman stops a handheld camera—often apparent. It is patched with excerpts from Bach's *Matthäus-Passion*
and with Pasolini's voice-over commentary adding to, and at
times commenting on, the few sync-sound dialogues in the film.

The dominant impression, repeatedly articulated in the
Sopralluoghi in Palestina, is of the *humility*—that is Pasolini's
term—of the places that the Gospel designates as the original
grand stage of the preaching and Passion of Jesus. Nazareth,
Mount Tabor, the Jordan River, Capernaum and the Sea of
Galilee, Bethlehem, Jerusalem with its sites of Gethsemane,
the Via Dolorosa, and the Holy Sepulcher—Pasolini had envisioned all of these as manifesting the archaic grandeur not only
of the Gospel text but of the accumulated weight of centuries of elaboration and representation. Pictorial renderings of
local, effectively familiar, or else idealized or fantastic European
landscapes as the settings of emblematic Gospel scenes had
not prepared Pasolini for what he found. The modern, industrial aspect of Israel was only, he states, a predictable, "practical

Figure 4.1. Pier Paolo Pasolini, *Sopralluoghi in Palestina per il Vangelo secondo Matteo* (Locations in Palestine for *The Gospel according to Matthew*), 1963.

Figure 4.2. *Sopralluoghi in Palestina*.

disappointment": this became the ostensible rationale for locating his *Gospel* elsewhere. The ambivalent attitude to modernity and progress that accompanies Pasolini's nostalgia for the archaic is also apparent in the gentle irony that tinges his image, in the *Sopralluoghi,* of the rationally organized communal kibbutz: his interview with an Italian family living there on the subject of child care may be implicitly juxtaposed with the resonant biblical image of mother and child. Yet despite the secular vision of the kibbutz, despite the dissonance of new building developments, highways, electric poles, the plain material concreteness of the holy places in Palestine, the modesty of their dimension and placement—bearing neither a "scenic" nor spectacular impact that Pasolini had expected—ultimately did add up to "an aesthetic revelation": one that has left its traces in the ultimate choices of locations and shooting style of *The Gospel according to Matthew.*

> I think my image of the holy places was completely transformed. Thus, rather than adapt the places to my imagination, I will have to adapt my imagination. . . .
> I'm thinking of the great Italian artists of the past centuries, of the painters, of Pollaiuolo, of the others who depicted the Baptism of Christ, who had had to imagine it, the Jordan River—and for whom the Jordan was far away, beyond the seas, the mountains, something unattainable—and for me it is right here. Now I feel . . . embarrassed for aesthetic reasons.

And again:

> Thus, my hope was already a little cracked, because of the evidence of certain elements not entirely conforming to what I had imagined for the setting of my film. Here, these are small Israeli houses that you could very well see in the Roman Agro. . . . The first impression was of a great modesty, a great smallness, a great humility.

Here we are halfway to the top of the Mountain of the Beatitudes. Here the crowd was probably gathered to listen to Christ. And up over there, where you see that small church with that black cupola, there Christ probably stood talking to the multitudes. The area is frightfully desolate, arid. It seems one of those abandoned places in Calabria or Puglia. And down over here is the Sea of Galilee, tranquil under the sun. What impressed me most is the extreme smallness, the poverty, the humility of this place. And for me—who was expecting this place, this Mountain of the Beatitudes, to be one of most fabulous places in my film and in the spectacle that Palestine would have offered me—it has been an incredible impression of smallness, I repeat, of humility. A great lesson in humility. After all, I am thinking that all that Christ did and said—four small Gospels, preaching in a small land, a small region that consists of four arid hills, a mountain, the Calvary where he was killed—all of this is contained in a fist.[9]

The repeated emphasis, pressing toward an oxymoron, of the "great humility" of the Christian sights recalls Pasolini's most characteristic trope. The sublime grandeur identified in the desolate "smallness" of a contemporary ruinous landscape pertains to Pasolini's notion of "contamination," borrowed from his linguistic studies of that period, where it describes the interlacing of voices—high and low, literary Italian and dialect—intertwined in free indirect discourse that maintains the specificity of diverse voices without neutralizing them in a median or standard idiom.[10] Nor would Pasolini want to compromise the connotations of impurity, tainting, contagion, violation that accompany this term, setting it most emphatically against the sanitized Italian of Fascism or the technocratic language of neocapitalism. Contamination in Pasolini's film practice finds its primary moment in his first use of Bach's *Matthäus-Passion* over the scene of a pimp's fight in the dust in

Accattone. Here, in the *Sopralluoghi,* Pasolini alludes to this trope as already immanent in the landscape. A shadow of the grandiose, archaic world of the Bible appears in the bare and desolate ruins punctuating a small geographical entity: "Both in Israel and then in Jordan the Biblical world indeed appears, but it emerges like a wreckage."[11] The contamination of humility and grandeur perhaps describes, on the most fundamental level, the impregnation of actual archaeological remains—apparently just scattered, dusty, "wretched fragments"—by a mythic-visionary charge whose claim to authenticity and value is of an altogether different order than that of the ruins themselves. Where a truly secular artist might have located in archaeological evidence a debunking of theological dogma or else a rationale for ignoring altogether the continued presence of the archaic, Pasolini embraces both the material concreteness of these traces and the grand resonance of the myth. Their mutual contamination—more emphatic than he had previously envisioned—forms the basis for an adaptation in which a landscape of poverty and ruin, and the gorgeous riches of Christian art, the contemporary and the archaic, the actual and the phantasmic intersect and interpenetrate but do not neutralize each other. It may also be seen to reflect, we will see, the oscillation of the cinematic image as such between its photographic-realist claim and its amenability to myth.[12]

Pasolini's notion of contamination evokes Erich Auerbach's analysis of the Gospel according to Mark in terms of a mingling of voices: Auerbach demonstrates how realistic "low life" elements, traditionally used for comedic modes, are here endowed with "high" design and purpose. The interweaving of styles serves to portray "the birth of a spiritual movement in the depths of the common people, from within the everyday occurrences of contemporary life." This, Auerbach suggests,

was rooted from the beginning in the character of Jewish-Christian literature; it was graphically and

harshly dramatized through God's incarnation in a
human being of the humblest social station, through
his existence on earth amid humble everyday people
and conditions, and through his Passion which, judged
by earthly standards, was ignominious; and it naturally
came to have—in view of the wide diffusion and strong
effect of that literature in later ages—a most decisive
bearing upon man's conception of the tragic and the
sublime.[13]

This model of biblical contamination is adopted by Pasolini,
informing his work of adaptation at every level. His film production of the Gospel will not aspire to historical and anthropological truth or philological precision but employ instead
a heterogeneous mode—a deliberate mingling of Christian
and other cultural references, of high and low voices, of periods and stylistics, quotidian detail and a visionary stance—
articulating the contamination embedded in the very notion
of incarnation and that Auerbach identified at the heart of the
biblical text. Adaptation involves, then, not *reconstruction* but
a new amalgam of materials, modes, frames of reference that,
on one level, are synecdochically tied to the Holy Land and, on
another, are analogous to its biblical rendering.

For early on, and possibly prior to his trip, Pasolini realized that the "actual" sites of Jesus' life and Passion in the Holy
Land will not do. The expedition to Palestine comes, instead,
to inform Pasolini's notion of analogy, which, complementing
contamination, qualifies the Christological groundings of this
film project. Analogy—by re-siting, displacement, temporal
leaps—will sustain Pasolini's adaptations throughout his career,
shedding light, we will see, on his idiosyncratic theories of film.
North Africa as well as northern Italy for *Oedipus Rex*, Anatolia
for *Medea*, Naples for the *Decameron* (1971), and the town of Salò
for *The 120 Days of Sodom* are among the celebrated examples
of Pasolini's practice of analogy. In the *Appunti per un'Orestiade*

africana Pasolini contemplates how to "export" the Greek-Mediterranean myth to contemporary sub-Saharan Africa as well as to African American ghettos. In Pasolini's treatment of the life of Saint Paul, contemporary New York would stand for ancient Rome, Paris for Jerusalem, modern Rome for ancient Athens, London for Antioch, and the Atlantic Ocean for Paul's "theater of voyages": the Mediterranean.[14] But it is the *process* of re-siting, the *movement* of analogy that acquires body and meaning in the Gospel project. The *Sopralluoghi in Palestina* emerges as, in effect, a pilgrimage wherein the impressions, indeed filmic imprints, of the original location are gathered to then be "imported" to southern Italy. The model of pilgrimage rehearses a more established analogical trajectory than what his other adaptations take up, but this transitional film also opens up a more radical gesture of contamination than that afforded by the "great humility" of the Holy Land itself. In personally, physically retracing Christ's journey Pasolini already projects the prospect of returning whence he came, bearing the sacred loot of his pilgrimage. This loot, inscribed in the *Sopralluoghi,* is in this way comparable to the transportable value of relics and icons that the pilgrim brings home. It will in turn serve to consecrate the Italian sites through which Pasolini will perform a second, covert, location hunt: the *Comizi d'amore* (*Love Meetings,* 1964). Ostensibly a documentary reportage based in interviews on prevailing attitudes and mores regarding love and sex in contemporary Italy, *Comizi d'amore* might first appear as a sensationalist journalistic inquiry on worldly love to match, as it were, the divine love taught by the Gospel. Profits from this film were in fact intended for production of *The Gospel,* while it served Pasolini, perhaps most importantly, for an exploration of landscapes and physiognomic types toward the feature production.[15] Only following this second, covert *sopralluogo* will Pasolini finally turn to the actual production of his *Gospel* in a few selected sites in Calabria, Basilicata, Puglia, and the Lazio region. Upon this second, Italian terrain—whose geographical and anthropological features are recalled repeatedly during the earlier Palestine tour—Jesus' movements will be rehearsed.

Standing by the small stream that is the Jordan River, touching the tall reeds, Pasolini confesses in the *Sopralluoghi* conversation with his guide Don Andrea that confronting the views that Jesus himself might have seen exerts a sense of presence and at the same time, he worries, a literalist reduction for which his own film will have to compensate: his vision of a "sacred place" would have to be adjusted in light of these humble sights. What Pasolini perceives as an aesthetic problem, Don Andrea then articulates from a religious outlook:

> But given that it is here that these scenes took place—
> on these locations, on this land—here the earth had
> been treaded [by Christ]. . . . There is a sort of geogra-
> phy of Palestine, a geography of the *Terrasanta*. And
> I think that one has to walk over it, thinking, reflect-
> ing, meditating, in order to absorb its spirit. Only then
> could one reinvent it in some other place, reimagine it,
> adapting it even to one's own sensibility, to one's own
> imagination. Then it will become a new thing; because
> I really believe that one cannot speak of a "photograph"
> of these places.[16]

What underlies this meditation is of course the notion of *terra sancta*:[17] a sacred topography, a configuration of sites locating a religion in the mapping of its founding myths. The attachment of value to a geography, and more specifically the sacral attributes of Palestine, is clearly not the singular domain of Christianity. Most religions privilege certain sites as meeting places between heaven and earth: typically, elevated spots (e.g., Mount Sinai, Golgotha) are associated with events paradigmatic to the religion. Christianity has also come to designate catacombs and saints' tombs as bridging this and another world. The spaces of ritual, structured according to hierarchies of sacred and profane, privilege and prohibition, are among the common constitutive characteristics of religious practice, organizing the world by its order and orienting the believer in its apprehensible cosmos.[18]

Pilgrimage to the Holy Land, in particular the passage through the stations of the Cross culminating in the Holy Sepulcher as part of a liturgical order wherein one retraces with one's own body the sacred topography, rehearses a trajectory well established in Christianity. But actual pilgrimage to Jerusalem is only the most literal form in which the *Terra Sancta* serves the believer. The holy places are incorporated in other modes of veneration: the bringing of relics from original sites to European churches, the placement of small replicas of the Holy Sepulcher on the altars of local churches, or the construction of models of the Sepulcher to scale. A celebrated replica, complete with pilgrimage relics, is to be found in Le Sette Chiese, around the corner from Pasolini's birth place in Bologna.[19] By "translating" the specificity of place and its spatial connotations into the narrative-temporal dimension of the liturgical order, a re-siting of the sacred becomes possible. The original pilgrimage gives way to procession between local European sites in an established ceremonial order that, in the liturgical year, retraces the trajectory from Annunciation through Pentecost.[20] These possibilities of the transposition of the sacred may be identified at the heart of Christian theology and have played a major role in its historical dissemination.

Peter Brown describes a historical shift from pilgrimage, "the movement of people to relics," to "the movement of relics to people"—a movement of "translation" that holds center stage in late antiquity and early-medieval piety.[21] Pilgrimage posited the sites of the Holy Land as themselves sacramental, but the theological possibility of "translation," the migration or displacing of the sacred, allowed for the dissemination of the faith through multiple secondary sites that partake in the sacramental value of the remote original location. Christianity is indebted in this to the growth of monasticism in the fourth century and to popular and pagan influences and practices associated with the veneration of both relics and holy men. Catacombs outside city walls, as well as remote and desolate places where hermits had retreated, were thus consecrated, serving to shift the balance of earlier maps of civilization toward a new holy geography. Sacred places became more common by virtue of the sheer number of saints and the distribution of relics that was soon authorized by the church. By stressing the popular roots of these cult practices and their profound impact on Christianity, Brown questions simple dichotomies that distinguish official Christian history, dogma, and hierarchy from popular manifestations initially associated with pagan or "vulgar" superstition such as the veneration of relics and icons. We may identify here, in effect, another model for "contamination" whereby high and humble, dogmatic and domestic or popular intermingle. The secondary, local site tied to accidents of place and history, even to regional folklore, can be consecrated and hence endowed with the sacred value of the original. The sacred is thus made available. The very tenet of Christian culture, the doctrine of the Incarnation, is informed by this paradigm: the historical and the eternal, mortal flesh and holy spirit are identified in the Christian sacraments under God's generous allowance of a sacred *praesentia* and bear upon the Christian understanding of time, of place, and of the image.

With the displacement of the sacred and the tracing thereby of new holy topographies, one may gloss Pasolini's specific notion of analogy as it complements his principle of contamination. Pasolini can now approach the most humble of sites in southern Italy, places quite remote from official holy centers—Jerusalem *or* Rome—and endow them with an authentic sacral value personally *translated,* as it were, from the *Terra Sancta.*

I had decided to do this even before I went to Palestine, which I only did to set my conscience at ease. I knew

I would make the Gospel by analogy. Southern Italy
enabled me to make the transposition from the ancient
to the modern world without having to reconstruct it
either archaeologically or philologically. . . . [Jerusalem]
was the old part of Matera, which now, alas, is falling
into ruin, the part known as the *Sassi*. Bethlehem was a
village in Apulia called Barile, where people were really
living in caves, like in the film, only a few years ago. The
castles were Norman castles dotted round Apulia and
Lucania. The desert part where Christ is walking along
with the apostles I shot in Calabria. And Capernaum is
made up of two towns: the part down by the sea is a village near Crotone, and the part looking away from the
sea is Massafra.[22]

And elsewhere, a temporal register enters this discussion of locations, engaging a deliberate strategy of anachronism as a mode
of historical thinking. This is also where we encounter Pasolini's
conscious confrontation of the archaic and the modern—at the
two ends of the historical process—simultaneously imagined,
animating each other:

I should say that I continuously felt the need to refer
to contemporary life, so that things would never be
historically reconstructed, but always in reference to
our experience of history. Not the past disguised as the
present but the present disguised as the past.
  For the major choices this was not difficult once the
mechanism of analogy had been established. For the
pastoral, agricultural, feudal world of the Jews I substi-
tuted wholesale the analogous world of the Italian south
(with its landscapes of the humble and of the powerful). . . . But for the small, minor choices, that often
come up unexpectedly on the set on a given day—that
was much more difficult. So, for the Roman soldiers at

Christ's preaching in Jerusalem, I had to think of the
Celere [Italian police units for the control of demon-
strations, strikes etc.]; for Herod's soldiers before the
Massacre of the Innocents I had to think of the Fascist
mob; Joseph and the Madonna as refugees were suggested to me by refugees in many analogous tragedies
in the modern world (for example, Algeria) etc. etc.[23]

The sites visited in Palestine have been rejected, ostensibly, because of the obtrusive modernity of 1963 Israel; in the Italian
south Pasolini seeks instead spaces of underdevelopment grasped
as premodern remnants and therefore in no need of reconstruction. For, Pasolini emphasizes, it is not reconstructed history
that interests him but rather the persistence of archaic forms
within the contemporary world: these forms he locates on the
margins of Italy of the early 1960s, in a chronically disinherited
world denied active participation in hegemonic culture. He
further suggests that this overlapping of historical moments is
also a way for the present to experience, to *think,* history. Recall
how, in the heart of *Comizi d'amore,* while interviewing Oriana
Fallaci sunbathing on the Riviera, Pasolini cuts, as by ironic
juxtaposition, to an extreme long shot of the Calabrian landscape: arid fields, distant mountains, a peasant with a primitive
plough and a mule. This is that "other planet" of the Italian
south, worlds away from Fallaci's progressive discussion of
"free love" (Figures 4.3–4.5). The sudden biblical vision foreshadowing the *Gospel* stands out in *Comizi d'amore,* accentuat-
ing Pasolini's ambivalent conception of modernity as bound
up with an aesthetic preference: the scorched features of the
peasant immersed in the landscape of his life and labor for generations rather than Fallaci's Riviera suntan, the "innocent" archaism of southern ignorance and, even, prejudice rather than
urbane, bourgeois-liberal sophistication and, Pasolini would
later conclude, consumerist promotion of "free love" as of in-
sincere tolerance. The archaic is understood as a condition; it

is a geographical, more so than a chronological, designation; it bears an ideological charge. In an exchange with Jean-Paul Sartre after the international release of *The Gospel according to Matthew* Pasolini explained the role of the archaic in his analogical mode by drawing a comparison between his choice of the Italian south and what Algeria as location for a film of the Gospel would mean to a French audience.[24] The Italian south is still perceived here as a colonized, Third World entity, bypassed by modernity even as it is exploited by northern industrial and consumer culture. It is here, Pasolini implies, that one may locate an authentic revolutionary potential that is not contradicted by the enduring power of the Christian myth in the rural subproletariat. Rather than posit the archaic against progress, Pasolini embraces it as a vital and even dialectical force, analogous to what he reads in Matthew's Gospel as Christ's challenge to *his* contemporary establishment. In both historical and art-historical terms Pasolini seeks, then, a location that—by virtue of having escaped, somehow, bourgeois-capitalist culture and the desacralizing rationality of the Enlightenment—in its cinematic rendering, can propel modernity to a more advanced consciousness. Only in such a place can an act of consecration

Figure 4.3. Pier Paolo Pasolini, *Comizi d'amore (Love Meetings)*, 1964.

Figure 4.4. *Comizi d'amore.*

Figure 4.5. *Comizi d'amore.*

have any meaning. As an aesthetic project it can even be grasped as, somehow, *realistic*.

The Face of the Earth

The concept of analogy now assumes breadth that sustains it as a practical working principle, as an ideology and an aesthetic. Leafing through Pasolini's film-theoretical writings one encounters that term repeatedly. It may be employed to read his theory for what it is: not really a semiology but a theology of the cinematic image. According to Pasolini, film partakes of reality through the photographic impression, even as reality— "being," "living"—is already a potential "cinema": a "language of action" that partakes of an expansive notion of cinema that includes specific filmic instances of "audiovisual techniques" in a continuum reality-cinema. "Res sunt nomina"—things are names—Pasolini declares, is the lesson that cinema teaches about the total semiology of reality itself. Reality speaks; it is spoken *through*; it is being and expression, flesh and word, at once, and may thus be transcribed in any particular film as the "written language of reality."[25] Both represented and representation, reality and its inscription in film are understood as analogical sections of a single continuum: both participate in reality, grasped not as some raw natural entity but always an expressive, human, cultural, and ideological domain. Analogy, then, defines the relation between the particular audiovisual cinematic sign and its source in the camera's field of vision: the profilmic that Pasolini grasps as an already formed textual and aesthetic entity, inscribed by death as the ultimate editing device, endowing meaning. Within specific filmic instances articulating techniques such as framing and editing propel the analogical imprint beyond transparent "naturalism" (that Pasolini abhors) to a different level, a potentially higher order. In this film-theoretical system— "scandalous from a linguistic point of view," Pasolini acknowledges—the sign does not stand for an absent referent but rather makes it manifest, legible: the cinematic sign is reality's *own* heightened articulation.[26] Following this logic, reality possesses an immanent human meaning embodied in everything and available to specific poetic or filmic expression. At its best film assumes reality's expressivity, its fullness of meaning, and thereby approaches a sacral plenitude.

Pasolini recognizes how this account of cinematic signs as meaning incarnate rehearses an archaic, religious, one might even say infantile perception:

> My fetishistic love of the "things" of the world makes it impossible for me to consider them natural. Either it consecrates them or it desecrates them violently, one by one; it does not bind them in a correct flow, it does not accept this flow. But it isolates them and adores them, more or less intensely, one by one.[27]

And again:

> Along with this method of reconstruction by analogy, there is the idea of the myth and of epicness which I have talked about so much: so when I told the story of Christ I didn't reconstruct Christ as he really was. If I had reconstructed the history of Christ as he really was I would not have produced a religious film because I am not a believer. . . . I am not interested in deconsecrating: this is a fashion I hate, it is petit bourgeois. I want to re-consecrate things as much as possible, I want to re-mythicize them.[28]

The mythicizing veneration, the "fetishistic love" that isolates, that cathects the object, that violently disrupts the "correct flow" of the discourse, positing in its place a consecrating imprint—this interferes with a transparent cinematic style of continuity editing but also with the neorealism of the long take. This is one way to read Pasolini's modernist appropriation of realist ground that infuses a plenitude in the static embossing of the shot via palpable camera work and disjointed editing.[29] His investment in the "'things' of the world" as in their incarnate images is manifest in the twofold commitment to the "realist" and the "reverential," deeply intertwined in Pasolini's thinking, the one contaminating the other. We note, once again, that these fetishized "things" are not some raw natural entity or flow but pertain to an (always) already "written language of reality," transcribed or imprinted on film. The cinematographic imprint—that causal bind between image and object, representation and represented—implicates "a certain realism,"[30] a motivated, spatial analogue; it affords, as well, the temporal leap to the archaic. Importantly, for Pasolini, the access through the cinematic image to the radiant light of an articulate reality and to the past also effects an attitude of veneration. The art-historical models underlying such a vision, and its attendant techniques, may now be explored.

The cinematographic impression can be seen to bind, then, Pasolini's realism with a reverential perception. Pasolini's archaistic imagination aspires to a primal sense of the cinematic image as reality's direct emanation—one that carries the evidentiary force of an imprint but also the magical resonance of a temporal bridge to the past, as to an altered state: a simultaneity of different temporalities, different orders of being.[31] In the context of an adaptation of the Gospel, this confronts us with the doctrine of the Incarnation and, more specifically, with the theology of the icon. Pasolini's aesthetic system draws on the potency of the devotional image, whose reverential archaism also carries a realist claim. This he approaches in an archaistic reading of Giotto and, more boldly, of Masaccio and Piero della Francesca as taught by the art historian Roberto Longhi. The rhetoric of the icon—which, like the relic, claims to provide visual, material evidence for the incarnation of the sacred in the world—asserts Christianity's redemptive vision of God's materialization in Jesus. The iconic image is not simply "symbolic" or "allegorical" in relation to its divine referent, as it would be in a Protestant system that severs the manifest and the hidden, the flesh and the spirit. Rather, it is grasped as participating in what it represents: it is an index of Christ's humanity; in partaking of his body it incarnates God.[32] The "materialism" of popular, even pagan, cult veneration inflected official monotheistic dogma in forging the rhetoric of the icon, which itself evolved in the same period in which the transposition of the sacred to new sites in Europe triggered the dissemination of Christianity; this I described earlier as a model for Pasolini's move from Palestine to the Italian south.[33]

It is, most forcefully, the *acheiropoietic* icon, the icon "made without hands," that proclaims an evidentiary, causal link in an original instance of contact or direct emanation, to reinforce the claim of resemblance between the sacred image and its referent. Following the Eastern Mandylion the Veronica, or *vera icona,* is the Western rival to the status of archetype of the sacred portrait of Christ from the early thirteenth century (Figure 4.6). The *acheiropoietic* icon, typically depicting the Holy Face on a cloth, is believed to have received the image by direct physical impression, sustaining the sacral presence, the original moment of contact, of identity, between represented and representation: whence its claim of causal, indexical link between the image and its referent.[34] This is why art historians, but even eminent church figures in modern times, have been drawn to consider the photographic image in relation to this tradition and have embraced, as well, the possibilities of cinema. Foremost among these is Pope Leo XIII, who, in the shots taken of him at the Vatican by W. K. L. Dickson in 1898, gives his benediction to the movie camera—and through it to the spectators of early cinema. Consider also the cult surrounding one Dr. Giuseppe Moscati (d. 1927) whose larger-than-life photograph is venerated at the altar of the church of Gesù Nuovo in Naples.[35] Like a photographic reproduction the *acheiropoietic*

Figure 4.6. *Mandylion* (Genua, S. Bartolomeo, thirteenth-century icon). Kunsthistorisches Institut in Florenz / Max-Planck-Institut.

icon, itself a mechanical reproduction of sorts, lends its testimonial value to its copies: the contact of image and image, like the "original" contact of body and image, is seen as retrospective proof of the first image's origin, endowing the copy, too, with miraculous power. The icon has, by implication, the properties of what it represents: hence it is expected to heal and to perform miracles, it participates in processions, it is venerated like a holy personage.[36]

The sacral value ascribed to the icon is articulated in anthropomorphic terms, associated with a predominantly upright, frontal depiction. In its purest form the icon isolates the face of Christ upon a veil whose surface is synonymous with that of the icon as an object of veneration. The ceremonial frontality of the icon, which it shares with ancient and imperial portraiture, offers itself to the devout's bowing and prostration. It does not draw the viewer into its space but is directed forward: depth is conceived not as interior to but in front of the icon, in the space of the devout.[37] But the otherworldly disposition effected by the frontality and formal stasis of the iconic figure has evolved as devotional portraits have come to incorporate expressive and narrative elements within increasingly realistic settings. In *Icon to Narrative* Sixten Ringbom has shown how, in the fifteenth century, the relation between cult images and empathetic, dramatic narrative representations is not that of rigid opposition but of rich and varied reciprocity, spanning from the emblematic Holy Face, through the half-length and popular "window" aspect portraits, increasingly opened to reveal detailed, realistic environments. While the half-length icon, a close-up of sorts, has given rise to nuances of intimate expression, landscapes came to afford a sense of unfolding depth in the vivid siting of the sacred instant. Landscapes, at times enframed through a window along with the holy figures, finally came to occupy entire backgrounds. Likewise, historical themes and narrative scenes, used in church decoration to edify the public, themselves came to inform even as they coexisted alongside the portrait icon: "the devotional image *par excellence*" of Eastern origin. Ringbom suggests how, in the logic of this reciprocity, a devotional image can be produced "by subtraction from a narrative or by the augmentation of a representational image."[38] A sacred portrait may be isolated or extracted from narrative, and conversely the static formal character of a holy figure can be "softened" by the introduction of additional figures, as of expression and sentiment that themselves carry narrative weight. In this reciprocity the timelessness, the otherworldly gaze, the abstract spatiality of the pure icon are altered, though not obliterated, in a turn to the created world that now informs the figure and its relation to setting and viewer. Remnants of an attitude of veneration from the portrait icon, and even the frontality and isolation of its more archaic forms, thus continue to inform some of the boldest pictorial forces of the Quattrocento, and it is to them that Pasolini is drawn in negotiating the archaic and the modern in his adaptation of the Gospel.

Pasolini's sense of a reverential attitude in the camera's relation to the visual field summons this art-historical context that inflects the plastic properties of his work. A frontal organization of mise-en-scène and framing, a ceremonial distinctness of figures in relation to each other and to the settings, are pervasive in his compositions and made even more emphatic by his employment of lenses and camerawork. The frontal assault of his camera endows its objects—figures, landscapes—with a corporeal, incarnationist presence projecting forth, imprinted, onto the screen. It yields a sense of the material world as itself already a pictorial surface, not inconsistent with Pasolini's theoretical conception of reality as already inherently articulate, semiotic, cinematic. The landscape, enframed by the movie camera as if it were a backdrop, supports an elaborate figuration of faces, bodies, headgear, and costumes. Though the camera ostensibly reproduces verbatim a perspectival field in translating spatial depth via an enframed two-dimensional image, Pasolini's mise-en-scène works against this translation to evoke, in exemplary instances, an upright surface or indeed the frontality of the icon receptive to the incarnation of a divine—that is, human—figure. In submitting figures and background alike to such pervasive frontality, and in grafting upon it the thematics of the Gospel, Pasolini in this film defined and historicized his cinematic aesthetic as a whole. Those are fundamental theological-aesthetic principles grasped at the very source of his art-historical allusions that Pasolini succeeds in adapting on film and that he identifies, moreover, as traversing the cinematic and the Christological tradition of the image in a bold, even scandalous anachronism. While explicitly thematized in *The Gospel*, these principles may be traced almost throughout his work and underlie, we have seen, his theory of film. They may also account for that other archaism of his cinema: its frequent affinities with early, "primitive" (or we might say, *archaic*) film practices whose frequent privileging of frontal mise-en-scène, so often attributed to theatrical influence, may itself be associated with the frontality of the devotional image.[39]

In the 1966 "Confessioni tecniche," his "Technical Confessions," Pasolini describes the inception of this aesthetic already in *Accattone*, leading to the conscious choice of techniques in *The Gospel according to Matthew:*

> Inexpert in cinema I simplified to the maximum, in *Accattone*, the medium's objective simplicity. And the result appeared to me—and in part, was—that of sacrality: a *technical sacrality* that then deeply affected the landscapes and characters. . . . Sacrality: frontality. And hence religion. . . . Also the lenses were, rigorously, the 50 and the 75: lenses that render the materials heavy, exalt the modeling, the *chiaroscuro*, give weight and often an unpleasantness of worm-eaten wood or porous stone to the figures, etc. Especially when one uses them with "stained" lighting, backlighting (with the Ferrania camera!), that hollows out the orbits of the eyes, the shadows under the nose and around the mouth, to the effect of widening and graining of the images, almost as in a dupe print, etc. Thus was born, in the ensemble of the film *[Accattone]*, in its figurative machinery, that "grave aestheticism of death." . . .

The principal lens [in *The Gospel*] had suddenly become the 300. Which obtained simultaneously two effects:
that of flattening and then rendering the figures even
more pictorial (Quattro- and Cinquecento), and at the
same time endowing them with the casualness and immediacy of a news documentary.[40]

The increase of focal length in *The Gospel* does not always allow
for centralized compositions, but the sense of frontality is
nevertheless accentuated. Interestingly, frontality becomes almost independent here of the sheer positioning of the actors
and their attitudes. It is effected through the deliberate efface-
ment of illusionistic depth and the collapsing together of figure
and ground by means of focal length and framing—so much
so that even a vast and spacious landscape that would allow a
penetrating, perspectival view is transformed into a backdrop
pressing up in front of the camera. The landscape surfaces
thereby optically collide with those of the figures and, in turn,
with the screen surface itself. Yet this colliding of surfaces—
enforcing the reciprocity of human and natural forms, of figure
and landscape—does not produce a dynamic, organic field that
embraces the viewer but maintains distinctness of elements,
turned forth in ceremonial stasis.

Already in the 1962 notes accompanying the published script
of *Mamma Roma,* Pasolini envisioned the biblical landscapes of
his *Gospel* through pictorial models in which the opposition
between figure and landscape, narrative articulation and devotional iconicity, movement and stasis is elided.

I cannot conceive of images, landscapes, compositions
of figures outside of my initial Trecento pictorial passion, which has man as the center of every perspective.
Hence, when my images are in motion, it is a bit as if
the lens were moving over them as over a painting: I always conceive of the background as the background of
a painting, as a backdrop, and therefore I always attack it

frontally. . . . The figures in long shot are a background and the figures in close up move in this background, followed with pan shots which, I repeat, are almost always symmetrical, as if within a painting—where, precisely, the figures cannot but be still—I would shift the view so as to better observe the details. . . . I seek the plasticity, above all the plasticity of the image, on the never-forgotten road of Masaccio: his bold *chiaroscuro*, his white and black—or, if you like, on the road of the ancients, in a strange marriage of thinness and thickness. I cannot be Impressionistic. I love the background, not the landscape. It is impossible to conceive of an altarpiece with the figures in motion. I hate the fact that the figures move. Therefore, none of my shots can begin with a "field," that is with a vacant landscape. There will always be the figure, even if tiny. Tiny for an instant, for I cry immediately to the faithful Delli Colli to put on the seventy-five: and then I reach the figure: a face in detail. And behind, the background—the background, not the landscape. The Capernaums, the orchards of Gethsemane, the deserts, the big, cloudy skies.[41]

Pasolini speaks of suspending the opposition of surface and depth, motion and stasis, pictorial color and photographic black and white. Like the flat surface of a painting, the visual field is "attacked frontally": figure and landscape converge in a ceremonial composition. This convergence evokes, on the one hand, Franciscan worldliness in the tradition of Giotto. But it might also be taken back in the devotional tradition of the altarpiece, where the landscape is interchangeable with the thickened, gilded ground of the icon. The fluid shifts in Pasolini's thought between Tre-, Quattro-, and Cinquecento frames of reference suggest the archaistic (and thereby willfully anachronistic) contamination of an embracing vision that will assert itself even against the conditions of his modern medium, motion pictures.

In accounting for this grasp of the visual field not only as an already *cinematic* but, first, as a pictorial surface, one must cite Pasolini's apprenticeship under the art historian Roberto Longhi at the University of Bologna before the war.[42] In Longhi's eloquent descriptions of Quattrocento painting one immediately identifies the critical source of Pasolini's frontality and its archaistic connotations. Longhi's 1927 monograph on Piero della Francesca draws particular attention to the role of landscape as effecting, precisely, an archaic, ceremonial frontality: a frontality described independently, moreover, of the sheer attitude of figures. Longhi's forceful *ekphrasis* establishes in this way a reciprocity of human and natural forms, suspending the opposition between figure and setting. Having noted Piero's indebtedness to Masaccio's sense of "corporeal existence in a physical world ennobled by action," Longhi characterizes the "archaic" order of Piero's figures as following Masaccio's "austere and primitive humanity."[43] This archaism, which Longhi associates with Egyptian and classical tomb painting, is modified but not contradicted by Piero's "metrical" preoccupations with perspective. Longhi provides the following account of *St. Jerome and a Devotee* (Figure 4.7).

> Its [the composition's] mathematical centre is occupied by the distant apparition of the city white-washed by men. Persons and things insert themselves everywhere freely into space, from the hewn trunk in the foreground to the tree standing behind the devout suppliant and to the vibrant zones of hills and sky. . . . The kneeling figure, for example, would be described in common phrase as given in profile, and yet it is the "prospect" or full view of him which spreads itself out at this moment before the spectator's gaze and stamps itself upon the many-coloured landscape. If we were to be faithful to the concept "profile"—valid, in truth, solely in an art of mere lines—we might attempt to apply it, not only to the man, but to the tree as well: and failing now to dis-

tinguish in the case of the tree a "profile" from a "front view," we should come very near to discovering the secret of the stylistic unity in this painting by Piero. This unity is in fact created by nothing else than by this very immanence of the perspective "front view" composed upon the plane.[44]

Figure 4.7. Piero della Francesca, *St. Jerome and a Devotee*, ca. 1450 (tempera on panel). Galleria dell'Accademia, Venice / The Bridgeman Art Library.

Just as a tree has no "profile" so too does Piero's figure offer itself here, Longhi suggests, in its fullest prospect, the frontal impact of its masses eclipsing the ostensible designation of its lines:
it appears *stamped* upon the landscape so that its profile posture
does not detract from the totality and thereby the frontality of
its presentation. Like bodily imprints, Piero's figures appear
stamped upon the background and the picture plane, equating
all surfaces before the viewer. Bodies, flesh, clothing, the natural
landscape and the architecture that reflects it, all seem adapted
to each other, coinciding in a full frontal scene. Longhi's lesson
for Pasolini here opens up not only the formal possibility of an
equilibrium of figure and ground, one inserted into the plane of
the other, but, as human and inanimate forms are leveled, as it
were, the world at large becomes—Franciscan fashion—an object of veneration. Yet the humanity of this consecrating vision
still resonates with the ceremonial, ritualistic disposition of an
acheiropoietic presentness. Such oscillation between the worldly
and the sacred, joined in an image, might have itself served as
an excellent model of contamination for Pasolini.

Pasolini repeatedly acknowledges Masaccio as prime pictorial referent: it is the Masaccio who descends from the
Franciscan Giotto, and the Masaccio whose archaic grandeur
will inform Piero della Francesca (as Longhi observed) that
Pasolini inherits.[45] In this genealogy one identifies, once again, a
confluence of narrative-pictorial and iconic dispositions, of perspectival space and archaic frontality, articulated in Masaccio's
overlapping planes and complex orientation of figures, adding up to a hieratic totality. It may be anachronistic to describe
Masaccio's Peter in the *St. Peter Healing with His Shadow* as *acheiropoietic,* yet this figure's departure from the realistic, mobile,
narrative impetus of the fresco, his corporeal frontality in a
distinct spatial order that seems to have left behind—as befits
a miraculous instance—the worldly space-time of the setting
with its diagonal flow, constitutes an archaic, hieratic intrusion
upon a contemporary scene of quasi-reportage: the ordinary
street corner, the beggars, the sense of something happening

"in passing" (Figure 4.8).[46] While Peter's glance seems directed to the viewer (rather than the hypothetical "elsewhere" in the divine address of the icon), and while his corporeal presence could suggest a material, worldly roughness, one clearly discerns here the archaic grandeur that distinguishes his frontal, hovering spatiality against the setting and that monumentalizes the imposition of his figure as casting that miraculously healing shadow. In moving beyond mere pictorial allusions and iconography, toward an understanding of Pasolini's interiorizing of Masaccio's archaism and its translation to a cinematic language, I would suggest that something akin to the visual oxymoron I have described above is approached in Pasolini's rendering of the Last Supper. Here a repeated, static frontal close-up of a radiant Christ—who has just established the Transubstantiation of the bread and wine—looking straight out toward the camera, is intercut with the comparatively natural, mobile reactions of the Apostles (Figures 4.9–4.10). The repeated portrait shot of Christ departs, in its almost freeze-frame arrest, from the malleable spatiality of the sequence. Though the Apostles glance at Jesus, *his* glance is directed away from their space and outward, breaking the flow of what first appears like a shot/reverse shot organization with the intrusion of an alien dimension: the taboo zone implicated by the direct look at the camera. Despite Pasolini's attention to a world of ordinary material detail—the bowls, the fingers scooping up wet meat, the drinking, the chewing and swallowing of food—the sequence's departure from illusionistic cinematic space and time through the isolated shots of Christ elicits an iconic gaze in the midst of the domestic scene.[47]

This segment echoes Masaccio's colliding of diverse spatial orders, receding and frontal, contemporary and archaic, realist and ceremonial. For even as his modeling of figures and foreshortening of architectural elements already belong to a modern perspectival order, even as his use, elsewhere, of the natural landscape would allow for a more leisurely, or at least more *reasonable,* distribution of figures, Masaccio's intensified

Figure 4.8. Masaccio, *St. Peter Healing with His Shadow*, ca. 1427 (fresco). Brancacci Chapel, Santa Maria del Carmine, Florence / Alinari / The Bridgeman Art Library.

Figure 4.9. Pier Paolo Pasolini, *The Gospel according to Matthew*, 1964.

Figure 4.10. *The Gospel according to Matthew*.

compression of groupings in a shallow foreground posits that setting as backdrop. The hills in the *Tribute Money* and in the *Baptism of the Neophytes,* the architectural elements in the *Story of Theophilus,* and even the receding street in *St. Peter Healing with His Shadow* (all in the Brancacci Chapel) convert natural or urban landscapes to backdrops against which figures and groupings are amassed, intensified, imprinted, projected forth—even when not bodily turned toward the viewer. A focused instance of Pasolini's lesson from Longhi might also juxtapose Masaccio's *Adoration of the Magi* (from the predella to the Pisa altarpiece) with Pasolini's camera work on this very theme.[48] Masaccio's *Magi* renders the processional scene laterally (Figure 4.11). The bare mountainous background, with only a sliver of sky at the top, suggests some atmospheric depth but this is not constituted as a space offered to the figures, which all appear ceremoniously laid out vis-à-vis the surface of the painting. In this ritual summation of a voyage that has reached its sacred object—a poor mother and child—the crowded group of attendants and horses on the right struggles for breathing space in a relatively shallow area thus occupied by anecdotal, quotidian detail that nevertheless intensifies the entire panel. The ceremonial frontality of the whole can be described, following Longhi's example, as quite independent from the ostensibly profile depiction of the majority of the figures. Pasolini's equivalent Gospel scene shifts from a similar processional organization set up against a nearby hillside (Figure 4.12) to a consummating high-angle shot taken from behind the Madonna and Child (Figure 4.13). A boy bearing gifts approaches from the back of the procession to the front, the camera tilting down and zooming in toward him as he kneels in front of the young Mary. From this second, over-the-shoulder shot—which no longer connotes a pictorial but a properly cinematic order—the figures now appear to crowd the frame as if the length of the procession, grasped from up front, was suddenly pressed forward. Between the lateral view of the processional spectacle

Figure 4.11. Masaccio, *Adoration of the Magi*, 1426 (central panel of predella, oil on poplar wood). Gemaeldegalerie, Staatliche Museen zu Berlin / Bildarchiv Preussischer Kulturbesitz / Art Resource, New York.

Figure 4.12. *The Gospel according to Matthew.*

Figure 4.13. *The Gospel according to Matthew.*

wherein the relation to the landscape suggested a ceremonial pictorial space, and this condensed elevated view that transports us to an explicitly cinematic space, we witness in a nutshell Pasolini's aesthetic of frontality. A history of the hieratic image breathes into the basic devices of Pasolini's medium a hallowed tradition of representation—but it is at the same time a modernist cinematic consciousness that emerges in this process.

The most mechanical and graceless of devices, the pronounced zoom motion, itself enacts the colliding of figure and ground, endowing the contemporary device with consecrating connotations. Pasolini's contamination of the reverential style by such newsreel machinations underlines a frontality already prescribed by the mise-en-scène and, as we will see, by the choice of the landscape itself.[49] The deliberate effacing of depth, the collapsing together of figure and ground by means of focal length and framing—so much so that even a vast and spacious landscape that would allow a penetrating, perspectival view is pressed up in front of the camera—effect a backdrop upon which even moving figures seem imprinted or, one might simply say, projected. In the opening of the baptism scene a mountainous landscape is traversed as the camera seems to plunge from its high-angle position by means of a series of zoom-in motions into the deeply set Chia Creek near Viterbo: features of the landscape appear to spread and flatten in their optical approach toward the screen surface. All sense of depth, of the distance just "traversed" by the zoom, is optically eliminated as figures and ground are crowded in the shallow, compressed, enclosed space that remains at the end of the lens's motion. The curious spatiality, the distinctness of figures, and the postures of the Baptist in these surroundings recall, once again, Pasolini's prime pictorial referent as the final position of the lens in very long focal length

obtains effects even dearer to my boy's-eyes trained on Masaccio, flattens the images even more, renders them

more warm and burdened. It leavens them like loaves,
massive and light . . . just as the painter's brush is light,
almost sparkling in creating the most massive *chiaroscuri*
of the modeling, that has man as its center and as its
light, the Universal Light.[50]

A "casual" effect of immediacy that Pasolini described as borrowed from sports or news reportage results, paradoxically,
in an icon-like presentness of the image. This is compounded
by a deliberate subduing of movement even in mobile shots:
Pasolini's camera tracks characters in close or medium shots
in such a way as to keep them in a practically steady relation
to the frame. In the first shot of the adult Jesus as he appears in
the baptism scene the busy narrative exposition does not, therefore, negate even as it may be said to "contaminate" a stunning
hieratic portrait, at once mobile and static. But even Pasolini's
deliberate severing of sound and image throughout the film,
his isolation of voices, his frequent use of music to displace all
natural sounds, and most radically the moments of completely
silent soundtrack, so rare in narrative cinema—all these far exceed the practices of the Italian post-sync tradition, depriving
the cinematic space of its illusionistic resonance. Beyond the
erratic shifts of a handheld camera, beyond the heterogeneous
texture, the contamination of techniques and effects, mechanical and reverential, Pasolini achieved an unforeseen contemplative detachment and calm that envelops the sense of the whole
in his *Gospel according to Matthew*. A hieratic disposition, even
in a perspectival frame of reference, allows him to bypass the
illusionist fallacy in favor of an immanence of vision that per-
meates not only the represented world but the materiality of
the medium itself.

From the very first images a consciousness of the perfect thematization of an archaistic imagination makes itself
apparent in Pasolini's *Gospel*. Consider that opening mute
frontal shot of the young pregnant Mary, modeled perhaps on

Piero's *Madonna della Misericordia,* against a blind arch that enframes her as would the iconic beam or panel structure (Figure 4.14). Such enframed areas as suggested by arches, windows, and doorways, often used in the cinema to enhance additional planes in deep-focus compositions—we have seen this in Visconti's *La terra trema*—are usually blocked in Pasolini's film. Rather than lead the eye into depth, they serve here to enframe a figure imprinted upon the ground that, oriented toward our space, compresses the figure onto the screen surface. Pasolini compounds this hieratic disposition with an almost silent soundtrack over the first few shot/reverse shots of Joseph and Mary. Even as the narrative is thus launched, Pasolini's bold treatment maintains this dominant orientation: Joseph is framed a few shots later in medium shot from the back, his torso a dark shape against the bright background, his silhouette stamped upon the view of Barile, the Apulian hilltown that serves as Pasolini's Bethlehem. The landscape, which seems projected right up in front of him, fills the frame almost entirely with very little definition of sky at the top to barely suggest distance and dimension. Throughout the film the framing of the landscape rarely allows more than this bit of sky to define the contours of a hillside. Indeed, wherever there is a sky over the landscapes of Pasolini's *Gospel according to Matthew,* it is usually overcast to maintain an opaque and flattened surface. Preparing for Joseph's dream, a pan tracing the undulating rhythms of the hill describes the expanse of natural features and architectural elements—ruins, caves, paths—blending into each other upon the surface. Joseph's own motion of turning and kneeling to sleep bodily repeats the movement of the descending pan: the human body is rendered synonymous with the unfolding landscape, which thus partakes in the dream. Following this logic of identity, indicated by camera work, between figure and landscape, the Angel's appearance seems "naturalized" in the humble setting: it is barely distinguishable from the children shown playing here a moment earlier, as if it had been all along part of this setting (Figures 4.15–4.16). It is as if the landscape has been waiting for this instance to offer to

Figure 4.14. *The Gospel according to Matthew.*

Figure 4.15. *The Gospel according to Matthew.*

Figure 4.16. *The Gospel according to Matthew.*

view its sacred burden, its own underlying *figure*: the natural, the everyday, and the miraculous apparition "contaminate" each other.[51] Already in these opening shots, then, Pasolini's camera seeks relations of repetition, identity, and reciprocity between the landscape and the figures, as if these were drawn by a single hand with no abyss, no shadow separating one from the other but as overlapping, colliding on the screen, pertaining to a single hieratic totality.

The importance of hillside landscapes, similarly enframed, which reappear in variation throughout the film, cannot be overemphasized. It is the archetypal ground of Pasolini's *Gospel according to Matthew,* rising vertically like an iconic backdrop, filling the frame with little or no sense of depth, confronting the viewer; upon it, figures, faces, often static and portrait-like, appear to be imprinted. Mountains and jagged rocky precipices, terraces and slopes, crevices, cave mouths and archways served iconic traditions and their Italian descendants well through the fourteenth century. Such landscape elements have traditionally been coupled with a high horizon line, so that the background would appear to rise vertically as the unifying ground where different dimensions, far and near, high and low, heaven and earth, join. The dense hillside architecture crowding some of Giotto's frescoes in San Francesco at Assisi can be seen to make such "backdrop" use of the elevated facets and structures, each plane seeming to emerge out of the other as the lot confronts the view of the surface as a whole (Figure 4.17). These hilltown depictions appear to be modeled *after* the natural conditions of such environments, yet their vertical frontality also refers back to the gilded or veiled iconic surfaces before narrative elaboration and the windows of linear perspective were opened. Pasolini's camera technique responds to such landscape features as support the crowd at the marketplace of Matera— Jerusalem's analogue—with its hill slopes, ascending paths, or *gradoni* (hillside ramps and terraced paths) leading toward the city gates (Figure 4.18). From a relatively high position, the

Figure 4.17. Giotto, *The Expulsion of the Devils from Arezzo*, 1297–99 (fresco). San Francesco, Upper Church, Assisi, Italy / Giraudon / The Bridgeman Art Library.

narrow-angle telephoto lens inhibits depth and motion, flattens the view, magnifies our sense of an upright, opaque backdrop, its negative spaces full in the thick of the figures and objects that crowd the frame. In this tapestry-like impression a multitude of elements are compressed: the image is rendered concrete, full, offering itself to view. It is not a simple morphological or iconographic allusion to his preferred pictorial sources—noted in so many commentaries on Pasolini—that is at stake but an

Figure 4.18. *The Gospel according to Matthew.*

affinity in the deeper structure, in the foundation of the image and, I would say, in Pasolini's grasp of cinema as such that we identify here. Even as Pasolini's location hunt has informed the Christological constitution of this aesthetic, so its cinematic modes of articulation find their perfect object in the southern Italian landscape.

The choice of Matera, an ancient hilltown in the Basilicata region, as the setting for Jerusalem is an emblematic instance in Pasolini's use of the southern Italian landscape; we locate here, as well, the historical specificity and ideological bearing of a charged location grasped as *terra sancta*. Its constitution in the film will serve to bring together and conclude many of the themes explored in this chapter: contamination and analogy by which the modern and the archaic, the humble and the sacred are negotiated; the film's consecrating grasp of its objects; its homologizing of figure and landscape; and the iconic rhetoric that underlies this cinematic aesthetic as a whole. The status of Matera in monastic culture—the early dissemination of Christianity wherein hermits from Palestine, Syria, and Cappadocia who escaped persecution found precisely here features "analogous" to their native lands—is accounted for by the isolated and inaccessible perch of the town just off the arid section of the *murge,* the rocky plateaus leading toward the heel of the Italian peninsula. Eastern Byzantine influences coexisted in Matera with Western, Latin culture: excavations have uncovered some 115 churches, chapels, and sanctuaries built in the rock, many containing frescoed icons of Old and New Testament figures. Major archaeological work was in fact in progress here from 1959 though 1966—surrounding the production of *The Gospel.*[52] The bringing to light of early Christian remnants that had endowed Matera with cult value must have suggested to an artist like Pasolini a strong sense of *praesentia* that would be analogically bequeathed upon his Jerusalem. Obviously, the actual icons within the rock and cave churches of Matera are not incorporated in the film, but Pasolini may have sought to articulate their embedded presence through the landscape's own anthropomorphic, auratic resonances.

Intersecting these Christological connotations of a privileged location is another discourse that reflects Pasolini's valorization of the archaic within modernity, inserting his intervention in an important contemporary debate. For Matera was seen to epitomize in the postwar era the massive neglect and underdevelopment of the Italian south: the ancient rock dwellings, the Sassi, still inhabited in the 1950s by a peasant population but completely bereft of sanitation, were deemed "the shame of Italy."[53] Matera became, thereby, an emblematic site of urban renewal specifically geared toward the preservation of vernacular, regional values within an advanced housing program. This too, we have seen, was neorealism: the reclamation of marginal and underdeveloped terrains for postwar modernity; the attentive reconstruction of the local and humble detail in a would-be organic forging of shared communal values and historical continuity out of indigenous patterns and vernacular traditions. Such concerns informed the housing project of La Martella, erected in the hinterland just

beyond Matera, joining to make it one of the crowning achievements of neorealist urban planning. This regionalist-modernist
approach to the Italian landscape surely informs Pasolini as he
comes to make new cinematic use out of the old town. Fearing
the eclipse of the archaic by aggressive modern developments
and neocapitalist speculation, Pasolini was attentive to the
harmonious, empathetic binding of the contemporary urban
fabric and the archaic peasant past so vital, he thought, for the
constitution of a not entirely disenchanted modernity. Such
concerns punctuated Pasolini's career and are still evident in his
contribution to the short 1974 television documentary on the
hilltown of Orte, in the Lazio region: *La forma della città* (The
Form of the City, directed by Paolo Brunatto). His commentary
and his guiding of the camera's controlled shifts of focal length
in the framing and reframing of the panoramic skyline and
discrete landscape elements directly address concerns we have
discerned in the *Gospel* project. Pasolini speaks for the protection of the most humble detail—a stone path, a gate—from the
threatening deformation of aggressive development that does
not take account of the town's age-old organic formation. A
decade after *The Gospel* and the *Sopralluoghi in Palestina*, he criti-
cizes here the ways in which recently erected workers' dwellings thoughtlessly "disturb the relationship between the city's
form and nature."[54] In the fabric of his own cinema Pasolini
sought instead, and with remarkable consistency throughout
his work, to explore potent continuities in the embrace of a
disappearing but still vital archaic domain, and the modernism
of a social and political, indeed, revolutionary possibility.

Pasolini's first panoramic shots of Matera—placed at the center of *The Gospel according to Matthew* and signaling the beginning of the Passion—link it to the film's opening in Barile, the
location for Bethlehem that I described earlier. The geographical
proximity of Jerusalem and Bethlehem in the Judea Mountains
accounts in part for this pairing of southern Italian hilltowns,
as does Pasolini's evident fascination with the severe beauty of

the Sassi side of Matera, where the hillside *gradoni* lead the eye, and the camera, across cave mouths interspersed with arches, windows, and doorways (Figure 4.19). The local stones that have sectioned and terraced the hillside for centuries to prevent landslides, the fusion of rock surfaces and stone houses with the natural rhythms of the place—those are traced, caressed, by the camera. These cinematic landscapes of Matera thus support our view of the Mediterranean hilltown as itself fully inserted in the landscape, a landscape that, while arid and hard to cultivate, has nonetheless been inhabited, tamed for centuries—if only, at times, by the sheer repetition of footsteps along the same paths—into a reserved moderation that is the root of its beauty. Densely built on top, thinning out down the hill, such towns—like Arab and Druze villages in the pre–Six-Day War Palestine that Pasolini had observed in the *Sopralluoghi*—seem to emerge out of the landscape, like an articulation of the place itself. The town repeats and embodies the landscape, which is in turn crystallized in the duration of a film shot.[55]

In one of the few shots in the film so explicitly designated as Jesus' point of view, such an undulating, caressing pan over

Figure 4.19. *The Gospel according to Matthew.*

the Matera landscape is matched in a delayed reverse shot with a close-up of Christ, the movement of his funereal yet gentle glance repeating the camera's movement. As in the earlier matching of Joseph's bodily movement with that of a descending panning shot over Bethlehem/Barile, there is in this reciprocity of the human look and the landscape a sense of full recognition and submission, marked by Christ's ultimate lowering and shifting of the eyes away from the view—a view at once so humble and so charged. And as his movement is responsive to the view, so the landscape appears here as if touched by the look, as if responding to the consecrating glance—of Jesus as of the camera—turned upon it. In this way is a landscape figured: Pasolini's own cinematic perception equates itself here with divine vision for which the "things of the world," touched by that charged glance, incarnate the sacred. In this quintessential instance—the shot/reverse shot reciprocity of Jesus facing the view of Matera as a whole, "taking it in" as he caresses it with his eyes—a spirit of place may be understood as incarnated in his human features, even as his charged glance is figured in the landscape. Like the iconic screen, Matera becomes at once backdrop to the impending Passion, its compassionate witness, and itself an object of divine contemplation. In this it reflects our own role opposite it. Béla Balázs eloquently described just such reciprocity between the landscape and human physiognomy, between the look and its objects in the cinema:

> The film, like the painting, thus offers the possibility of giving the background, the surroundings, a physiognomy no less intense than the faces of the characters. . . . It is as though the countryside were suddenly lifting its veil and showing its face, and on the face an expression which we recognize though we could not give it a name.[56]

This is the face of the earth. Its expression, its return look, its *praesentia*, is unraveled by a consecrating perception, now identified with that of the movie camera.

As the sacred is transported from the *Terra Sancta* to this place, so does its incarnation in the humanity of Christ bear upon the archaic landscape that grounds his image, affording a more enduring expressivity than that of one human face alone. Pasolini seeks to capture in the filmed surface, in the "things of the world," a glimpse of the iconic image of God: seen but not quite nameable, exceeding the particular and the historical in its apotheosis in the landscape. It is not abstracted as text, it denies the arbitrariness of signs, it transpires on film. According to such a theology, analogy as working principle is complemented by anagogy,[57] the work's participation in divine meaning, where what has been told in darkness is screened in light.

The Ends of the Land

The cinematic consecration of a landscape in reciprocity with the human glance, the human visage, comes to express in Pasolini's work a modern resurrection of archaic vitality. His dream of a revolutionary potential embedded in this plenitude, and set against a depleted, homogenized, commodified Italy, yields forceful anachronisms in the disruptive—dare I say magnificently flawed—fabric of Pasolini's film theory and practice. By the mid-1970s its promise collapses in the face of Pasolini's dreaded incursions of neocapitalism: the relentless all-consuming, all-emptying of things, actions, people, places. For all their differences of temperament and form, Pasolini and Antonioni share this recognition in the search for a new figural order in late modernity. Antonioni's perception of the depletion of modernity's promise does not explicitly compare, as did Pasolini's, the face of contemporary Italy with the atrocious phenomena surrounding the Second World War. But his latest work too is fully engaged in the environmental and cultural shifts sweeping Europe. Antonioni's trust in the prospects of art and cinema—fully informed by science and technology—to negotiate such transitions must be greater, for we find an astonishing capacity for renewal in his recent recasting of a documentary glance upon Italian landscapes that persist as bulwarks in the face of this transmutation. The cinematic intelligence of place by which an earlier modernism was assimilated and transfigured, as we have seen, in Antonioni's formative period echoes in a bold return in the early 1990s to several resonant locations. Having formulated in the interim some of the most penetrating observations that cinema has ever offered on industrial society, Antonioni recapitulates but also profoundly transforms that earlier formulation in his return. On the eve of the twenty-first century, in a transition perhaps no less acute than the one he had witnessed across the divide of the world war, Antonioni refigured cinema's glance upon the Italian landscape: a glance that enfolds the past in projecting an uncertain future.

These Sicilian landscapes (Figure A.1) seem offered in a long planetary view, perhaps from the removed perspective of a survivor of a no longer seen but yet sensed cataclysm, a view oscillating between the archaic earth and the phantasmic order of science fiction. The eight-minute documentary short *Noto Mandorli Vulcano Stromboli Carnevale,* produced by ENEL (Italy's national electric company) for the Italian pavilion at the Seville Expo of 1992, incorporates extensive aerial cinematography of extraordinary color and resolution in the last three of its five Sicilian landscape vignettes. In its *impegno* with industrial civilization, in its perceptual feat, in the choice of landscape objects, the film echoes Antonioni's neorealist assimilation of earlier avant-gardes as a late-modern recollection. Antonioni

Figure A.1. Michelangelo Antonioni, *Noto Mandorli Vulcano Stromboli Carnevale,* 1992.

returns here to *L'avventura*'s locations in the Aeolian islands and in Noto's elevated bell tower, invoking as well such neorealist locations as Visconti's Sicily, Rossellini's Stromboli, and even, in the closing images, Fellini's crowded piazzas. The filmed location is not a landscape painting, not a still photograph. As moving image, the fuming earth seems to heave and pulsate like a corporeal presence, an immanence waiting to unfold. Whatever film-historical or regional connotations are at work here, they are transfigured by the aerial cinematography in smooth gliding motions, enhanced by synthesized music. Such views still have the power to transform our sense of orientation, dimension, depth: the mouths of volcanos, the precipices and folds of earth that appear in one instance as small dunes in tight framing are revealed in the next as voluminous mountainous expanses (Figure A.2). The iridescent sulfuric cracks, vast or minuscule (it is often unclear which) emit fumes that at times envelop the frame entirely (Figure A.3). Empty and full,

Figure A.2. *Noto Mandorli Vulcano Stromboli Carnevale.*

Figure A.3. *Noto Mandorli Vulcano Stromboli Carnevale.*

deserted and populated views, the primeval and the devastated become strangely alike in this short film. Does such perception replenish these marginal sites? Does it elicit new energy, a new life therein? The celebrated, named Sicilian locations are altered; seen from outside itself, the eruptive landscape is raised to a new figural order. Or should one simply say that its exhilarating alien aspect is predicated on the superb technology that confronts it—from a distance? And if so, even in a new image order, ever more removed, cinema is at home in this world.

In the half century that separates Antonioni's work across the Second World War—his early photographic essay and first documentary—from these late Sicilian landscapes, the tense relation between modernity (or late modernity) and its conditions of representation in motion pictures has not been resolved. But its attendant anxieties have perhaps been augmented by a still altering environment, as by the progress of image technologies—the displacements of the very notion of reference and reproduction, photographic and actual. Even further removed in the digital sublime, the index, the real, the body, the historical trauma haunt new technologies with ghosts from the past, never put to rest. A fundamental ambivalence about their implication still informs the most eloquent instances of fiction and documentary, in cinematographic, digital, and virtual spaces. Arguably, we inherit these discourses, with few detours, from the ruinous grounds of the world war: debates propagated by neorealism are still with us. In the wake of the Cold War, on the margins of Europe, do Antonioni's images speak of an exhaustion of resources as impending crisis, or of some new age transformation of consciousness vis-à-vis a still living, breathing earth?

It should not dispel the historical lesson of neorealism to see in its strongest articulations of the Italian landscape a premonition of Antonioni's glance, at once mature and anxious, removed and demiurgic, upon these Mediterranean isles. Pasolini, in his "desperate vitality," had already envisioned—also on a coastal landscape of an increasingly marginal country, and where the land ends—such a divided look enfolding ruin and immanence, emblematically historical in its Janus turn to departures and returns, past and future:[1]

> "As to the future, listen:
> your Fascist sons
> will sail
> towards worlds in the New Prehistory.
> I will be there
> as one who dreams that he is harmed
> on the coast of the sea
> in which life recommences.
> Alone, or almost, on the old beach
> among ruins of ancient civilizations,
> Ravenna
> Ostia, or Bombay—it is the same—

> with Gods who have flaked away, old problems
> — such as the class struggle—
> that
> dissolve . . .
> Like a partisan
> who died before May 1945.
> I will start very slowly to decompose,
> in the painful light of that sea,
> forgotten poet and citizen."[2]

Perhaps in a disenchanted world these strong—divisive and divided, erupting, eroding—observations of a poet, a filmmaker, a partisan, a citizen, thus come to represent our own glance upon the landscape in a time of transition, and in some of cinema's most vital expressions.

Acknowledgments

Italian Locations evolved through different phases and places, and with the help and inspiration of many. Institutional, professional, and personal support at Yale University sustained an academic pursuit of my passions: I have been most indebted at the Department of the History of Art and in the Film Studies Program to Dudley Andrew, Edward S. Cooke Jr., Thomas Crow, David Joselit, Charles Musser, and Brigitte Peucker. The A. Whitney Griswold Faculty Awards supported my forays into Italian archives for the first half of the book. Much of the rest draws on a dissertation written in New York University's Department of Cinema Studies, where the Jay Leyda Memorial Fellowship and the George Amberg Memorial Award provided support. At NYU, I have been grateful for the guidance of Richard Allen and William Simon and cherish the continued intellectual example and support of Annette Michelson. In developing my research the help of several Italian institutions has been indispensable: in Rome I am grateful to Sergio Toffetti and staff at the Cineteca Nazionale, and to Edoardo Ceccuti and staff at Istituto Luce; at the Cineteca di Bologna and the Archivio Pier Paolo Pasolini it has been my special privilege to be helped by Anna Fiaccarini and Roberto Chiesi. Sandro Bernardi, Marco Bertozzi, Francesco Casetti, and Jacopo Chessa opened doors and were also the first to extend an Italian readership for my work. While in residence at the American Academy in Rome, sponsored by a National Endowment for the Humanities Postdoctoral Fellowship, I filled gaps in this project while laying the foundations for another. Several expert readers on this side of the Atlantic—Peter Brunette, Angela Dalle Vacche, P. Adams Sitney, and one anonymous reviewer—offered constructive advice at different stages of revision of the manuscript. I was fortunate to have the heartening support of Edward Dimendberg and of Douglas Armato and his wonderful staff at the University of Minnesota Press.

Also at Yale I relied on the expert help of Helen Chillman at Visual Resources, Michael Kerbel and Ann Horton-Line at the Film Study Center, Tom Klute and friends at Photography and Media Services, and all manner of assistance from Nicole Chardiet, Susan Emerson, Marilyn Green, and Susan Hart. The lively, bright feedback of students and assistants was most meaningful in all different phases: Jess Atwood-Gibson, Lance Duerfahrd, Mariano Prunes, Alessandra Raengo, Lutz Robbers, Irene Small, Eric Stryker, and many others deserve my thanks.

My closest colleagues and friends Sean Anderson, Tim Barringer, Hisham Bizri, Moshe Elhanati, Romy Golan, Flavia Marcello, Ivone Margulies, Joe McElhaney, Mira Perlov, John-David Rhodes, Michal and Harold Rose, Katie Trumpener, Chris Wood, and Claire Zimmerman inspire me at those luminous intersections of the intellectual and the personal. Most generous is always the conversation of David Jacobson: for many years he has been the most rigorous and sensitive reader, friend. I am ever grateful for the open doors, and hearts, of my extended families in the Galilee and in the Po Valley.

No longer living is David Perlov, whose filmmaking and mentorship have inspired my ways of seeing and thinking about cinematic locations in these pages.

Gone is my adored father, the painter Avigdor Steimatsky, who taught me the intense, vulnerable pursuit of intuition in the visual encounter: how to follow it now but without him, and even where language fails?

The indelible strength and love of my mother, Tamar Gotlieb-Steimatsky, from far and very near, sustains me always.

Nadja and Aram, my children: the happiness they inspire puts all things in place daily, and joins everything together.

Paolo Barlera: ironic and constant man, and river-boy. To you this book is dedicated, after all.

Notes

Introduction

1. "Una disperata vitalità" is the title of Pasolini's 1963 cycle of poems, published in the collection *Poesia in forma di rosa* (Milan: Garzanti, 1964). The first part of this poem invokes this same Roman periphery; I quote from the translation by Norman MacAfee and Luciano Martinengo in Pier Paolo Pasolini, *Selected Poems* (London: John Calder, 1984), 149: ". . . as in a film by Godard—rediscovery / of romanticism in the seat of / neocapitalistic cynicism and cruelty— / at the wheel / on the road from Fiumicino . . ."

2. In *Stupendous, Miserable City: Pasolini's Rome* (Minneapolis: University of Minnesota Press, 2007) John-David Rhodes offers the most advanced treatment of the urbanist critique embedded in Pasolini's first feature films as bound up with a critique of neorealism. Rhodes's work has enhanced my thinking in these pages.

3. After her "pink neorealist" beginnings as a *mondina*—the bare-legged rice picker in Giuseppe De Santis's *Bitter Rice* (*Riso amaro,* 1949) but also as a Miss Italy candidate—Mangano became a figure of commercial celebrity, wife of Dino De Laurentiis, the powerful producer of *Le streghe,* where she stars in all the episodes. Her work on *La terra vista* is the first in a string of important roles that she played for Pasolini. Pasolini memorably brought forth multiple connotations in Mangano's persona—innocent and sophisticated, serenely archaic and neurotically modern. Thus she emerges as a figure for mediating anachronisms in such diverse roles as Jocasta in *Oedipus Rex* (*Edipo Re,* 1967), the industrialist's wife in *Teorema* (1968), and the Madonna of Giotto's dream in the *Decameron* (1971). I am grateful to David Jacobson for insights on this topic.

4. Roberto Chiesi of the Centro Studi–Archivio Pier Paolo Pasolini at the Cineteca di Bologna argued (in personal conversation) that Pasolini was no cinephile, and that much of the iconography of

this short film derives from the popular children's comics weekly *Il corriere dei piccoli* on which generations of Italians were raised. I see no contradiction between this comic's inspiration and the evocation not only of Italian sources but of Clair, Pasolini's old favorite, and Vigo's intense poetics in *L'Atalante* (1934).

5. A comparably bold palette of industrial, plastic, and fabric colors may be found in a temperamentally opposed film of that era: Michelangelo Antonioni's *Red Desert* (*Il deserto rosso*, 1964).

6. "Io sono una forza del Passato" is a famous line from Pasolini's 1962 poem of the sequence *Poesie mondane,* written during the production of *Mamma Roma* (1962). The section including this line is recited by Orson Welles in the role of film director in Pasolini's short *La ricotta* (1963). Except where otherwise indicated, translations in this book are my own, with the help of Paolo Barlera.

7. My use of "modernity" and "modernism" generally follows consensus: modernity in reference to the broad historical period at least since the late-eighteenth-century decline of the aristocracy and the rise of the middle classes, or since the beginnings of the industrial revolutions, and the effects of these revolutionary forces upon geography, demography, politics, and culture. Modernity might be periodized differently: traced back to include the Renaissance, or else mapped onto different cultural contexts. In fact it arrives in Italy with a relative delay, of which I will remind the reader in the first chapter. "Modernism" too is notoriously polysemic: as the following discussion implies, it is the cultural and aesthetic self-consciousness applied to a late stage of modernity. While not quite as fluid as the various "realisms," modernism can encompass a variety of styles across the arts. The transgressive modernisms whose programs traversed artistic practice, politics, and life are often classified among the avant-gardes.

8. "Pink" neorealism is often how the "exploitation" dimensions of such films as, most famously, De Santis's *Bitter Rice* were sometimes denigrated for their sensationalist materials, even as their achievements have been acknowledged in the criticism.

9. The periodizing proposed in this "obverse" historiography of neorealism via the case of the Cinecittà refugee camp, largely glossed over in the literature, carries historical and symbolic weight that I address in an essay forthcoming in *Bianco e nero* 560/61 and 562 (2008) and in *October* (Fall 2008). The requisition of Cinecittà may have been

not unrelated to the Allied Film Board's immediate flooding of the market with American films that had had little or no European distribution during the war. I might cite at least one other periodizing framework of the decade launched by Visconti's *Ossessione* in 1943, the first film to which a neorealist epithet was attached, and capped on the other end by Visconti's historical melodrama *Senso* of 1954. Beyond these narrow periodizations, however, the farther horizons of neorealism are discussed in what follows.

10. David Overbey's introduction to *Springtime in Italy: A Reader on Neo-Realism,* ed. and trans. David Overbey (Hamden, Conn.: Archon Books, 1978), 1–33, develops a comparable critique, though it sometimes risks throwing out the baby with the bathwater. Though De Sica's use of location does not tear at its cinematic fabric in the ways that engage me in this book, his attention to urban spaces is not without interest and has been acknowledged by Bruno Reichlin in "Figures of Neorealism in Italian Architecture," part 2, *Grey Room* 6 (Winter 2002): 110–33.

11. See Mario Cannella's essay, originally published in 1966, "Ideology and Aesthetic Hypotheses in the Criticism of Neo-Realism," *Screen* 14, no. 4 (Winter 1973–74): 5–60.

12. On the film industrial circumstances and politics of this period, see Callisto Cosulich, "Neorealismo e associazionismo 1944–1953: Cronaca di dieci anni," in *Il neorealismo cinematografico italiano,* ed. Lino Miccichè (Venice: Marsilio, 1999), 90–97.

13. Some of these stars, like Amadeo Nazzari, were inherited from Fascist and wartime production; others, like Anna Magnani, achieved star stature as neorealist archetypes.

14. Gian Piero Brunetta cites and analyzes Barbaro's preface to Pudovkin in *Storia del cinema italiano,* rev. ed., vol. 2 (Rome: Riuniti, 1993), 203. This citation can be compared with Barbaro's earlier comment from a 1930–31 survey of Russian literature: "Although drawing on 19th century literature, [Russian] neorealism cannot be considered a proper return but has, rather, innovative, even avant-garde, characteristics somewhat analogous to the German neorealism of Döblin in literature and of Dix in painting, more so than to our Moravia or to the 'magical realism' of Bontempelli" (Umberto Barbaro, "Letteratura russa a volo d'uccello," *Neorealismo e realismo,* vol. 1 [Rome: Riuniti, 1976], 108).

15. The importance, for Visconti, of his assistantship on Renoir's costume film cannot be overestimated. One recalls, at the same time, the film's uncertain finale—in part the result of production circumstances but certainly also subject to directorial choices—as its brief narrative dissolves in the almost abstract pictorial expanses of the Marne River landscape. I will describe something similar in chapter 1, regarding Antonioni's Po River film.

16. Visconti recalled in a later interview that Serandrei wrote to him upon receiving the rushes: "I don't know how I could define this type of cinema except with the term *neorealist*." In "Vita difficile del film *Ossessione*," *Il Contemporaneo* 4, supplement to *Rinascita* 22, no. 17 (April 24, 1965): 7–8.

17. Gian Piero Brunetta analyzes Barbaro's art-historical contextualizing of *Ossessione* in "Longhi e l'Officina cinematografica," in *L'arte di scrivere sull'arte: Roberto Longhi nella cultura del nostro tempo,* ed. Giovanni Previtali (Rome: Riuniti, 1982), 47–55.

18. The ideological pitfalls of antimodernist nostalgia were symptomatic of many modernist traditions. Cf. Romy Golan's nuanced treatment of comparable tensions in *Modernity and Nostalgia: Art and Politics in France between the Wars* (New Haven, Conn.: Yale University Press, 1995). This conflicted identity of neorealism has also been the pretext for its sometime wholesale critical dismissal as naive and retrograde by British *Screen* critics in the 1970s, whose theoretical and ideological agendas collapsed distinctions between all liberal-humanist and reactionary positions and did not bring into consideration specific historical circumstances of the Italian postwar. See, for example, Christopher Williams, who seeks to kill two birds with one stone in "Bazin on Neo-Realism," *Screen* 14, no. 4 (1973): 61–67. I see no need to enter into direct argument with this body of criticism, which is of greater interest for the analysis of 1970s film theory itself than for shedding significant light on postwar Italian culture.

19. The notion of "restricted" versus "elaborate" codes Jameson borrows from Basil Bernstein. Jameson's examples for an oppositional realism range from Chantal Akerman's *News from Home* (1977) to the work of dialect minorities or other marginalities—as in Deleuze and Guattari's notion of a minor literature that adopts a hegemonic language and transforms it into an intensified dialect that cannot, itself, become hegemonic. See Fredric Jameson, "The Existence of Italy,"

Signatures of the Visible (New York: Routledge, 1990), 155–229. Also informing this discussion is Jameson's "The Realist Floor-Plan," in *On Signs,* ed. Marshall Blonsky (Baltimore: Johns Hopkins University Press, 1985), 373–83. In fact cinematic neorealism itself went on to inspire nations, minorities, and ethnic groups in comparable moments of the re-formation of new identities: see Lino Micciché's introduction, "Sul neorealismo, oggi," to *Il neorealismo cinematografico italiano,* xiv–xv. Micciché dwells here on the Italian movement as a frame of reference for new wave "cinemas of underdevelopment" in Africa, Latin America, Eastern Europe, India, and East Asia.

20. Yet it is of course also possible to apply Jameson's cultural periodization wholesale, working toward an evolving postmodern logic, for example in Pasolini's *La terra vista dalla luna.* It is so as not to enmesh my discussion in more theoretical baggage than what is most essential that I have avoided using this third term, preferring instead to consider a realist-oppositional and realist / modernist / antimodernist variants, though hinting here and there at a historical and cultural late modernity, or postmodernity, that some would trace back to the Second World War but whose logic is certainly intensified from the 1960s onward.

21. T. J. Clark, *Farewell to an Idea: Episodes from a History of Modernism* (New Haven, Conn.: Yale University Press, 1999); see both his introduction, especially 10–11, and the conclusion, 405–8. In *The Emergence of Cinematic Time: Modernity, Contingency, the Archive* (Cambridge, Mass.: Harvard University Press, 2002), Mary Ann Doane focuses on the earliest cinematic explorations of contingency, preceding institutional cinema's measures of controlling the representation of time. She makes apparent the ideological stakes—the capitalist economic logic—in the control of contingency, as through continuity editing in narrative cinema.

22. Clark further quotes from Calvino, who observed that "Italian literary and figurative culture had missed the appointment with expressionism in the post–World War I period, but it had its great moment after World War II" (*Farewell,* 405–7).

23. André Bazin's "An Aesthetic of Reality: Neorealism" was first published in 1948; see *What Is Cinema?* vol. 2, ed. and trans. Hugh Gray (Berkeley: University of California Press, 1971), 16–40. For Bazin's further elaboration of comparable practices of opacity and interruption,

see also his essays in *What Is Cinema?* vol. 1, ed. and trans. Hugh Gray (Berkeley: University of California Press, 1967), especially "In Defence of Mixed Cinema," 53–75, and *"Le Journal d'un curé de campagne* and the Stylistics of Robert Bresson," 125–43.

24. In "Stile, realismo e modernità nella teorizzazione di André Bazin," pp. 25–50 in *Il concetto di modernità nel cinema* (Parma: Pratiche Editrice, 1993), Giorgio De Vincenti emphasizes the ways in which this confrontation is comparable to that of the Bazinian notion of "impure cinema," where the material inscription of other media— literature, theater—in certain cinematic adaptation conforms to the ontological photographic realism that Bazin promoted throughout.

25. That certain neorealist locations emerge as spectacular ensembles, themselves apparently coherent, readable within rich cultural contexts—we will think this way about Visconti's *La terra trema*— poses no difficulty for Bazin. Rather, it may be compared with his promotion of the interference of a literary text or of theatrical space in cinematic adaptation. Such extraneous entities brought into the film serve, in Bazin's other writings, to authenticate the act of adaptation itself. There are however dissonances between the discussion of neorealism via the discrete Rossellinian "fact," the ornateness of Visconti, and the transparency of De Sica across Bazin's diverse essays: they implicate a differentiation of neorealist styles that the Rossellini essay does not foresee. See the selection of essays on neorealism in *What Is Cinema?* vol. 2.

26. Gilles Deleuze, in Bazin's footsteps, dwells on neorealism's intervention as more fundamental to cinema's epistemology, he claims, than the transition from silent to sound film in the late 1920s. See *Cinema 1: The Movement-Image,* trans. Hugh Tomlinson and Barbara Habberjam (Minneapolis: University of Minnesota Press, 1986), 211–12, and *Cinema 2: The Time-Image,* trans. Hugh Tomlinson and Robert Galeta (Minneapolis: University of Minnesota Press, 1989), 1–24. The notion of "cronaca"—the chronicle—that punctuates neorealist discourses in this era itself exceeds this cinema's lesson from contemporary reportage. It is perhaps most consciously marked in Antonioni's titling of his first feature film, *Cronaca di un amore* (*Chronicle of a Love Affair,* 1950), which departs altogether from neorealist thematics even as it radicalizes some of the narrative and formal techniques addressed here.

27. Antonioni's "interstitial" perception, as Roland Barthes will dub it—see his 1980 lecture translated in Geoffrey Nowell-Smith, *L'avventura* (London: BFI, 1997), 63–68—infuses an anxious contingency even in the classically charged site or the natural landscape. Yet it is also apparent that Antonioni did not "need" the French theorization of neorealism in order to interiorize and radicalize its lessons—my first chapter addresses another modernist lineage that informs his work. For a politicized reflection on the postwar arenas of the everyday that might inform Antonioni's work one nevertheless looks to the French example with such thinkers as Henri Lefebvre and Michel de Certeau.

28. I rely here on De Vincenti's account of the links between Zavattini's neorealism and New Wave modernisms in *Il concetto di modernità*, 157–75.

29. For a translated synthesis of Zavattini's ideas drawn from articles of the early 1950s, see his "Thesis on Neo-Realism" in Overbey, *Springtime in Italy*, 67–78; certain details stand out in another translation, cited above, from some of the same sources: "Some Ideas on the Cinema," in *Film: A Montage of Theories*, ed. Richard Dyer MacCann (New York: Dutton, 1966), 216–28.

30. In both his writing and later documentary projects Zavattini drew a link between neorealism and New Wave practices baptizing Jean-Luc Godard, in the early 1970s, as a neorealist. Critics later noted affinities between Zavattini's work and such filmmakers as Jean Rouch and Chantal Akerman. Other than De Vincenti's seminal essay, see also Gianni Rondolino's "Cinema del dopoguerra: Uno sguardo d'insieme," in *Storia del cinema italiano*, vol. 7, *1945–1948*, ed. Callisto Cosulich (Venice: Marsilio; Rome: Scuola Nazionale di Cinema, 2003), 58–72; and Ivone Margulies's *Nothing Happens: Chantal Akerman's Hyperrealist Everyday* (Durham, N.C.: Duke University Press, 1996), 21–41. Margulies's work has done much to advance my thinking on these neorealist/modernist intersections.

31. "Man is but a mold of his native landscape" translates a famous line from a Hebrew poem of the 1920s—at the dawn of another national consciousness—"Ha'adam eino ela" by Shaul Tchernichovsky, *Poems*, vol. 1 (Tel Aviv: Dvir, 1966), 306.

32. Pasolini's position here, echoed through many of his pronouncements over the years, is confirmed by David Forgács's analysis that marks the true departure of postwar modernization in the

Land Reform of 1950, which broke old landholding patterns in the south, and whose consequences are deeply bound with the effects of the economic miracle upon the Italian landscape; see Fogács's "Post-War Italian Culture: Renewal or Legacy of the Past," in *Reconstructing the Past: Representations of the Fascist Era in Post-War European Culture,* ed. Graham Bartram et al. (Keele, Staffordshire, England: Keele University Press, 1996), 49–63.

I. Aerial

1. "Per un film sul fiume Po," *Cinema* 68 (April 25, 1939): 254–57. Although I offer in the citations that follow my own translations from this text, these have been informed, as well, by David Overbey's version, "Concerning a Film about the River Po," in *Springtime in Italy: A Reader on Neo-Realism,* ed. and trans. David Overbey (Hamden, Conn.: Archon Books, 1979), 79–82. Some of the ideas raised in the *Cinema* essay are prefigured in an earlier article, "Documentari," in the *Corriere padano,* January 21, 1937, rpt. in Michelangelo Antonioni, *Sul cinema,* ed. Carlo di Carlo and Giorgio Tinazzi (Venice: Marsilio, 2004), 65–67.

2. On neorealism *avant la lettre,* see the several essays under the heading "Il neorealismo e il cinema italiano degli anni trenta" in *Il neorealismo cinematografico italiano,* ed. Lino Micciché (Venice: Marsilio, 1999), 331–414.

3. The juxtaposition of "commercial need" and "intelligence" is not original, of course, and could have been raised by diverse ideological fronts. Speaking for a rigorous political cinema and privileging documentary over traditional fiction, the futurist photographer, film critic, and theater director Anton Giulio Bragaglia, in a 1931 contribution to Gentile's *Educazione fascista,* cites from René Clair a warning that in the "battle between capital and intelligence . . . intelligence would inevitably lose out." Cited by Victoria de Grazia in *The Culture of Consent: Mass Organization of Leisure in Fascist Italy* (Cambridge: Cambridge University Press, 1981), 220. Antonioni himself, in an article for *Corriere padano,* December 17, 1937, criticized the stagnation of Italian cinema that cannot disengage itself from financial considerations on the one hand and literary models on the other, to discover its own properly cinematic "intelligence." See "Assente: L'intelligenza," rpt. in Antonioni, *Sul cinema,* 67–70.

4. While some heroic rhetoric survived, even when transfigured, in neorealism, it was largely subsumed under an ideology of would-be "anti-rhetoric": see Mino Argentieri's chapter "Confusi desideri di realismo e di antiretorica" in his *Il cinema in guerra: Arte, comunicazione e propaganda in Italia, 1940–1944* (Rome: Riuniti, 1998), 269–96.

5. The "interstice" is Roland Barthes's key term from a 1980 lecture in the form of a letter; see the English translation, "Dear Antonioni," in Geoffrey Nowell-Smith, *L'avventura* (London: BFI, 1997), 63–68.

6. This attribution conforms to that of Carlo Di Carlo in his introductory essay, "Vedere in modo nuovo," to *Il primo Antonioni* (Bologna: Cappelli, 1973), 11. I present it only tentatively since I believe it unlikely that Antonioni personally took the last photograph in the sequence, though he obviously chose to include it in his sequence; I speculate on its provenance in what follows.

7. This screening device that reorganizes and flattens the image is comparable, with just a slight stretch of the imagination, to the fashion shoot compositions in *Blow-Up* (1966) whose concern is, again, still photography.

8. Rosalind Krauss noted to me the Impressionist lineage of these first eight photographs. Photogrammetry is that branch of aerial photography that serves cartography. The term "instrumental" I borrow from Allan Sekula, who uses it to discuss the aesthetic-ideological bind that informs the relation between the realist, scientific, primarily military applications of aerial photography, its aesthetic appreciators, and its progeny; see "The Instrumental Image: Steichen at War," *Artforum* (December 1975): 26–35.

9. See *Vues d'en haut: La photographie aérienne pendant la guerre de 1914–1918* (Paris: Musée de l'Armée; Nanterre: Musée d'Histoire Contemporaine, 1988).

10. Among the numerous examples, it may suffice to cite Robert Delaunay's 1922 painting of the Eiffel Tower modeled on a 1909 balloon photograph, which also Le Corbusier used for the cover of his book *Decorative Art Today* (1925). See Beaumont Newhall, *Airborne Camera: The World from the Air and Outer Space* (New York: Hastings House, 1969), 104–5, for juxtaposition of these images. In the Soviet Union Alexander Rodchenko, El Lissitzky, and Kasimir Malevich pursued new spatial explorations in painting, sculpture, and photography explicitly informed by the altered views of the airborne camera.

Aaron Scharf summarizes these trends in *Art and Photography* (1968; London: Penguin, 1986), 294–97. The vertical city views taken from Berlin's radio tower by Lászlò Moholy-Nagy suggest the continuity between aerial photography and the modernist potentiality of high-angle composition generally.

11. We may associate this aerial revelation with the "optical unconscious," described by Walter Benjamin as the gift of photography that captures fundamental relations and phenomena, hitherto unavailable to ordinary perception, upon the optical surface of the world. See "The Work of Art in the Age of Mechanical Reproduction," in *Illuminations,* ed. Hannah Arendt, trans. Harry Zohn (New York: Schocken, 1969), 235–37.

12. In his *Theory of Film: The Redemption of Physical Reality* (New York: Oxford University Press, 1960), 13–18, Siegfried Kracauer sees amplified in the aerial view a "precarious balance" between what he calls the "realist" and the "formative" affinities of the photograph. In the photography essay of 1927 Kracauer has already implied, more radically, that the formal possibilities of photography, emblematized in the aerial view's "reduction" or abstraction of its objects, are *inseparable* from its privileged access to modern reality. The ambivalence of the photograph is transposed in the aerial view to another order that enables tensions of surface and depth, alienation and identification, abstraction and referentiality to inform modern consciousness regarding the material basis of phenomena. The "mass ornament" is Kracauer's emblem of modernity drawn from mass gymnastics, military parades, and music hall shows whereby the spectacle, typically seen from a distance, allows a larger surface pattern to emerge in another dimension from that of its parts: it is consistent, then, with aerial photography's grasp of the landscape as an abstract optical surface. The mass ornament can represent to consciousness its condition in modernity, but taken as a finite, mythified unity that obscures the concrete observation of things, it embodies a fascist outlook. "As linear as it may be, there is no line that extends from the small sections of the mass to the entire figure. The ornament resembles *aerial photographs* of landscapes and cities in that it does not emerge out of the interior of the given conditions, but rather appears above them." Siegfried Kracauer, "Photography," and "The Mass Ornament" in *The Mass Ornament: Weimar Essays,* trans. and ed. Thomas Y. Levin

(Cambridge, Mass.: Harvard University Press, 1995), 47–63, 75–86. I quote from p. 77, emphases in the original.

13. Originally in Vittorio Mussolini, *Voli sulle Ambe* (Florence: Sansoni, 1937). English translation of this passage is in A. J. Barker, *The Civilizing Mission: A History of the Italo-Ethiopian War of 1935–36* (New York: Dial Press, 1968), 234. Sekula cites this passage as part of his eloquent analysis of the conflation of the aesthetic pleasures of aerial photography and its militarist substance. One of the many and more recent examples of the haunting power of aerial photography to dissociate such visual pleasures from their most urgent human meaning was brought home to CNN viewers who, in the first days of the 1991 Gulf War, could witness how a vehicle approaching a bridge comes under the direct line of bombardment by the very aircraft that carries the camera. As the line of fire and the camera's view coincide one realizes that this "hit," so familiar from video games, involves not abstracted pleasure of technological mastery but the direct deathly consequence of military aggression. The only reason it can be seen time and again on television is due to the distant, alienating perspective that empties the view of any anthropomorphic identification, abstracting it as a chillingly spectacular tool of propaganda.

14. This was still on the pages of *Corriere padano,* October 26, 1938, and December 10, 1938. The first of these, "Luciano Serra italianissimo pilota," is anthologized in Michelangelo Antonioni, *Sul cinema,* 27–29. Sam Rohdie translates segments from these reviews in *Antonioni* (London: BFI, 1990), 30. Alessandrini's film was conceived by another fighter pilot who turned to cinema, the aerophotographer Filippo Masoero, whom I discuss below.

15. In retrospect we might associate the rising smoke in two points in the last photograph not with factory chimneys but with smoke bombs used in military aerial exercises.

16. Walter Benjamin famously cites Marinetti's 1936 manifesto celebrating "the fiery orchids of machine guns" in war's aesthetic forging of a "new architecture, like that of the big tanks, the geometrical formation flights, the smoke spirals from burning villages." See the "Epilogue" and last footnote to "The Work of Art," 241, 251.

17. This summary is based on Gian Piero Brunetta's account of the *Cinema* group in his *Storia del cinema italiano,* vol. 2, *Il cinema del regime, 1929–1945* (Rome: Editori Riuniti, rev. ed. 1993), 220–30.

18. E.g., Ennio Flaiano, "Le ispirazioni sbagliate," *Cinema* 61 (January 10, 1939): 10–11; Domenico Purificato, "L'obiettivo nomade," *Cinema* 78 (September 25, 1939): 196. The introduction to my dissertation, "The Earth Figured: An Exploration of Landscapes in Italian Cinema" (New York University, 1995), dwells on these and related texts of the period.

19. I am grateful to the historian Frank Snowden for his discussion of these topics with me: Snowden reads Mussolini's important "Ascension Day" speech (May 26, 1927) as identifying ruralization at the very heart of the "Fascist revolution"; see Benito Mussolini, *Opera omnia*, vol. 22, *Dall'attentato Zaniboni al discorso dell'Ascensione* (Florence: La Fenice, 1957), especially 366–67. One conspicuous regionalist movement was *strapaese* ("ultra-country"), which coexisted alongside *stracittà* ("ultra-city") as Fascist themes in response to the rapid industrialization and first full experience of modernity in the Italian 1920s and 1930s. *Strapaese*'s regionalist cult posited itself as the pure Italian alternative to technology and to the internationalist modern culture of the city, which it understood as un-Italian and thereby un-Fascist. James Hay describes the documentary and fiction films of the 1930s devoted to the myths of *stracittà* and *strapaese* in *Popular Film Culture in Fascist Italy: The Passing of the Rex* (Bloomington: Indiana University Press, 1987).

20. Ruth Ben-Ghiat offers a lucid summary of this subtle cultural policy in the introduction to her *Fascist Modernities: Italy, 1922–1945* (Berkeley: University of California Press, 2001), 1–15.

21. Antonioni's brief period of work at E-42 is cited from an interview, but without specified references, by Pierre Leprohon, *Michelangelo Antonioni: An Introduction*, trans. Scott Sullivan (New York: Simon and Schuster, 1963), 16. EUR's residential neighborhoods constitute one of the two main locations of Antonioni's *L'eclisse* (1962). Perhaps, in the field of architecture, it was Giuseppe Terragni's Casa del Fascio, completed 1936 in the northern lake town of Como, that best exemplified the ways in which an official Fascist building— beyond the imperial center of Rome, however—could join rationalist design with classical allusions to satisfy a Fascist vision of empire, incorporating as well Mediterranean vernacular, even rural elements. See Richard A. Etlin, *Modernism in Italian Architecture, 1890–1940* (Cambridge, Mass.: MIT Press, 1991), 439–79.

22. My main sources on *aeropittura* are Enrico Crispolti, *Il mito della macchina e altri temi del futurismo* (Rome: Celebes, 1969); Crispolti, *Aeropittura futurista aeropittori* (Modena: Galleria Fonte D'Abisso Edizioni, 1985); Crispolti, "Second Futurism," in *Italian Art in the Twentieth Century: Painting and Sculpture, 1900–1988*, ed. Emily Braun (Munich: Prestel Verlag, 1989), 165–71; Franco Passoni, *Aeropittura futurista* (Milan: Collezione "Le presenze" della Galleria Blu, 1970).

23. This is the editorial opinion of Giovanni Lista in "La création photographique futuriste" in the catalogue *Photographie futuriste italienne, 1911–1939* (Paris: Musée d'art moderne de la ville de Paris, 1981), 5–22.

24. See Crispolti, *Aeropittura futurista aeropittori*, 127–30.

25. Cristpolti, "Second Futurism," 168–69, cites Marinetti's claim of "five hundred Italian *aeropittori*" in his 1934 presentation at the Venice Biennale. Among them Crispolti counts the Ligurian ceramist Tullio D'Albisola, who trained Lucio Fontana and, at the other end of Italy, the Sicilian futurist Pippo Rizzo, who was an influence on the young Renato Guttuso.

26. The manifesto, dated April 11, 1930, was published on the first page of a special issue of *Il Futurismo*, January 11, 1931. It was signed by Marinetti and the *aero*-painter and photographer Tato, pseudonym of Guglielmo Sansoni. See the translation in *Photography in the Modern Era: European Documents and Critical Writings, 1913–1940*, ed. Christopher Phillips (New York: Metropolitan Museum of Art and Aperture, 1989), 299–300.

27. See Lista, *Photographie Futuriste Italienne*, 74–75.

28. Giovanni Lista, *Futurism and Photography* (London: Merrell, 2001), 145.

29. I discuss this pictorial tradition in chapter 3.

30. Brunetta, *Storia*, 151, emphasizes this "anthropocentrism" of the film, reporting as well that, perhaps for its relatively "antirhetorical" stance, it was not well received by the Fascist press.

31. While Calligraphism—which flowered in the early 1940s, ostensibly as an escape from the colossal gestures and propaganda of the regime—often attended to regional land- and cityscapes, neorealism eventually came to define itself against its hermetic reflexivity and retreat from contemporaneity in ornamental engagement with literary adaptation and historical themes. A prime example of

Calligraphism in feature production is Luigi Chiarini's *Via delle cinque lune* (1942), with the collaboration of Pasinetti and Umberto Barbaro, as well as Visconti's editor, Mario Serandrei.

32. I differentiate this LUCE body of work from the *auteur* documentaries cited earlier, but it is also to be distinguished from the category of *cinegiornali,* newsreels proper that would consist of shorter reportage pieces.

33. Sean Anderson, historian of Fascist colonial architecture, tells me that regarding aerial reconnaissance guidelines were clear: round structures are indigenous, rectangular ones are Italian.

34. Argentieri, *Il cinema in Guerra,* 290–91, reports on some of the oppositional voices among those presiding over this documentary (though not newsreel) production of Istituto LUCE.

35. See my account of Rossellini's episode in the Introduction. Geoffrey Nowell-Smith dwells on this return to the Po Valley by those who will become the most significant postwar Italian filmmakers, in "Away from the Po Valley Blues," *PIX* 1 (Winter 1993–94): 24–30. Sergio Toffetti too traces the metonymical charge of the Po for Italian cinema in "Il cinema corre sul fiume," *Catologo del Festival Cinemambiente* (Turin, 2004).

36. I find it significant that although Antonioni professes to have planned *Gente del Po* as a short of some twenty minutes, none of his subsequent documentaries of that first period, through 1950, exceed ten minutes, while twenty minutes would perhaps be the more conventional length for documentaries of that era.

37. See my introduction regarding T. J. Clark's discussion of contingency in *Farewell to an Idea: Episodes from a History of Modernism* (New Haven, Conn.: Yale University Press, 1999), 10–11.

38. Elements of this film—the intimate spaces in the belly of the barge versus the smooth horizontality of exteriors, the striking use of high-angle, even perpendicular shots of the barge passing—are reminiscent of Jean Vigo's *L'Atalante* (1934), while the river views might bring to mind Jean Renoir's *Day in the Country (Partie de campagne,* 1936/1946), on which I comment in the Introduction.

39. Antonioni will return to De Chirico's "metaphysical" compositions and iconography—itself gesturing to the two artists' shared native province of Ferrara—in the years to come.

40. Carlo Di Carlo, Antonioni's close associate and curator over

many years, kindly showed me the short fragment titled *Vertigine* (Vertigo, 1950), where Antonioni's camera was mounted on a cable car to achieve plummeting aerial views. This fragment is all that survived of a ten-minute documentary *La funivia del Faloria* (The Faloria Cable-Car, 1950).

41. It is revealing that in the peak period surrounding *L'eclisse* Antonioni recalled the formative era between the Po River article and the production of *Gente del Po*. In a key essay, "The Event and the Image," he articulates the fundamentals of his aesthetic in light of a landscape image, recalled from his 1942 stay in Nice. He describes a long "establishing" view of a beach evocative of his images of the Po River: wide expanses of water, an opaque sky, scattered figures defined against an emptiness. This is followed by a narrative fragment based on a narrowing down of the view to particulars of action and reaction surrounding the discovery of a corpse in the water. Antonioni then envisions a film that would remove dramatic events from the scene, condensing its impact instead in a suspended image of place, at once empty of action and full of potential, the force of unfolding anxiety by comparison to which narrative intrigues are superfluous. This essay's vivid *ekphrasis* corresponds to the Po River essay's photographic illustrations, echoing its appeal to an "intelligence" of place on film, an intelligence that discloses the tensions of a historical moment, thus spatialized. "Il fatto e l'immagine" was first published in *Cinema nuovo* 164 (July 1963); see the translation in Michelangelo Antonioni, *The Architecture of Vision: Writings and Interviews on Cinema,* ed. Carlo Di Carlo and Georgio Tinazzi, American edition by Marga Cottino-Jones (New York: Marsilio, 1996), 51–53.

42. In one peculiar instance a documentary production based in a revisitation to the locations of an earlier fiction film performs a second-level fracturing operation: the *Ritorno a Lisca Bianca* (1983) traces in color the camera positions of *L'avventura* in the island location, not so much to continue the search for a lost character as to envision the earlier feature film's production as *itself* an event now sunk into the landscape. Antonioni went on to make another documentary of a great river, the Ganges, in *Kumbha Mela* (1989), a film largely structured along extensive lateral traveling shots taken from a boat moving with the stream. These predefined movements serve as foil to the punctuation of bathing procedures, gestures, and chance

expressions as the bathers—some emerging in their recurrence as protocharacters—pass through the frame. The use of the grand landscape figure of the river as correlative to the film's central mode of articulation—the traveling shot—amplifies duration, setting what persists or recurs *within* against what passes *outside* the field of vision as pertaining to the procedures of ritual and to its altered temporal order. In one part of the film the camera enframes the gathering places on the riverbank in near perpendicular shots. Carlo Di Carlo recounts (in personal conversation) that Antonioni asked Indira Gandhi for a helicopter to shoot this ritual spectacle of some ten million people, and she granted his wish, though it is not clear that the high-angle shots here are, in fact, aerial proper.

2. Ruinous

1. One thinks here, retroactively, of the scene in Godard's *Les Carabiniers* (1963) where one of the protagonists, Michelange, out to conquer the world, intrudes upon the projected image and wreaks havoc in a movie theater. Rossellini is acknowledged in the script credits of Godard's film, which is punctuated with neorealist allusions.

2. Rossellini will return to this location in his short *Napoli '43* where, among a large crowd seeking shelter during bombardments, the intense encounter and love at first sight of a soldier and an actress (dressed up as a fairy) is cut short by the soldier's death. This color episode is part of the compilation film *Amori di mezzo secolo* (Love Stories of Mid-Century, 1954)

3. It is Gilles Deleuze who describes comparable instances in postwar cinema as "limit situations": these powerful instances are not necessarily divorced from the everyday, in that they may occur not only in the face of, say, a volcano but of a factory or a school. They are "limit situations" in that their power—their beauty, their pain—outstrips action and thus partake of Deleuze's notion of the "time-image." See *Cinema 2: The Time-Image*, trans. Hugh Tomlinson and Robert Galeta (Minneapolis: University of Minnesota Press, 1989), 18–20.

4. I am aware how, in the chapter title as in subsequent uses, the adjective "ruinous" may appear ambiguous, connoting both a passive condition and an active, destructive disposition. Since my primary use of "ruinous" is to describe a landscape or an edifice, I do not think that

such ambiguity interferes with the principle meaning that one must infer in this case; my choice imparts, rather more so than the simpler "ruined," the connotation of a pervasive condition of collapse, a terrain made up of ruins, this beyond the subjection to a specific aggressive agent at a particular, limited point. "Ruinous" may add, as well, a nuance of the haunting, traumatizing impact of this terrain on the viewer, on the image, on the postwar experience broadly conceived.

5. Erwin Panofsky, "Style and Medium in the Motion Pictures," in *Three Essays on Style,* ed. Irving Lavin (Cambridge, Mass.: MIT Press, 1995), 96. This version of the essay was first published in 1947.

6. Walter Benjamin, *The Origin of German Tragic Drama,* trans. John Osborne (London: Verso, 1977), 178.

7. See the Introduction for my discussion of Jameson's notion of realism as the symbolic "production of the referent of daily life" (Fredric Jameson, "The Realist Floor-Plan," in *On Signs,* ed. Marshall Blonsky [Baltimore: Johns Hopkins University Press, 1985], 373–75). One also considers here the French theorists of the everyday, principally Henri Lefebvre and Michel de Certeau.

8. This is from the title of André Bazin's 1949 review of a bullfight documentary, "Death Every Afternoon." See Mark A. Cohen's translation in *Rites of Realism: Essays on Corporeal Cinema,* ed. Ivone Margulies (Durham, N.C.: Duke University Press, 2003), 27–31.

9. Gian Piero Brunetta claims that "in the war [namely, postwar] trilogy Rossellini constructs a true and proper *historiographic monument* whose internal tensions and weight of moral and conceptual energy is unsurpassed in the entire narrative and documentary system of the postwar." *Identità italiana e identità europea nel cinema italiano dal 1945 al miracolo economico* (Turin: Fondazione Giovanni Agnelli, 1996), 39–40. In splitting up and reperiodizing the neorealist trilogy I will rework some of these terms.

10. It is well known how in Italy, as in France and elsewhere throughout postwar Europe, reconstructions of recent events pictured a much broader participation in the Resistance specifically, and in anti-Fascism generally, than history could really account for.

11. In fact "the war trilogy" is often used to reference not Rossellini's actual wartime films but his postwar work, e.g., Stefano Roncoroni, ed., *La trilogia della guerra: Roma città aperta, Paisà, Germania anno zero* (Bologna: Cappelli, 1972), or Peter Brunette, *Roberto Rossellini*

(New York: Oxford University Press, 1987). In "North and South, East and West: Rossellini and Politics," in *Roberto Rossellini: Magician of the Real,* ed. David Forgacs et al. (London: BFI, 2000), 7–11, Geoffrey Nowell-Smith scans Rossellini's career to describe the director's political consistency, set against other parameters of his oeuvre. Nowell-Smith starts with the "first" Rossellini as that of neorealism, a choice based on Rossellini's international reception, and relegates to a footnote—perhaps as a best forgotten prehistory—Rossellini's propagandistic wartime films under Fascism.

12. Ruth Ben-Ghiat, "The Fascist War Trilogy," in *Roberto Rossellini,* ed. Forgacs et al., 20–35.

13. André Bazin's seminal article on Rossellini, "An Aesthetic of Reality: Neorealism (Cinematic Realism and the Italian School of the Liberation)," in *What Is Cinema?,* vol. 2, ed. and trans. Hugh Gray (Berkeley: University of California Press, 1971), 16–40, was probably the first to invest *Paisà* with a new consciousness more momentous in its implications than the thematics of the war and liberation posited in *Open City. Germany Year Zero* will take us away from Italy to Germany, purporting to tackle the particular aberration that was Nazism, but its dedication to the memory of Rossellini's young son Romano suggests that it is in this belated moment, following the son's death, that the binding of historical reality with the most personal, and universal, implication of irrecoverable loss really "landed" on Rossellini. One need not overinterpret this biographical element to gather that the son's death brought to his work a rift more profound than Rossellini's relatively secure wartime experience had effected.

14. André Bazin, *"Germany, Year Zero," Bazin at Work: Major Essays and Reviews from the Forties and Fifties,* trans. Alain Piette and Bert Cardullo, ed. Bert Cardullo (New York: Routledge, 1997), 124. The essay was first published in 1949.

15. Cf. Bazin, "An Aesthetic of Reality," 37: "The unit of cinematic narrative in *Paisà* is not the 'shot,' an abstract view of a reality which is being analyzed, but the 'fact.' A fragment of concrete reality in itself multiple and full of ambiguity, whose meaning emerges only after the fact, thanks to other imposed facts between which the mind establishes certain relationships."

16. See Jeffry Diefendorf's summary of the data on rubble clear-

ance in *In the Wake of War: The Reconstruction of German Cities after World War II* (New York: Oxford University Press, 1993), 18–30.

17. Edmund's killing of his father can be interpreted as an effect of this impulse to clear up a space for a "healthy" future, obviously under a doubly perverted ideology of the "survival of the fittest."

18. Karl Jaspers was among the most articulate philosophical voices in these debates; see Rudy Koshar's summary in *From Monuments to Traces: Artifacts of German Memory, 1870–1990* (Berkeley: University of California Press, 2000), 152–53. I am grateful to Jeffrey Olick for his expert advice on this cultural history.

19. To this string of ambiguities one might add, as Sandro Bernardi observes, the oscillating status of Rossellini's location between urban setting and landscape proper, though Walter Benjamin perhaps resolves this in describing the ruin as, precisely, the sinking of history back into nature (*Origin of German Tragic Drama*, 178). See Bernardi's essay "I paesaggi nella 'trilogia della guerra': Realtà e metafora," in *Storia del cinema italiano*, vol. 7, *1945/1948*, ed. Callisto Cosulich (Venice: Marsilio; Rome: Edizioni di Bianco and Nero, 2003), 97–114, as well as his "Rossellini's Landscapes: Nature, Myth, History," in *Roberto Rossellini*, ed. Forgacs et al., 50–63.

20. The first citation describes Cologne, the second Berlin, in Stephen Spender, *European Witness* (New York: Reynal and Hitchcock, 1946), 14–17, 240.

21. Ibid., 15.

22. For example, Martin Wagner, the emigré architect banished from Berlin's Board of Works in 1933, suggested that Berlin's rubble should not be rebuilt at all; see Wolfgang Schivelbusch's account of these positions in *In a Cold Crater: Cultural and Intellectual Life in Berlin, 1945–1948*, trans. Kelly Barry (Berkeley: University of California Press, 1998), 14–18.

23. *L'An Zéro de l'Allmagne* was the title of Edgar Morin's contemporary book (Paris: Éditions de la Cité Universelle, 1946), which must have been the inspiration for Rossellini's title, though the notion of Germany's zero hour was already current in reference to the May 8, 1945, surrender. Morin spent that first year after the surrender of Germany to study, interview, and project what forms the country's future might take; one of his chapters is devoted specifically to the German youth.

24. Koshar, *From Monuments to Traces*, 171. A prime example in the debate surrounding the fiction of continuity in reconstruction, largely won by traditionalists, must be the Frankfurt house where Goethe was born. Itself apparently undistinguished and modified in the nineteenth century with period furniture, it was reduced to rubble in Allied bombing. Diefendorf (*In the Wake of War*, 72) cites Walter Dirks's lucid argument against its restoration: "That the Goethe house collapsed in rubble has its own bitter logic. It was not an oversight that one could have corrected, not some sort of mistake in the course of history; there is justness in its ruin. And therefore one should acknowledge it. The destruction of this house belongs just as much to German and European cultural history as does its construction. . . . We should not try to erase this last chapter—the destruction—of its long history." But Goethe's house was faithfully rebuilt, as copy, to keep intact this symbol of German Enlightenment—and as if nothing had happened.

25. Spender (*European Witness*, 242) reports and Koshar (*From Monuments to Traces*, 170) confirms the account of Hitler's private spaces in the bunker. Koshar deems the subsequent "recycling" of the Chancellory rubble the most radical form of reconstruction.

26. After all, as Koshar reminds us in *From Monuments to Traces*, 124, the Reichstag ruin from the fire of February 27, 1933, was itself preserved as monument to Nazi victory over the chaos of parliamentary politics.

27. Lewis Mumford, *The Culture of Cities* (New York: Harcourt, Brace, 1938), 433–40.

28. See J. L. Sert, F. Léger, and S. Giedion's 1943 statement "Nine Points on Monumentality," in *Architecture Culture, 1943–1968: A Documentary Anthology*, ed. Joan Ockman (New York: Columbia University Press and Rizzoli, 1993), 27–28; Ockman's introduction has also informed my discussion here. On the tensions between the practical and symbolic functions of the monument, and between its deliberate commemorative use and the heritage of cultural edifices that come to constitute "unintentional monuments," see the seminal essay by Alois Riegl, "The Modern Cult of Monuments: Its Character and Origin," trans. Kurt W. Forster and Diane Ghirardo, *Oppositions* 25 (Fall 1982): 21–51.

29. Giuseppe Pagano, "Presupposti per un programma di po-

litica edilizia," part 3, "Restauro dei monumenti," first published in *Costruzioni-Casabella* 186 (June 1943), anthologized in *Architettura e città durante il fascismo,* ed. Cesare De Seta (Roma-Bari: Laterza, 1990), 285. Pagano's convoluted style is in the original Italian, which I tried to clarify at points without wishing to oversimplify or distort his voice in the translation. Pagano's bold pronouncements against grandiose Fascist architectural projects on the pages of a prestigious journal evidence the relative freedom of critical debates even in this period, in the midst of the war. Yet they may have played a part—alongside his Resistance activities and contributions to the clandestine press—in the ire of the establishment that ultimately led to the deportation of Pagano to Mauthausen where he perished in 1945. See De Seta's biographical introduction in *Architettura e città.*

30. Ibid., 287.

31. See Italo Insolera, *Roma moderna: Un secolo di storia urbanistica* (Turin: Einaudi, 1962), 189–90, for details and a critique of this particular course of urbanist work, all of which involved continued destruction of old Roman neighborhoods. This included, among other plans, the realization of Mussolini's project, with all its symbolic charges, for the via della Conciliazione leading to the Vatican, and the Termini train station with its monumental piazza. While for the Termini facade a new solution was sought in postwar competition, Insolera is critical that no one had the courage to tear down the enormous "Nazi style" back wings of the station.

32. I mentioned in the Introduction the documentary compilation film *Giorni di Gloria* (1945) by Mario Serandrei, Luchino Visconti, and others: its sequences devoted to the exhuming of corpses and their identification at the Fosse Ardeatine, followed by the trial and execution of the Fascist chiefs who supported the Nazi massacre, may be considered as a first monument to that traumatic event.

33. See Insolera, *Roma moderna,* 192–208; Bruno Reichlin, "Figures of Neorealism in Italian Architecture," part 1, *Grey Room* 5 (2001): 78–101, and part 2, *Grey Room* 6 (2002): 110–33; Maristella Casciato, "Neorealism in Italian Architecture," in *Anxious Modernisms: Experimentation in Postwar Architectural Culture,* ed. Sarah Williams Goldhagen and Réjean Legault (Cambridge, Mass.: MIT Press and Canadian Centre for Architecture, 2000), 25–54.

34. In linking the culture of reconstruction to prewar modernisms

Tafuri refers here not only to rationalist architecture but also to "Persico and Nizzoli's trellis in the Gallery of Milan and to the 'captive objects' of Marcel Duchamp, Alberto Giacometti, and Melotti." All citations in the paragraph are from Manfredo Tafuri, *History of Italian Architecture, 1944–1985,* trans. Jessica Levine (Cambridge, Mass.: MIT Press, 1989), 4–5. For my description of these monuments I have relied, beyond personal observation, on both Tafuri and Reichlin (part 2) and on conversations with Flavia Marcello, historian of modern Italian architecture.

35. One must pass by Francesco Coccia's heroic figurative statue (not visible in Figure 2.8) to approach the concrete slab at the Fosse Ardeatine. The statue flies in the face of the "antirhetorical" stance of neorealism but is also symptomatic of its contradictions.

36. Ernesto Nathan Rogers's "Program: Domus, the House of Man" was published in 1946; see Ockman, ed., *Architecture Culture,* 78–79. Ockman's introduction to Rogers, p. 77 in this anthology, attends to the earlier article, "A House for Everyone." See also Casciato's account in "Neorealism in Italian Architecture."

37. Variants of these ideas entered into considerations of Berlin's development in later years when, with the Cold War and the division of Germany and of Berlin itself, a need for monumental gestures and countergestures, on the two sides of the Wall, found expression in massive residential projects, harnessing the dwelling toward larger cultural and symbolic values. See Francesca Rogier's comparison of the Eastern Stalinallee and the Western Hansaviertel projects in "The Monumentality of Rhetoric: The Will to Rebuild in Postwar Berlin," in *Anxious Modernisms,* ed. Goldhagen and Legault, 165–90.

38. See Roland Barthes, *Camera Lucida: Reflections on Photography,* trans. Richard Howard (New York: Hill and Wang, 1981), 93: "Earlier societies managed so that memory, the substitute for life, was eternal and that at least the thing which spoke Death should itself be immortal: this was the Monument. But by making the (mortal) Photograph into the general and somehow natural witness of 'what has been,' modern society has renounced the Monument." One might cite here Rossellini's reflection on the release of the photograph by the contingency of neorealist cinematography in the comical *La macchina ammazzacattivi* (The Machine to Kill Bad People, 1948–52). Here a magical camera freezes its subjects dead in their positions, monu-

ments of their own petty crimes and complicity, while the film finally releases them back into life's mutability and contingency. It is not a passive preservation of the profilmic but the camera's active, even violent intervention that is posited in this fable. With the failure of a definitive photographic monument, the workings of cinematography *as such* come to stand for the impossibility of perfect human judgment and for the vital necessity to go on despite the evidence.

39. This is I think impossible to deny despite Tag Gallaghar's best efforts in *The Adventures of Roberto Rossellini: His Life and Films* (New York: Da Capo, 1998), 66–88. But even if we forgo definite judgment on the precise politics of Rossellini's wartime films, it is evident that his survival in the system, like that of most of his colleagues in the Italian film industry, did not necessitate vast compromises after all. Given the relative tolerance of the regime, his work could juggle some wartime propaganda, plain Italian patriotism and nationalism, and general humanist sentiments that could be taken this way or that. See again Ben-Ghiat, "The Fascist War Trilogy," on this topic.

40. See note 3 to this chapter.

41. We find related ideas rigorously explored in later years, and in Rossellini's footsteps, in Jean-Marie Straub's *Not Reconciled* (based on Heinrich Böll's novel and co-scripted with Danièle Huillet),which concerns itself with generational debates in a family of architects over the question of Cologne's relationship to its past. Here a deliberate act of demolition is deemed a more adequate form of remembering than the reconstruction of monuments to their former glory. One might go on to associate Rossellini's example, and Straub-Huillet's, with the "negative" or "antimonument" positions that fully emerged in the last quarter of the twentieth century regarding the remembrance of the Holocaust and in view of the rebuilding of Berlin after unification. Neither blind restoration and continuity nor a consumable monument set apart from everyday life, the antimonument reframes the ruin as a persisting fragment, pointing to a past, to an absence that is still present. See a summary of these ideas by Charles Merewether, "Traces of Loss," in *Irresistible Decay: Ruins Reclaimed,* ed. Michael S. Roth (Los Angeles: Getty Research Institute for the History of Art and the Humanities, 1997), 33–37, and James E. Young's seminal essay "The Counter-Monument: Memory against Itself in Germany Today," *Critical Inquiry* 18 (Winter 1992): 267–96.

42. The emblematic suggestiveness of such landscapes, imagined via temporal inversion or collapse, is articulated in Walter Benjamin's memorable allegory of the angel of history who faces the past; there, "where we perceive a chain of events, he sees one single catastrophe which keeps piling wreckage upon wreckage and hurls it in front of his feet. The angel would like to stay, awaken the dead, and make whole what has been smashed," but a storm that we call "progress" "propels him into the future to which his back is turned, while the pile of debris before him grows skyward." See "Theses on the Philosophy of History," *Illuminations,* ed. Hannah Arendt, trans. Harry Zohn (New York: Schocken, 1969), 257–58.

43. Even as we witness Rossellini's neorealist work acquire symbolic dimensions, his "great Christian allegory" of the Ingrid Bergman cycle still maintains a remarkable weight of unsublimated, material presentness. Jacques Rivette defines in allegorical terms a dialectic of the didactic and epiphanic in *Journey to Italy;* see his 1955 "Letter on Rossellini," trans. Tom Milne, in *Cahiers du Cinema, the 1950s: Neo-Realism, Hollywood, New Wave,* ed. Jim Hillier (Cambridge, Mass.: Harvard University Press, 1985), 200. I dwell at length on the figurative import and cultural connotations of *Journey to Italy*'s landscape in my dissertation, "The Earth Figured: An Exploration of Landscapes in Italian Cinema," New York University, 1995. Since then this landscape has been revisited by Giuliana Bruno in her *Atlas of Emotion: Journeys in Art, Architecture, and Film* (New York: Verso, 2002), and by Laura Mulvey in "Vesuvian Topographies: The Eruption of the Past in *Journey to Italy,"* in *Roberto Rossellini,* ed. Forgacs et al., 95–111.

44. It is, again, that other northerner, Walter Benjamin, who considered the "porosity" of Naples as the "inexhaustible law of the life of this city, reappearing everywhere." See "Naples," in *Reflections: Essays, Aphorisms, Autobiographical Writings,* trans. Edmund Jephcott (New York: Schocken Books, 1986), 163–73.

45. For the making of the Pompeii sequence, Rossellini was in fact informed about an imminent discovery at the digs and hurried to shoot the actual unearthing process of what conveniently turned out to be a man and a woman. In turn this was intercut with Bergman's and Sanders's reverse shots and the didactic commentary. See the account of this in Alain Bergala, *Voyage en Italie de Roberto Rossellini* (Crisneé, Belgium: Editions Yellow Now, 1990), 131. The rough inter-

lacing of documentary and fictional modes recurs in the film, whose sustained marks of discontinuity were an object of admiration for Rossellini's New Wave followers. It is a juxtaposition of frames in Bergala (75) that sent me to examine the symmetry of these shots in the film. Bergala, an otherwise thorough reader, does not comment on the astonishing formal symmetry and implications of his own choice and juxtaposition of frames.

46. Philippe Dubois thereby calls Pompeii "une véritable *ville photographique*," *L'Acte photographique et autres essais* (Paris: Nathan, 1990), 273.

3. Choral

1. Visconti's notes for the tri-part treatment are in *La terra trema di Luchino Visconti: Analisi di un capolavoro,* 2nd ed., ed. Lino Miccichè (Turin: Lindau / Associazione Philip Morris Progetto Cinema, Centro Sperimentale di Cinematografia—Cineteca Nazionale, 1994), 205–17.

2. Rosi's account of the production—his earliest film job— constitutes the introduction to the published script in Luchino Visconti, *La terra trema* (Bologna: Cappelli, 1977), 9–17.

3. Visconti must have appreciated some of this work, especially as practiced by Alessandro Blasetti, whose *Sole* (1929), *Terra madre* (1931), and *1860* (1934) exhibited a refined perception of the rich historical fabric of regionalist artistic traditions.

4. See Erich Auerbach's chapter *"Germinie Lacerteux"* in *Mimesis: The Representation of Reality in Western Literature,* trans. W. R. Trask (1946; Princeton, N.J.: Princeton University Press, 1953), 493–524. Conversely, Lukács discredits naturalism for its descriptive methods that fail, in his view, to deeply integrate persons in their historical milieu as did the realist novels of Balzac; see "Narrate or Describe?" in Georg Lukács, *Writer and Critic, and Other Essays,* ed. and trans. Arthur Kahn (London: Merlin Press, 1978), 110–48. On stylistic distinctions between naturalism and verismo, see the translator's introduction to Giovanni Verga, *The She-Wolf and Other Stories,* trans. Giovanni Cecchetti (Berkeley: University of California Press, 1962), especially vii and xv.

5. Biographical materials in this chapter are largely drawn from Gianni Rondolino, *Luchino Visconti* (Turin: UTET, 1981).

6. As told by Gianni Puccini in "Storia di *Cinema*," in *Il Lungo viaggio del cinema italiano: Antologia di "Cinema," 1936–1943*, ed. Orio Caldiron (Padua: Marsilio, 1965), lxxxiii.

7. See Romano Luperini, *Simbolo e costruzione allegorica in Verga* (Bologna: Il Mulino, 1989), 103–45. "I Malavoglia is a harshly realistic but also courageously experimental novel; it appeals to the materiality of factual data and to the investigation of the real, but reveals also a lyrical-symbolic component; above all it presupposes an avant-garde attitude that negotiates the rupture principally on a formal level" (104). Zola, too, considered his own naturalistic methods "experimental," but implied therein the spirit of scientific investigation perhaps more than an artistic-poetic ambition.

8. Mario Alicata and Giuseppe De Santis, "Truth and Poetry: Verga and the Italian Cinema," in *Springtime in Italy: A Reader on Neo-Realism*, ed. and trans. David Overbey (Hamden, Conn.: Archon, 1979), 134–35.

9. Mario Alicata and Giuseppe De Santis, "Ancora di Verga e del cinema italiano," reprinted in *Il lungo viaggio*, ed. Caldiron, 446.

10. Alicata's text of 1942 is cited in Rondolino, *Luchino Visconti*, 98. His example of lyricizing and thereby politically suspect realism is Robert Flaherty's *Man of Aran* (1934); compare this to Antonioni's 1939 criticism of Flaherty's hybrid form, cited in the first chapter.

11. Visconti, "Tradizione e invenzione," cited by Rondolino, *Luchino Visconti*, 92. The Faraglioni are the perpendicular volcanic rocks scattered opposite the shore of Aci Trezza. I return to them later.

12. It seems to me that the boldness of such an enterprise—the ambitious yoking of tradition and revolution—might equal that of an iconoclastic avant-garde intervention, even as it appears as its opposite.

13. Gianni Puccini recounts this initial inspiration of the old postcard in Caldiron, *Il lungo viaggio*, lxxxiii. I have found the postcard, whose whereabouts were hitherto unconfirmed and, to the best of my knowledge, never before reproduced, in the Visconti archive at the Istituto Gramsci in Rome, Box C-14: 003872. I am deeply grateful to the staff at the archive and institute for their help.

14. Visconti, "Tradizione e invenzione," quoted in Rondolino, *Luchino Visconti*, 91.

15. Roland Barthes, "The Realistic Effect," trans. Gerald Mead, *Film Reader* 3 (1978): 131–35.

16. Giovanni Verga, "Gramigna's Mistress," in *The She-Wolf,* 86–88. Emphases in the original.

17. Luperini, *Simbolo e costruzione allegorica,* 15–59.

18. Among the best English-language commentaries on this subject are Millicent Marcus, *Filmmaking by the Book: Italian Cinema and Literary Adaptation* (Baltimore, Md.: Johns Hopkins University Press, 1993), 38–39, and P. Adams Sitney, *Vital Crises in Italian Cinema: Iconography, Stylistics, Politics* (Austin: University of Texas Press, 1995), 72–77.

19. From Verga's preface to *I Malavoglia,* in the translation by Judith Landry: *I Malavoglia (The House by the Medlar Tree)* (London: Dedalus, 1985; New York: Hippocrene, 1987), xviii; my emphases.

20. Giovanni Verga, "Fantasticheria," *Tutte le novelle,* vol. 1, ed. Marco Buzzi Maresca (Milan: Mursia, 1986), 163–71.

21. Verga to Luigi Capuana, March 14, 1879, in Giovanni Verga, *Specchio e realtà,* ed. Wladimiro Settimelli (Rome: Magma, 1976), 174; my emphases.

22. Visconti, "Tradizione e invenzione," cited by Rondolino, *Luchino Visconti,* 91.

23. Verga to Capuana, May 29, 1881, *Specchio,* 175.

24. Verga must have encountered members of the Macchiaioli during his frequent visits to Florence beginning in 1865, followed by his residence there between 1869 and 1872. It is there, as well, that he strikes up the friendship with Capuana. See "Chronology" in Verga, *I Malavoglia,* iv.

25. From an 1852 *Vocabolario Universale della Lingua Italiana,* cited by Norma Broude in *The Macchiaioli: Italian Painters of the Nineteenth Century* (New Haven, Conn.: Yale University Press, 1987) 4; my emphasis. On the optical experiments of the Macchiaioli, see also pages 62 and 107; consider in particular the example of such artists as Telemaco Signorini and Odoardo Borrani.

26. It is Verga's contemporary C. S. Peirce who categorized the indexical sign, using the photograph as one of his examples, in "Logic as Semiotic: The Theory of Signs," in *Philosophical Writings of Peirce,* ed. Justus Buchler (New York: Dover, 1955), 98–119.

27. Verga, "Gramigna," 86–88, emphasis in the original. This citation may be readily associated with André Bazin's observation of 1945 that "photography effects us like a phenomenon in nature." Bazin's subsequent formulation articulates a sensibility that will perfectly

match, to my mind, Visconti's landscape sensibility: "By the power of photography, the natural image of a world that we neither know nor can know, nature at last does more than imitate art: she imitates the artist." "The Ontology of the Photographic Image," *What Is Cinema?* vol. 1, trans. Hugh Gray (Berkeley: University of California Press, 1967), 13, 15 respectively.

28. Verga dedicated a copy of *I Malavoglia* to Capuana, the "illustrious photographer" who had introduced him to photography. See the "Nota bio-bibliografica" in Verga's *Tutte le novelle,* 31.

29. The photographs have been published in *Verga fotografo,* ed. Giovanni Garra Agosta (Catania, Italy: Giuseppe Maimone Editore, 1991). As compared with Verga's extant four hundred photographs, Zola produced several thousand exposures with no fewer than ten cameras during the eight years between 1894 and his death in 1902. See François Emile-Zola and Massin, *Zola Photographer,* trans. Liliane Emery Tuck (New York: Seaver Books/Henry Holt, 1988), 3–4.

30. That Verga's cataloging, or archiving, mode in these types of photos appears even more emphatically "instrumental" than that of Eugène Atget or August Sander may also be ascribed to the simple fact of his more humble capacities as a photographer—yet the deliberately self-limiting approach to human subjects and settings and the comparative approach to topographic views suggest a consciousness at work here. In juxtaposing photography's aesthetic and sociological, or otherwise instrumental, discursive modes I draw on the seminal essays by Rosalind Krauss, "Photography's Discursive Spaces," and Allan Sekula, "The Body and the Archive," both in *The Contest of Meaning: Critical Histories of Photography,* ed. Richard Bolton (Cambridge, Mass.: MIT Press, 1989), 287–302, 343–89 respectively.

31. Roland Barthes, "The Photographic Message," in *Image Music Text,* ed. and trans. Stephen Heath (New York: Hill and Wang, 1977), 15–31; in what follows I also allude to Barthes's observation in the same essay that the "'denotative' status of the photograph, the perfection and plenitude of its analogy, in short its 'objectivity,' has every chance of being mythical" (19).

32. Verga considered cinema as a continued life for his narratives—though, it appears, chiefly for economic reasons. For a chronicle, starting in 1909, of Verga's exchanges regarding cinematic adaptation of his work, see Gino Raya, *Verga e il cinema* (Rome: Herder Editore,

1984). See also the more recent book with an identical title, *Verga e il cinema*, ed. Nino Genovese and Sebastiano Gesù (Catania, Italy: Giuseppe Maimone Editore, 1996), for further commentary on this front as on Visconti's adaptation of Verga. The editors' introduction to the more recent book cites Verga's photography but does not address its emblematic possibilities as a *verista* link to *La terra trema*.

33. These are the terms by which Sekula charts the photographic predicament in "The Body and the Archive."

34. Visconti, "Tradizione e invenzione," quoted in Rondolino, *Luchino Visconti*, 91. I have added quotation marks to the phrase Visconti cites from Manzoni's celebrated description of the Lombard sky in Bruce Penman's translation, Alessandro Manzoni, *The Betrothed* (London: Penguin Books, 1972), 324. Millicent Marcus (*Filmmaking by the Book*, 26) cites Visconti's text, alongside Alicata and De Santis's writing on Verga, to support her analysis of the ideological contradictions at the heart of verismo and neorealism.

35. See detailed descriptions of the frescoes and reproductions in W. J. T. Peters, *Landscape in Romano-Campagnian Mural Painting* (Assen, Neth.: Von Gorcum, 1963), 27–32. There are numerous other pictorial and literary connotations one might evoke in view of the eastern shores of Sicily: suffice it to cite among them Antonello's *Crucifixion* (ca. 1460–65) set against the background of Messina or, most eloquent among Grand Tourists in the modern age, Goethe, whose interest in volcanic phenomena drew him to Aci Trezza; see *Italian Journey, 1786–1788*, trans. W. H. Auden and Elizabeth Mayer (San Francisco: North Point Press, 1982).

36. The full consciousness of a tradition of representation free from the pretense of supplanting it under the narrow imperatives of the moment is, I dare say, a mark of Visconti's artistic maturity. It is the approach that professes to expose a "reality behind the myth," *as if* independent of the layering of preceding representations, which is often the more naive and deluded one.

37. This is one of Gramsci's seminal themes in the *Quaderni* of the early twenties. See the section "Notes on Italian History" in *Selections from the Prison Notebooks of Antonio Gramsci*, ed. and trans. Quintin Hoare and Geoffrey Nowell-Smith (New York: International Publishers, 1971), 44–120.

38. Accounts of the altering and interlacing of spaces may be found

in *La città-set: La terra trema di Luchino Visconti: Reperti per una archeologia del cinema,* ed. Michele Mancini and Fiametta Sciacca (Rome: Theorema edizioni, 1981). See also Rosi's account in the introduction to Visconti, *La terra,* 9–17, and Visconti's sketches of settings and props in *La terra trema di Luchino Visconti,* ed. Lino Miccichè. These sources also inform Sandro Bernardi's refined analysis of the spatial effects of the film in *"La terra trema:* Il mito, il teatro, la storia," in *Il cinema di Luchino Visconti,* ed. Veronica Pravadelli (Rome: Biblioteca di Bianco e Nero Quadrini, no. 2, 2000), 65–88.

39. Glass windows that would allow in the light while providing some separation and blocking of sounds would be a luxury in such places until well into the 1940s and are practically nonexistent in the film except in such institutions as the local café.

40. I borrow this term from Bazin's characterization of theatrical, as juxtaposed with "centrifugal," cinematic space in "Theater and Cinema, Part Two," *What Is Cinema?* vol. 1, 95–124.

41. Cf. Alessandro Cappabianca, "Il teatro di posa: Scena/set/studio," in *La città-set,* 77–78: "The whole construction, in its globality of interiors and exteriors, places itself as a *total interior* (thus *studio,* thus *soundstage*) as opposed to the *radical exteriority represented by the sea.* . . . It should then be the presence of the sea, of the 'exterior-sea' set, that makes Aci Trezza in its entirety emerge as an interior, that renders it not only as set, but indeed as studio, soundstage." Cappabianca does not associate the effect of interiority with Visconti's camera work that, as I suggest, renders even the sea and, basically, the conception of reality as such, as a coherent and determinant theatrical space. This broader conception is fundamental, it seems to me, to Visconti's aesthetic and ideology at large.

42. While my classical connotations are consistent with my earlier contextualization of this location, one may also consider here the stagecraft of northern Italian Baroque theater, e.g., the marine backdrops of the designer Francesco Guitti where perspectival effect is enhanced by rocks to enframe the horizon. See Janet Southorn, *Power and Display in the Seventeenth Century: The Arts and Their Patrons in Modena and Ferrara* (Cambridge: Cambridge University Press, 1988), 133–39 and plates 99–111.

43. Once again we might refer here to the Greek or Hellenistic open theaters that typically projected toward a stage at least in part

open to the landscape beyond—this unlike Roman amphitheaters surrounded on all sides by tiers and stage buildings. Vincent Scully describes the remains of Greek and Hellenistic theaters scattered in comparable southern European sites and along this very coast. See *The Earth, the Temple, and the Gods: Greek Sacred Architecture* (New Haven, Conn.: Yale University Press, 1962) 192–94. John Brinckerhoff Jackson's "Landscape as Theater" also suggests the centrality of the theater to our grasp of the landscape; see *The Necessity of Ruins and Other Topics* (Amherst: University of Massachusetts Press, 1980), 67–75. Interestingly, in obeying the theatrical projection of the view, Visconti keeps the spectator's back to Etna, which must be visible from any point along these shores but makes only a few ghostly appearances in the film, and most prominently as a painted backdrop in the family photograph discussed earlier. Yet it is also the volcano that anchors the film's title, beyond its symbolic revolutionary connotation, in the physical landscape.

44. See Luchino Visconti, *Il mio teatro*, vol. 1, 1936–1953, ed. Caterina d'Amico de Carvalho and Renzo Renzi (Bologna: Cappelli, 1979).

45. My understanding of Visconti diverges here from that of Geoffrey Nowell-Smith, who posits the theatrical strain of *La terra trema* irreconcilably against its realist project. See his *Luchino Visconti* (1967; 3rd ed., London: BFI, 2003), 29–44. I also differ with Nowell-Smith's observation that Jean Renoir's mentorship seems to be forgotten in this film. Renoir's spectacular fruits of high realism, never lacking in ironic consciousness, themselves encompassed literary, theatrical, and historical adaptations set on location. Renoir's long take and depth-of-field cinematography, while dubbed realist by Bazin, enfolds theatrical and cinematic spaces to achieve a modernist consciousness of the medium and its limits; their influence is, I believe, strong in the visual style of *La terra trema,* especially in the built environments and interior scenes. See Bazin's essay "The French Renoir" in his *Jean Renoir,* ed. François Truffaut, trans. W. W. Halsey II and William H. Simon (New York: Simon and Schuster, 1973), 74–91; André Bazin, "Theater and Cinema, Part Two," in *What Is Cinema?* vol. 1, 95–124; see also Giorgio De Vincenti's commentary on the modernism of Renoir's practice and Bazin's theory in *Il concetto di modernità nel cinema* (Parma: Pratiche Editrice, 1993).

46. Such a conception of landscape is suggested by Adrian

Stokes's remark that just as human works organize and resolve the Mediterranean landscape so, "upon this sea and land the creations of men look natural, acceptable to the play of Nature." *Stones of Rimini* (1934; New York: Schocken, 1969), 64. In "Visconti a tourné *La Terre tremble*," *L'Ecran Français* 176 (November 9, 1948): 5, Jean-Charles Tacchella exhibited great foresight at a time when critics still measured the film by moralistic dichotomies: "For the author of *La terra trema* 'life is a work of art.'. . . Having chosen to 'take nature as a model' . . . Visconti seeks to poeticize this nature." This before Visconti went on to explore even more boldly just what a notion of "life as a work of art" might entail in the cinema and beyond.

47. Visconti's production left a lasting mark, finally, on the very life of Aci Trezza, though perhaps not quite in the ways he might have intended. See Mancini and Sciaccia, eds., *La città-set,* on the hopes and frustrations effected by this production.

4. Archaic

1. Pasolini's archaism may be compared with certain "primitivisms" in modernist art. Thomas Crow suggested to me that "archaic" may connote a higher consciousness of "legitimized" artistic practice as distinct from the broader range of ethnographic objects appropriated by the modern taste for "primitive" production.

2. André Bazin, "Pour un cinéma impure," is undated in the collection of Bazin's writings, *Qu'est-ce que le cinéma?* vol. 2: *Le cinéma et les autres arts* (Paris: les Éditions du Cerf, 1959), 7–32. I cite the original here rather than the translation, "In Defence of Mixed Cinema," *What Is Cinema?* vol. 1, trans. Hugh Gray (Berkeley: University of California Press, 1967), 53–75, since "mixed" does not carry the meaning and connotations of "impure" that are relevant to Pasolini's aesthetic.

3. As has been noted often, the film's original title omits (as does the Gospel itself) the "Saint" added in the American release version. I have chosen to ignore this distortion, distasteful also to Pasolini himself. In what follows I italicize the title of the film, leaving unitalicized—as is the tradition—references to the biblical text.

4. In using "Palestine" I follow Pasolini's designation for Israel and sections of Jordan. By this he wishes to designate a larger geographical area than that of Israel before the Six-Day War. In reference

to more specific locations, he does name Israel and Jordan as such: that is, his usage is not politically inflected, nor is mine in this text.

5. Barth David Schwartz notes in the biography *Pasolini Requiem* (New York: Pantheon, 1992), 360, that in January 1961, having just started work on *Accattone,* Pasolini traveled to India with Alberto Moravia and Elsa Morante. Impressions of this trip were collected in Pier Paolo Pasolini, *L'odore dell'India* (Milan: Longanesi, 1962).

6. P. Adams Sitney describes the hagiographic models of Pasolini's early work in *Vital Crises in Italian Cinema: Iconography, Stylistics, Politics* (Austin: University of Texas Press, 1995), 173–84.

7. An advisor of the Pro Civitate Christiana confirmed that *La ricotta* does not manifest contempt but rather a serious contemporary exploration of the subject—see "Lettera di P. Grasso S.J. a Pier Paolo Pasolini," Pier Paolo Pasolini, *Il Vangelo secondo Matteo, Edipo Re, Medea* (Milan: Garzanti, 1991), 13–14 and 17–18. It is indeed only upon superficial view that Pasolini's short would appear to "deconsecrate." Its conceit describes the Passion of a starving film extra tormented by the indifferent powers of a film industry that, even in producing a film of the Crucifixion, cannot tell a Passion when it sees one.

8. See Paul Ginsborg, *A History of Contemporary Italy: Society and Politics, 1943–1988* (London: Penguin, 1990), 259–61.

9. *Sopralluoghi in Palestina* soundtrack.

10. See, for example, Pier Paolo Pasolini's essays "New Linguistic Questions," "Comments on Free Indirect Discourse," and "Dante's Will to Be a Poet," all from 1964–65; in *Heretical Empiricism,* ed. Louise K. Barnett, trans. Ben Lawton and Louise K. Barnett (Bloomington: Indiana University Press, 1988), 3–22, 79–101, 102–12 respectively. Also on the subject of contamination, consider Pasolini's own account of the amalgam of cinematographic styles in *The Gospel* vis-à-vis the more consistent texture of *Accattone* in the interviews with Oswald Stack, *Pasolini on Pasolini* (London: Thames and Hudson; BFI, 1969), 84. One might hypothesize that it is only his last film, *Salò, or The 120 Days of Sodom* (*Salò o le 120 giornate di Sodoma,* 1975)—which constitutes such a despairing turning-of-the-back to Pasolini's lifelong celebration of a happy contamination of the archaic and the modern—that is dominated by a homogenous, symmetrical, and thereby morbid style.

11. *Sopralluoghi* soundtrack.

12. André Gaudreault's essay "La Passion du Christ: Une forme, un genre, un discours," in *Une Invention du diable? Cinéma des premiers temps et religion*, ed. Roland Cosandey et al. (Sainte-Foy, Québec: Les Presses de l'Université Laval, 1992), 91–101, describes in such terms the ontology of filmed versions of the life and Passion of Christ.

13. Erich Auerbach, *Mimesis: The Representation of Reality in Western Literature*, trans. Willard R. Trask (Princeton, N.J.: Princeton University Press, 1953), 43, 41 respectively. Evidence of Pasolini's familiarity with this text may be found in *Les dernières paroles d'un impie: Entretiens avec Jean Duflot* (Paris: Pierre Belfond, 1981), 140–41.

14. See *San Paolo* (Turin: Einaudi, 1977). The *Appunti per un'Orestiade africana* is most revealing for the method of adaptation by analogy and its pitfalls, in that Pasolini sought to examine here cultures perhaps more remote vis-à-vis the original text than any of his films were to approach. Perhaps for this reason the tension between the filmmaker's design and the contemporary African setting becomes so apparent: aspiring to match contemporary indigenous physiognomies and landscapes to the tragedy of Orestes, Cassandra, Clytemnestra, and Agamemnon—with the trees shaking in the wind in the role of the Furies—Pasolini finally retreats from what seems to remain for him an impenetrable Other that overwhelms his ambitious projection of the myth. See Luca Caminati's analysis in *Orientalismo eretico: Pier Paolo Pasolini e il cinema del Terzo Mondo* ([Turin]: Bruno Mondadori, 2007), 68–79.

15. Also some technical devices, such as the *vérité* practice of a handheld camera—effecting a sense of unpremeditated but confrontational scanning of the visual field in search of the revelatory instance in *Comizi d'amore*—may be seen to prefigure certain stylistic strategies in Pasolini's *Gospel*, as analyzed below.

16. *Sopralluoghi* soundtrack. Don Andrea emphasizes "photograph" to imply surface resemblance divorced, as it were, from the authentic identity of the site.

17. Except when quoting directly from the Italian, "*terrasanta*," I employ "*terra sancta*" in the Latin as it is traditionally cited in English writings, capitalized when a definite article is employed to designate Palestine in particular.

18. On this topic, see Mircea Eliade's chapter "Sacred Space and Making the World Sacred," in *The Sacred and the Profane: The Nature*

of Religion, trans. Willard R. Trask (San Diego: Harcourt Brace Jovanovich, 1959), 20–65.

19. Thanks to Luciano Chessa for directing me to this sight, a famous pilgrim destination where embedded churches from diverse periods in fact evoke the enclosure of the Sepulcher in Jerusalem.

20. See Jonathan Z. Smith's account of this transposition in *To Take Place: Toward Theory in Ritual* (Chicago: University of Chicago Press, 1987), 94.

21. Peter Brown, *The Cult of the Saints: Its Rise and Function in Latin Christianity* (Chicago: University of Chicago Press, 1981), 88; my account that follows is based on this study.

22. Stack, *Pasolini on Pasolini,* 82.

23. Pier Paolo Pasolini, "Confessioni tecniche," in *Uccellacci e uccellini* (Milan: Garzanti, 1966), 49.

24. Maria Antonietta Macciocchi provides an account of Pasolini's meeting with Sartre, one of the few in the French left who did not reject Pasolini's adaptation of the Gospel: see *Duemila anni di felicità* (Milan: Mondadori, 1983), 332–33.

25. See Pasolini's essay of 1966, "The Written Language of Reality," in Barnet, ed., *Heretical Empiricism,* 197–222. Against Metz's qualification that the cinematic impression of reality cannot be described as a "language system," Pasolini may be seen to suggest here that everything—not only written or spoken languages but the transpiring of all experiences, actions, objects, appearances—is already semiotic. "Res Sunt Nomina" is the title of the 1971 essay in which Pasolini posits a "'philosophy' of cinema," in Barnet, ed., *Heretical Empiricism,* 255–60.

26. Pasolini's scandalous semiology provoked the negative response of contemporary semioticians such as Umberto Eco. But it is a thinker like Roland Barthes—if not the classical semiotic Barthes of the "Introduction to the Structural Analysis of Narratives," then the *photographic* Barthes—whose affinities with Pasolini's film theory come to mind, albeit in a more self-critical form: "Certainly the image is not the reality but at least it is its perfect analogon and it is exactly this analogical perfection which, to common sense, defines the photograph. . . . This purely 'denotative' status of the photograph, the perfection and plenitude of its analogy, in short its 'objectivity,' has every chance of being mythical." Or, "In Photography, the presence of the thing (at a certain past moment) is never metaphoric. . . .

The photograph is literally an emanation of the referent. . . . A sort of umbilical cord links the body of the photographed thing to my gaze: light, though impalpable, is here a carnal medium." The references are, respectively, Roland Barthes, "The Photographic Message," *Image Music Text*, ed. and trans. Stephen Heath (New York: Hill and Wang, 1977), 16–19; and Barthes, *Camera Lucida: Reflections on Photography*, trans. Richard Howard (New York: Hill and Wang, 1981), 78–81. For Pasolini, as for Barthes, reflections on the photographic or cinematographic image ultimately rebound their semiotics into frankly personalized, phenomenological—and in Pasolini's case, theological—grounds. The mutual acknowledgments of these men starting from the early sixties deserve a separate study.

27. Pasolini, "Quips on the Cinema," in Barnet, ed., *Heretical Empiricism*, 227.

28. Stack, *Pasolini on Pasolini*, 82–83.

29. Geoffrey Nowell-Smith's essay "Pasolini's Originality," in *Pier Paolo Pasolini*, ed. Paul Willemen (London: BFI, 1977), 4–20, was perhaps the first, and remains the best, to analyze Pasolini's practice against realist standards, both classical continuity editing and neorealist narrative models. Nowell-Smith's insights on Pasolini's assertive choices, in willful disregard for cinematic conventions, are confirmed in the testimony of Tonino Delli Colli, Pasolini's cinematographer, in an interview accompanying the 2004 Criterion DVD edition of *Mamma Roma* (1962). These observations may be juxtaposed with Pasolini's own professing of technical ignorance, as in some of the "Confessioni tecniche" excerpts cited in this chapter.

30. Maurizio Viano offers no source for this expression, which he credits to Pasolini. His *A Certain Realism: Making Use of Pasolini's Film Theory and Practice* (Berkeley: University of California Press, 1993) attends to some of the key terms that also animate my discussion.

31. The film-theoretical association of the cinematographic image with the notion of a luminous "impression" or "trace"—with a special claim to evidentiary but also magical, and specifically Christological, values—has its most celebrated advocate in André Bazin, whose seminal essay "Ontologie de l'image photographique," as first anthologized in vol. 1 of *Qu'est-ce que le cinéma?* (Paris: Editions du Cerf, 1958–62), 9–17, is illustrated with a photographic negative of the Shroud of Turin—which is how the bodily imprint upon the shroud

is visible. For an extensive discussion of "imprint" as a primal image-matrix, underlying paradigmatically facial and more generally corporeal resemblance as a prehistoric—and pre-art-historic—practice, preceding representational mediation and carrying both ritualistic and juridical functions, see Georges Didi-Huberman, *Devant le temps: Histoire de l'art et anachronisme des images* (Paris: Minuit, 2000), especially the chapter "L'Image-matrice: Histoire de l'art et généalogie de la ressemblance," 59–83. Didi-Huberman has excavated in several studies the theoretical potential of *empreinte* and the contact-image, dwelling also on its Christological uses; see "The Index of the Absent Wound (Monograph on a Stain)," trans. Thomas Repensek, *October* 29 (Summer 1984): 63–81; the exhibition catalog *L'Empreinte* (Paris: Centre Georges Pompidou, 1997); and "Face, proche, lointain: L'empreinte du visage et le lieu pour apparaître," in *The Holy Face and the Paradox of Representation,* ed. Herbert L. Kessler and Gerhard Wolf (Bologna: Villa Spelman Colloquia, vol. 6 / Nuova Alfa Editoriale, 1998), 95–108. Also in this last collection is Hans Belting's essay "In Search of Christ's Body: Image or Imprint" (1–11), which differentiates the representational function of the portrait from the Christological investment in the icon, on which I dwell below.

32. My summary relies on Hans Belting, *Likeness and Presence: A History of the Image before the Era of Art,* trans. Edmund Jephcott (Chicago: University of Chicago Press, 1994), and the *New Catholic Encyclopedia* (New York: McGraw-Hill, 1967) under "Icon."

33. Belting's emphasizing of popular cult influences upon official dogma is comparable to Peter Brown's account of the cult of saints and relics.

34. In the Peircean categorization the indexical sign is causally tied to its referent in distinction from the iconic sign defined by resemblance. Iconicity as a Peircean category should be distinguished here from the historical and theological designation of the icon. Indexicality, meanwhile, can often combine with iconic characteristics. One of Peirce's examples for the indexical sign is the photograph.

35. On Pope Leo films, see Charles Musser, *The Emergence of Cinema: The American Screen to 1907* (New York: Scribner's, 1990), 219–21, and Aldo Bernardini, "Les catholiques et l'avènement du cinéma en Italie: Promotion et contrôle," in Cosandey, ed., *Une Invention du diable,* 3–11. That same pope also wrote a poem, in Latin, in praise of "Ars

photographica" (1877), wherein it is the human likeness that has the power to elevate the modern, mechanical device to the heights of Catholic art: "O shining image / Imprinted by the sun's rays / How well you reproduce / The noble brow, / The radiant eyes, the grace of visage. / / O wonderful power of the spirit / O new marvel! / Apelles who emulated Nature / Could not paint a more perfect image." This translation is from the epigraph to the catalog by Wendy M. Watson, *Images of Italy: Photography in the Nineteenth Century* (South Hadley, Mass.: Mount Holyoke College Art Museum, 1980). On the venerated photograph of Dr. Moscati, see Belting's account and the reproduction in *Likeness and Presence,* 11–13. Annette Michelson brings the *acheiropoietic* icon to bear on cinema in "The Kinetic Icon in the Work of Mourning: Prolegomena to the Analysis of a Textual System," *October* 52 (1990): 16–39. See also note 31 for related references.

36. See Belting, *Likeness and Presence,* 53, 208–9.

37. See Gervase Mathew's *Byzantine Aesthetics* (New York: Viking Press, 1964), 31.

38. Sixten Ringbom, *Icon to Narrative: The Rise of the Dramatic Close-Up in Fifteenth-Century Devotional Painting* (1965; rev. ed. Doornspijk, Neth.: Davaco, 1984), 39, 57 respectively. Ringbom surely borrows the notion of the close-up from cinema. He further observes that the "difference between the devotional image and public art is . . . primarily one of function and size. Formally and iconographically this difference is much less marked" (53). In this revisionist reading of the icon / narrative relation, which I go on to read, via Pasolini, also in Masaccio, I have greatly benefited from conversations with Christopher Wood.

39. François de la Bretèque discusses the iconic frontality of early film that rehearses, in its move from "face-to-face positioning" to "an oblique posture," the evolution of Western religious art. See his "Les films hagiographique dans le cinéma des premiers temps," in Cosandey, ed., *Une Invention du diable,* 121–30.

40. Pasolini, "Confessioni tecniche," 44–46. While Pasolini states here as in the Stack interviews that in a critical moment early in the shooting he chose to turn his back on the "sacred frontality," in fact he recognized retroactively the resolution and crystallization of this visual style in *The Gospel.*

41. From Pasolini's production diaries, published with the screen-

play of *Mamma Roma* (Milan: Rizzoli, 1962), 145–49. On Pasolini's "pastiche" of pictorial allusions, see Alberto Marchesini, *Citazioni pittoriche nel cinema di Pasolini (da "Accattone" al "Decameron")* (Florence: La Nuova Italia, 1994). Marchesini cites Pasolini's 1964 article "Marxismo e Cristianesimo," which admits to his disparate sources: "I thought principally of Piero della Francesca, from whom I took the costumes of the Pharisees, for example, but I also thought of the painter that I love the most, that is, Masaccio; I thought of the primitives, of Giotto. In the face of Christ you will see elements from El Greco and Byzantine elements," etc. (78–79).

42. Indeed, *Mamma Roma* is dedicated to this influential figure whom Pasolini acknowledges as inspiring his own "figurative conversion" (or "revelation"): "a Roberto Longhi cui sono debitore della mia 'fulgurazione figurativa'" (*Mamma Roma* screenplay, 8). Once again, Christological allusion—Saint Paul's conversion or *fulgurazione,* as the term is commonly used—seems inseparable here from Pasolini's aesthetic frame of reference.

43. Roberto Longhi, *Piero della Francesca,* trans. Leonard Penlock (London: Frederick Warne, 1930), 17.

44. Ibid., 42–43. Longhi attends to comparable effects on pp. 46 and 105.

45. Longhi dwells further on Piero's archaism, on Masaccio's "return to Giotto" and his "archaic figure-types," in "Masaccio and Masolino," trans. David Tabbat and David Jacobson, in Roberto Longhi, *Three Studies* (Riverdale-on-Hudson, N.Y.: Stanley Moss–Sheep Meadow Books, 1995), 3–92.

46. In this analysis of Masaccio I have consulted Paul Joannides, *Masaccio and Masolino: A Complete Catalogue* (London: Phaidon Press, 1993).

47. Observing the market scene by the gate of Damascus in the old city of Jerusalem in the *Sopralluoghi in Palestina,* Pasolini points out a comparable touch of "contamination" between the worldly and the divine that has perhaps found its way into the sequence under discussion, as into related juxtapositions: he describes an old lady chewing some sweets while passing the time waiting for Jesus to perform a miracle.

48. The predella, a horizontal band below the main panels of an altarpiece, typically incorporates small figures or scenes to form "part

of the integrated programme of the altarpiece, providing a visual commentary on the major images above and at the same time raising the main panels, and thus improving their visibility." It gives occasion therefore for the joining of different dimensions, narrative and iconic, realist and devotional elements in a kind of collage. See "Predella" entry by Ronald Baxter in *The Dictionary of Art*, ed. Jane Turner (New York: Grove, 1996).

49. Pasolini lists in "The Cinema of Poetry," his best-known essay published the year following *The Gospel* and implicitly describing it, the range of mechanical devices contributing to a poetics of contamination (*Heretical Empiricism*, 184): "The alternation of different lenses, a 25mm and a 200mm on the same face; the proliferation of wasted zoom shots, with their lenses of very high numbers which are on top of things, expanding them like excessively leavened bread; the continuous, deceptively casual shots against the light, which dazzle the camera; the hand-held camera movements; the more sharply focused tracking shots; the wrong editing for expressive reasons; the irritating opening shots; the interminable pauses on the same image, etc."

50. Pasolini, "Confessioni tecniche," 45. The "Universal Light" is a term that Pasolini adopts from Longhi's "lume universale" to designate the even, omniscient, ideal light of Renaissance painting before it was naturalized, particularized, and rendered expressive in the transition to the Baroque.

51. This is paradigmatic of the representation of miracles throughout the film: the miraculous is inserted into the ordinary succession of events via editing, while the humble and mundane is thereby lifted out of its "flow" by virtue of such sudden cuts to otherworldly silence as we witness here. Pasolini observed (in *Les dernières paroles*, 39–40) that in this premodern rural landscape the miraculous is still part of the perception of the everyday, thus consistent with his "realist" refusal to reconstruct the biblical world. Still he was to regret his incorporation of miracles in the film as "almost counter-Reformation Baroque, repellent . . . disgusting pietism" (Stack, *Pasolini on Pasolini*, 87).

52. My geographical and archaeological account is largely based on Edward Allen's *Stone Shelters* (Cambridge, Mass.: MIT Press, 1969) and La Scaletta, *Le chiese rupestri di Matera* (Rome: De Luca Editore, 1966).

53. This was coined by both the Christian Democrat Alcide De Gasperi and by the Communist opposition leader, Palmiro Togliatti.

Carlo Levi paused in this place even earlier, bringing it to attention in 1945 with *Christ Stopped at Eboli*. See Maristella Casciato's account in "Neorealism in Italian Architecture," in *Anxious Modernisms: Experimentation in Postwar Architectural Culture,* ed. Sarah Williams Goldhagen and Réjean Legault (Cambridge, Mass.: MIT Press and the Canadian Centre for Architecture, 2000), 25–54. Thanks to John-David Rhodes, who pointed out to me the relevance of Matera's postwar urbanist history to a discussion of Pasolini.

54. From the soundtrack to *La forma della città*. Pasolini goes on to compare this instance of bad urban planning in Orte with similar occurrences in the Third World, in places where he has been shooting his films for years: Persia, Morocco, Eritrea, Yemen, and, he might have added, Israel. His own documentary in the form of an appeal to UNESCO, *Le mura di Sana'a* (The Walls of Sana'a, 1970–71), is concerned with similar issues of preserving the integrity of the ancient town in North Yemen, saving it from all manner of foreign speculation and indifferent "developments." Here, as in *La forma della città,* the intertwining of a nostalgic aesthetic vision with political-ideological critique is explicit.

55. My account of this landscape type is indebted to Norman F. Carver Jr., *Italian Hilltowns* (Kalamazoo, Mich.: Documan Press, 1979), and to my own experience.

56. Béla Balázs, *Theory of the Film,* trans. Edith Bone (1952; New York: Arno Press, 1972), 96–97. Balázs's writings were translated in Italy already during Fascism, as part of a series of film-theoretical publications carried out by *Bianco e nero* in the late 1930s. Comparable to Balázs's formulation and more celebrated is Walter Benjamin's description of the "ceremonial character" of the aura, associated with a distant, reverential contemplation, as resting on the return look of the inanimate or natural object in "On Some Motifs in Baudelaire," *Illuminations,* ed. Hannah Arendt, trans. Harry Zohn (New York: Schocken Books, 1969), 188.

57. Pasolini is certainly familiar with Dante's formulation of the fourth sense of reading in the *Convivio* 2.1.6: "The fourth sense is called anagogical, that is, transcending the senses: this is brought out when a work is expounded with regard to its spiritual meaning; even though the work is true in a literal sense, what is said there speaks also of things beyond our knowledge relating to eternal glory." *The*

Banquet, trans. Christopher Ryan (Saratoga, Calif.: Anma Libri, 1989), 43. Millicent Marcus defines the four levels of reading as the basis for Pasolini's work in *Filmmaking by the Book: Italian Cinema and Literary Adaptation* (Baltimore, Md.: Johns Hopkins University Press, 1993), 112–13.

Afterword

1. John A. Pinto described Janus's divided look as the historical gaze in a lecture titled "The Perspective of Janus," March 14, 2005, at the American Academy in Rome. In *Janus and the Bridge* (Rome: Papers and Monographs of the American Academy in Rome, 1961), 301, Louise Adams Holland comments on the ways in which new meanings have continuously been devised for the Janus symbol, one of whose basic themes is that of the gate or the passage: topographical tropes of territorial limits complemented by the temporal suggestion of Janus the sky god who journeys, with the sun and moon, across the sky. Janus is also the emblem of the American Academy in Rome, where I write these closing passages.

2. Pier Paolo Pasolini, "Una disperata vitalità," originally published in *Poesia in forma di rosa* (1964) and revised in Pasolini's *Poesie* (1970; Milan: Garzanti, 1999), 185–86. The quotation marks surrounding this stanza designate the direct address of the poetic voice, as in a mock-interview. "As one who dreams that he is harmed" translates Pasolini's borrowing of line 136 from Canto 30 of Dante's *Inferno*. While I tried to follow the logic of Pasolini's lines and syntax in my translation, I have also consulted Allen Mandelbaum's translation of *The Divine Comedy of Dante Alighieri* (Berkeley: University of California Press, 1980), 266. Pasolini first omitted, then corrected this line in the poem's various editions, and it has thus become a point of contention among scholars.

Publication History

A version of chapter 1 was previously published as "From the Air: A Genealogy of Antonioni's Modernism," in *Camera Obscura, Camera Lucida: Essays in Honor of Annette Michelson,* ed. Richard Allen and Malcolm Turvey (Amsterdam: Amsterdam University Press, 2003). Reprinted with permission. A version of chapter 1 appeared in Italian as "Dall'aere: Una genealogia del modernismo di Antonioni," *Il nuovo spettatore 7* (2003). A short version of chapter 1 was published as "Regionalism to Modernism: Antonioni, 1939," in *Deterritorialisations: Revisioning Landscapes and Politics,* ed. Mark Dorrian and Gillian Rose (London: Black Dog Publishing, 2003).

A version of chapter 3 was previously published as "Photographic Verismo, Cinematic Adaptation, and the Staging of a Neorealist Landscape," in *A Companion to Literature and Film,* ed. Robert Stam and Alessandra Raengo (London: Blackwell Publishers, 2004). Reprinted with permission.

Shorter versions of chapter 4 were published as "Pasolini on *Terra Sancta*: Towards a Theology of Film," *Yale Journal of Criticism* 11, no. 1 (1998); and as "Pasolini on *Terra Sancta*: Towards a Theology of Film," in *Rites of Realism: Essays on Corporeal Cinema,* ed. Ivone Margulies (Durham, N.C.: Duke University Press, 2003).

Index

Compiled by Denise E. Carlson

abstraction, 15, 69, 185n13, 192n15;
    in Antonioni's work, 31, 33,
    39; of objects, 6, 184n12
Accattone (Pasolini), 119, 143,
    207n10
acheiropoietic icons, 139–40, 147
Aci Trezza (Sicily), 90–91, 94,
    103–7, 200n11, 203n35; fisher-
    men of, 79, 86, 103, 105, 110–13;
    as location, 116, 204n41,
    206n47; postcard of, 85–86
actions, xxiv, xxv, xxvii, 86. *See
    also* cause and effect
adaptations: by analogy, 208n14;
    Bresson's, xxv; cinematic,
    117, 180n24; Renoir's, 205n45;
    Verga's, 94. *See also Gospel ac-
    cording to Matthew, The; Terra
    trema, La*
Adoration of the Magi (Masaccio),
    152, 153
Aeolian islands (Italy), 169
aerial trope, xxviii, xxix, xxxii,
    1–39, 167. *See also* cinematog-
    raphy: aerial; photography:
    aerial
aerofotografia, 22. *See also* pho-
    tography: aerial
aeropittura (aerial painting),
    20–23, 27, 120–23, 187n25

aesthetics: Antonioni's, 4, 6,
    26, 189n41; cinematic, 118,
    120, 160; Fascist, 37; mod-
    ern, xii, 176n7; natural, 115,
    116; neorealist, xxii, xxiv,
    47; northern Italian, 103;
    Pasolini's, x, 117–18, 136–39,
    142–43, 154, 206n2, 213n42,
    215n54; photographic, 101–2,
    108, 202n30; realist, 79–80,
    136; Rossellini's, 43, 49, 61;
    vernacular, 69; Visconti's,
    204n41; Zavattini's, xxvii
Africa: cinema in, 179n19; Italian
    exploits in, 16–17, 20, 28; as
    location, xxxi, 118, 120, 127,
    128, 208n14
airplanes, 14–15, 20, 22. *See also*
    photography: aerial
Akerman, Chantal, 178n19, 181n30
Alessandrini, Goffredo, 185n14;
    Luciano Serra pilota, 17, 23–24
Algeria, 134
Alicata, Mario, 81, 82–84, 200n10,
    203n34
alienation, 31, 117, 184n12, 185n13
Alighieri, Dante, 215n57, 216n2
allegory: Christian, 198n43; cine-
    matic, 76; ruins as, 43–44,
    71, 74

Allies, xiii, xv, 28, 41, 47–48, 176n9

altarpieces, 145, 213–14n48

"Amante di Gramigna, L'" ("Gramigna's Mistress," Verga), 81, 83, 86–93

Amori di mezzo secolo (Love Stories of Mid-Century, Rossellini), 190n2

anachronism, xvi, 118, 120, 132, 145, 167, 175n3

anagogy, 165, 215n57

analogy, 136–37, 165, 209n26; Pasolini's notion of, 120, 127, 128, 132, 160–61, 208n14

Anatolia, 118, 127

Anderson, Sean, 188n33

anecdote, 5, 18

angles, camera, 93, 94, 98–101, 109, 189n42. *See also* high-angle shots

anti-Fascism, xi, 19, 47, 191n10; in cinema, xiii–xv, 46. *See also* Fascism

antimodernism, xvi, xx, 25, 46, 178n18; realism and, 179n20. *See also* modernism

Antioch (Turkey), 128

antirhetoric, 183n4, 196n35. *See also* rhetoric

Antonello da Messina: *Crucifixion*, 203n35

Antonioni, Michelangelo, 1–39; aesthetics, 4, 6, 26, 189n41; interstitial mode, xxvi, 6, 181n27, 183n5; landscapes, xxix, 3, 7, 12, 38, 47, 167–69, 188n39; modernism of, xxii, 1–39, 118; neorealism

of, xxviii–xix, 1–7, 31–33, 35, 37–38, 168; photography, xxxii, 8–11, 35, 170, 183n6; vision of progress, 3–4; World War II work, 39, 116, 167–68, 170

Antonioni, Michelangelo, works: *L'avventura,* xxiii, 38, 169, 181n27, 189n42; *Cronaca di un amore,* 38, 180n26; documentaries, xv–xvi, 6, 14, 26–38, 167–68, 170, 188n36, 189n42; *L'eclisse,* 38, 186n21, 189n41; film reviews, 17, 182n3; "For a Film on the River Po," 1–14, 26–30, 31, 35, 38, 189n41; *La funivia del Faloria,* 189n40; *Gente del Po,* xiv, 31–38, 178n15, 188n36, 189n41; *Il grido,* 12, 38; *Noto Mandori Vulcano Stromboli Carnevale,* 168–70; *Red Desert,* 176n5; *Vertigine,* 189n40

anxieties, xvi, xx, 68, 88

Appunti per un film sull'India (Notes for a Film on India, Pasolini), 119–20, 127–28

Appunti per un'Orestiade africana (Notes for an African Oresteia, Pasolini), 120

Apulian region (Italy), 132, 156

Arabia, xxxi, 118

Arab villages (Israel), 163

archaic trope, xx, xxviii, xxx–xxxi, 101–2, 113–14, 117–65; Masaccio's, 149; within modernity, ix–xi, 119–20, 126, 132–34, 160–62, 207n10; Pasolini's, 145–46, 155–56, 167, 175n3, 197n10, 206n1 architecture: anti-Fascist, 46; Fascist, 186n21, 188n33; hillside, 158; Mediterranean, 107–10; modern, 19–21, 65, 149; neorealist, 69; postwar, xii, 55, 62; rationalist, 67, 196n34; regional, 65. *See also* housing; monumentalism / monuments

aristocracy: decline of, 176n7

art: abstract, 15; Baroque, 214n50,n51; Byzantine, 213n41; Catholic, 212n35; Christian, 126; cinema as, xii; Greek, 213n41; life and, 206n46; modernist, 1, 206n1; nature and, 3, 202n27; nostalgic, 116, 215n54; public, 212n38; realist, xx, 91–93, 101; regional, xvi, 104, 199n3; ruins as, 63; Weimar, xvii. *See also* painting

articulation, 43, 144; cinematic, xxv, 160, 190n42; of reality, xxvi, 137–38

"Ascension Day" speech (Benito Mussolini), 186n19

Asia, East: cinema in, 179n19

Atalante, L' (Vigo), 176n4, 188n38

Atget, Eugène, 202n30

Athens (Greece), 128

Atlantic Ocean, 128

Auerbach, Erich, 80, 126–27, 199n4, 208n13

aura, cinematic, xv, 215n56

auteurist motifs, xxviii, 29, 188n32

avant-garde, xx, xxvi–xxvii, 47, 200n7,n12; cinematic, 70, 71, 118, 168; European, 27; Italian,

xvii, 14, 20, 22; modernist, xxiii, 176n7; neorealist, 177n14; Soviet, 27; Verga's elements of, 82

Avventura, L' (Antonioni), xxiii, 38, 169, 181n27, 189n42

Bach, Johann Sebastian, *Matthäus-Passion*, 122, 125–26

Balázs, Béla, 164, 215n56

Bandito, Il (The Bandit, Lattuada), xv

Baptism of the Neophytes (Masaccio), 152

Barbaro, Umberto, xvii, xix, 177n14, 188n31

Barile (Italy), 132, 156, 162, 164

Barlera, Paolo, 176n6

Barthes, Roland, 70, 86, 98, 181n27, 183n5, 196n38, 202n31, 209–10n26

Basilicata region (Italy), 128, 160

Battaglia dell'Amba Aradam, La (The Battle of Amba Aradam, Istituto LUCE), 29

Bazin, André, xxiv–xxvii, 46, 49–51, 79, 117–18, 180n24,n25, 192n13,n15, 201n27, 205n45, 210n31

Beersheba (Israel), 122

Belting, Hans, 211n33

Ben-Ghiat, Ruth, 48, 186n20

Benjamin, Walter, 44, 184n11, 185n16, 193n19, 198n42,n44, 215n56

Bergala, Alain, 198–99n45

Bergman, Ingrid, 198n43

Berlin (Germany), xvi, 184n10,

196n37, 197n41; ruins in, 26, 49–61, 69, 70, 72, 193n22, 194n25

Berlusconi, Silvio, xxxii

Bernardi, Sandro, 193n19

Bernstein, Basil, 178n19

Bethlehem (Palestine), 122, 132, 156, 162, 164

Bible: in art, xix; landscapes of, 126–27, 143–44, 167, 214n51. *See also Terra Sancta*, the

Bicycle Thieves (*Ladri di biciclette*, De Sica), xiv, xxvii

Bini, Alfredo, 120, 121

Bitter Rice (*Riso amaro*, De Santis), 175n3, 176n8

black market, xv, 57, 59

Blasetti, Alessandro, 24–25, 199n1

blitz-film, xxvi–xxvii

Blow-up (Antonioni), 183n7

Böll, Heinrich, 197n41

Bontempelli, Massimo, 177n14

Bragaglia, Anton Giulio, 182n3

Braun, Eva, 59

Bresson, Robert, xxv; *Diary of a Country Priest*, 118

Bretèque, François de la, 212n39

Brown, Peter, 130–31, 211n33

Brunatto, Paolo: *La forma della città*, 162, 215n54

Brunetta, Gian Piero, xvii, 177n14, 191n9

Cabiria (Pastrone), 43

Cahiers du cinéma, xxvi, 46

Cain, James M.: *The Postman Always Rings Twice*, xix–xx, 81–82

Calabria (Italy), 125, 128, 132, 133

Calligraphism, 187n31

Calvino, Italo, xxiii, 179n22

cameras: airborne, 14–15, 22, 183n10; Ferrania, 143; hand-held, 122, 155, 208n15, 214n49; movements of, 27, 107–8, 110–12, 164–65; movie, 115; photographic effects of, xxiv–xxv, 183n7. *See also* angles, camera; cinematography; frontality; photography; shots

Capernaum (Israel), 122, 132

capital: intelligence and, 182n3

Cappabianca, Alessandro, 204n41

Capuana, Luigi, 91, 94, 201n24

Carabiniers, Les (Godard), 44, 190n1

Caravaggio, 25

Carraro, Don Andrea, 121, 122, 129, 208n16

cartography, 13, 14, 15, 183n8. *See also* mapping

Caruso, Dr., 121

Casa del Fascio (Como), 186n21

catacombs, 129–30, 131

Catania (Sicily), 100, 113

Catholicism, 121, 212n35

cause and effect, 38, 71, 80, 93, 109, 155

Cavalleria rusticana (Verga), 96

Celere (Italian police), 133

center: periphery and, xvi, 64

Certeau, Michel de, 181n27, 191n7

Chancellory (Berlin): ruins of, 26, 55–61, 69, 70, 72, 194n25

change, xxx–xxxi, 3, 44, 105,

197n38; documentary treatment of, 14, 35; in Europe, 167

characters: Manichaean, xiv, 48; relation to milieu, 80, 109; sacred, 143

Chessa, Luciano, 209n19

Chiarini, Luigi: *Via delle cinque lune,* 188n31

chiaroscuro, 143, 145, 155

Chiesi, Roberto, 175n4

children: amid ruins, ix, 49–53, 57, 59

choral trope, xxviii, 79–116

Christian Democrats, xiii

Christianity, 83, 121, 129–31, 134, 137, 138–39, 160–61

chronicle, the, 38, 180n26. *See also* reportage

Cielo è rosso, Il (The Sky Is Red, Gora), 44

Cimitero Monumentale (Milan), 65

Cinecittà refugee camp, 71, 81; Allied use of, xiii, 176n9

cinema: anti-Fascist, xiii–xv, 46; avant-garde, 70, 71, 118, 168; contingent, xx, xxvii–xxviii, 179n21, 181n27; European, 179n19; Fascist, 48, 71, 184n12; French, xviii, 134; images in, xi, xx, 136–37, 210n26,n31; impure, 117–18, 120, 180n24, 206n2; Italian, xiv, xviii, xxvii, 79–80, 182n3, 197n39, 207n7; literature and, xxvi–xxviii, 4, 6; modern, xxii, 13, 30, 116, 120, 170; narrative in, xxv, 155, 179n21, 192n15; nature

in, 79–116; neorealist, xv, 35, 45–47, 69, 82–83, 114–16, 137–38, 179n19, 196n38; Pasolini's theory of, 143, 160, 209n25, 210n29; post-Fascist, 30; postwar, vii–ix, xii, 79–80, 190n3; realist, xviii, xx, 86, 114, 118, 136–37, 209n25; reconstructive, xvi, xxiii, xxvi, xxxi, 35, 72, 105–6; Visconti's theory of, xix. *See also* filmmaking; films; locations: cinematic; representation(s): cinematic; space(s): cinematic

"Cinema of Poetry, The" (Pasolini), 214n49

cinematography: aerial, 24, 168, 169; depth-of-field, xix, 107, 205n45; documentary, 60–61; Pasolini's, xxix, 137–38, 142–49, 152–56; Rossellini's, 57, 59–61, 70–71; Visconti's, xxix, 101, 110, 113, 204n41, 205n43. *See also* photography

cinéma vérité, xxvii

Cinquecento frame of reference, 144, 145

cities. *See* corpse-cities; landscape(s): urban; urban areas

Clair, René, 182n3; *À Nous la liberté,* ix

Clark, T. J., xxiii

classicism, xxiv, 19, 82

close-ups, 71, 145, 155, 164, 212n38

Coccia, Francesco, 196n35

Cocteau, Jean: *Orpheus,* 44

codes/coding, xiv, xxi–xxii, 38, 178n19

coherence, 52, 57

Cold War, 172, 196n37

collectivity, postwar, 1, 68, 69

Cologne (Germany), 197n41

color films, xxii

Colosseum (Rome), vii, 56

Comizi d'amore (*Love Meetings*, Pasolini), 128, 133, 134, 135, 208n15

commemoration: monuments as, 67; postwar, 37, 71; ruins as, xxx, 45–46, 54, 62; symbolic, 43, 65

commerce, xxx, xxxii

communication, 3, 20

communists, xxiii, 48, 69, 116

communities, restoration of, 45, 52–53

Como (Italy), 186n21

Conquista della Somalia Inglese (Conquest of British Somalia, Istituto LUCE), 29

conscience: realist, 4, 104

consciousness: aesthetic, 101; altered, 43, 120; cinematic, 111, 115, 117–18, 154; historical, 2, 114; modernist, xxvi–xxvii, xxx, 6, 13, 27, 33, 37, 105–6, 205n45; oppositional, xi, 69; postwar, xxv, 4, 35; proto-neorealist, 81

construction, 26, 65, 68, 69, 196n37. *See also* reconstruction

consumerism, vii, viii, x, xxvi–xxvii, xxx–xxxii

contact-images, 211n31

contamination, 14, 131; Pasolini's notion of, 118, 120, 125–26, 154–55, 158, 160, 207n10, 213n47, 214n49

contemporaneity. *See* modernity; present, the

contingency, 72, 197n38; cinematic, xx, xxvii–xxviii, 179n21, 181n27; neorealist, 105; photographic, 14; postwar, xxiii–xxv, 29, 31, 35, 39, 43, 45

continuities, 37, 48, 52; in editing, xxv, 137–38, 179n21, 210n29; re-establishing, 57, 108, 194n24; ruptures and, xii, xv–xvi, xix–xx, xxviii, 72, 106, 114

Conversazione in Sicilia (*Conversation in Sicily,* Vittorini), xvii–xviii

Corbusier, Le, 14–15, 183n10

Corfu (Pagano), 64

corpse-cities, 41–78; ancient, 70–78; modern, 49–70

Corriere dei piccoli, Il (comics weekly), 176n4

courtyards: as locations, 108, 169

crime, xv, 54, 57, 59

Crispolti, Enrico, 187n25

Cronaca di un amore (*Chronicle of a Love Affair,* Antonioni), 38, 180n26

Crotone (Italy), 132

Crow, Thomas, 206n1

Crucifixion (Antonello), 203n35

culture: aerial, 20, 23; anti-Fascist, 18, 47; cinematic, xii–xiii, 113; consumer, xxx–xxxii; Fascist, xx–xxi, xxix, 1–2, 14–30; Italian, xii, xvi, xvii, xxviii, 7, 14, 39, 179n22; modern, 22,

45–46, 176n7; neorealist, 47,
114; populist, viii, 1; postwar,
xi–xii, xv, 18, 167; realist, 92–93;
regional, xii, 3–5, 19, 208n14;
urban, 25
Cyclops, 103–4, 111

D'Albisola, Tullio, 187n25
D'Annunzio, Gabriele, 20, 22
Davoli, Ninetto (actor), vii, x
*Day in the Country (Partie de
campagne,* Renoir), xviii, xix,
188n38
Dead Sea, 122
death, 44, 143; life juxtaposed
with, 72, 75, 76; signs of,
49–54, 71
Decameron (Pasolini), 127, 175n3
decay: regeneration and, 74
De Chirico, Giorgio, 188n39
deep-focus compositions, 156
defeat, xxiv, 59, 193n23
Delaunay, Robert, 183n10
De Laurentiis, Dino: *Le streghe,*
175n3
Deleuze, Gilles, xxv–xxvi, 72,
178n19, 180n26, 190n3
Delli Colli, Tonino, 210n29
departures, cinematic, xxviii
depth, xix, 107, 144, 154, 158, 159,
205n45; surface and, 101,
145–46, 184n12
De Robertis, Francesco: *Uomini
sul fondo,* 25
De Roberto, Federico, 94
D'Errico, Corrado, 27
De Santis, Giuseppe, 81, 82,
203n34; *Bitter Rice,* 175n3,

176n8; *Giorni di gloria,* xiv,
195n32
De Sica, Vittorio: *Bicycle Thieves,*
xiv, xxvii; locations of,
177n10; *Miracle in Milan,*
viii–ix; *The Roof,* ix; *Sciuscià,*
xxvii; transparency of,
180n25; *Umberto D.,* xxvii
destiny: narratives of, 3, 5
De Vincenti, Giorgio, 180n24;
neorealism of, xxvii
devotion, 144, 214n48. *See also*
veneration
dialect, xiv, 88–89, 106, 125, 178n19.
See also language
*Diary of a Country Priest (Journal
d'un curé de campagne,* Bresson), 118
Di Carlo, Carlo, 183n6, 188n40,
190n42
Dickson, W. K. L., 139
Didi-Huberman, Georges,
211n31
Diefendorf, Jeffry M., 194n24
digression, xxii, xxv, 71
dilation, xxvii; spatiotemporal,
xxv
Dirks, Walter, 194n24
discontinuities. *See* continuities:
ruptures and
discourses: anti-Fascist, 46;
modernist, xii; neorealist,
180n26
displacement, xvi, xxiv, 118, 120,
127; of the sacred, 130–32
dissolution, 33, 35, 39
distance, xxix, 7, 12; proximity
and, xxviii

Dix, Otto, 177n14
Doane, Mary Ann, 179n21
Döblin, Alfred, 177n14
documentaries, 182n3; Antonioni's, xv–xvi, 6, 14, 26–38, 167–68, 170, 188n36, 189n42; auteurist, 29, 188n32; fiction combined with, xxv, 1–2, 76, 199n45; landscape, 4–5, 13; Pasolini's, 118–36; photographic, xiv, 98–99, 101–2, 106, 108–9, 116; poetic, 27; postwar, 191n9; propagandist, 5, 22, 24, 26, 28, 30, 185n13; realist, 82–83; ruins in, 43, 44; Visconti's, 84–85, 110. *See also* newsreels; reportage
documentation: monuments as, 41, 63
domination: Pasolini's response to, xxxi
Dottori, Gerardo, 21; *Umbria,* 23
Druze villages (Israel), 121, 163
dwellings. *See* housing

Eclisse, L' (Antonioni), 38, 186n21, 189n41
Eco, Umberto, 209n26
editing, 107, 136, 214n49; in camera, 122; continuity in, xxv, 137–38, 179n21, 210n29
E-42, 19–21, 62, 186n21
Eiffel Tower: painting of, 183n10
1860 (Blasetti), 25, 199n3
Eisensteinian montage, 71
ellipses, xxiv–xxv, 46
ENEL (Italian electric company), 168–70

environment: airplane's effects on, 20; changing, 27–28, 167; modern, 3–4
epics. *See* myths
epistemology, xvi, xxi–xxii, xxvii
Etna, Mount (Italy), 103, 108, 111, 204n43
EUR (Italian World's Fair site), 19, 38, 186n21
Europe: avant-garde in, 27; changes in, 167; cinema in, 179n19; literature of, xxi–xxii; margins of, 118, 171; modernization of, 80–81, 167; neorealism in, xvi, xvii, xxiv; postwar, xxvi, xxxi, 191n10; ruins of, 44, 48, 53; twentieth-century, xvii, xxiv, xxxii
"Event and the Image, The" (Antonioni), 189n41
everyday life, 42; French theories of, 191n7; in *Gente del Po,* 33, 35; photographs of, 94–96; reconstruction of, 45, 59, 62, 68–69, 181n27; representations of, 14, 64; in Verga's work, 84
evidence: ruins as, 45–46, 49, 54; visual, 86
existentialism, xxiv
expressionism, xv, xvii, 179n22
Expulsion of the Devils from Arezzo, The (Giotto), 159
exteriors, 33, 74, 188n38, 204n41; cinematic, 107–8, 110–11; ruinous, 50–51, 54, 71

failure, 71–72
Fallaci, Oriana, 133

family values, xxx, 25

"Fantasticheria" (Verga), 90

Faraglioni, the (Sicily), 104, 111, 200n11

Fascism, xviii, xx–xxii, 37–38; aftermath of, xiii–xvi, xxix–xxx, 4, 44, 116; cinema of, 48, 71, 184n12; complicity with, 47–48; containment policy, 23; culture of, xix, xx–xxi, 1–2, 14–30; mobs, 133; modernization under, x, xxix, 4, 81; monumental projects, 61–63, 65, 71; propaganda, 28, 71, 192n11, 197n39; regionalism of, 80, 81, 82, 186n19; rhetoric of, xx, 6, 30, 125; trials of leaders, 195n32. *See also* anti-Fascism

feature films, xv, xxv

Fellini, Federico, 169; *Nights of Cabiria,* ix

Ferrara (Italy), xix, 12, 188n39

fiction: documentary combined with, xxv, 1–2, 76, 199n45; literary, 88–89

fiction films, xxv, 5–6, 13, 23–26, 182n3, 189n42

figure-ground dichotomy, xxviii, 7, 15, 39, 76; in Pasolini's work, 144–50, 152, 154, 156, 158, 160, 164

figures: allegorical, 43–44, 76; human, 15, 95–96, 98, 144, 146–48; landscape, 49; movements of, 12, 107–8; Pasolini's, 142, 159; withdrawal of, 38–39

film-lampo, xxvi–xxvii

filmmaking, x–xi, 2; capitalist modes of, xxvii; Fascist, 22–30; mythicized, 110; traveling and, 118–36

film noir, xv

films, xv, xxii; American, xiv, 71, 177n9; resemblance to paintings, 164–65. *See also* cinema; documentaries; newsreels; *and specific film genres*

First World War, 14, 82, 179n22

fishermen, Sicilian, 79, 86, 103, 105, 110–13

Fiumara di Fiumicino (Italy), vii, xxxi

Flaherty, Robert, 5, 200n10

flash-film, xxvi–xxvii

focal length, 144, 154. *See also* angles, camera; shots: duration of

folklore, 5, 18, 25, 80, 88, 131

Fontana, Lucio, 187n25

"For a Film on the River Po" (Antonioni), 1–14, 26–30, 31, 35, 38, 189n41

Forgács, David, 181n32

Forma della città, La (The Form of the City, Brunatto), 162, 215n54

fracturing, xxii, xxiv; in Antonioni's work, 189n42; of reality, xxvi, xxvii, 4; in Rossellini's work, 48, 70, 75

fragmentation: in Antonioni's work, 31–33, 35, 39; in Rossellini's work, 43, 71. *See also* ruins frames of reference: Pasolini's, 127, 213n42; Renaissance, 142, 144–46, 158; Visconti's, 25

framing: Antonioni's technique, 33; cinematic, 13, 99–100, 110–11, 113, 114–16; Pasolini's technique, 136, 142, 144, 154–56, 158–59; photographic, 98–101. *See also* reframing

France: cinema in, xviii, 134; naturalism in, 94; neorealism in, 181n27; realism in, 80; Resistance in, 191n10

Franciscans, 145, 148

freeze-frame shots, 149, 196n38

From the Airplane (Masoero), 24

frontality: cinematic, 112, 212n39; of icons, 141, 212n40; in Pasolini's work, xxxi, 142–49, 152, 154, 158; photographic, 95, 99

functionalism, ix, xi

Funivia del Faloria, La (The Faloria Cable-Car, Antonioni), 189n40

future, the, xxiii, xxx, 49, 92–93; vision of, 21, 23, 45, 53–54, 56, 193n17. *See also* Second Futurism

Galilee, Sea of, 121, 125

Gandhi, Indira, 190n42

Ganges River, 189n42

gangster films, xv

Gente del Po (People of the Po, Antonioni), xiv, 31–38, 178n15, 188n36, 189n41

geography, 176n7. *See also*

landscape(s); *Terra Sancta, the*; topography

Germany: neorealism in, 177n14; postwar, xxix, 196n37; reconstruction in, 57, 69; rubble-genre films, 44; ruins in, 26, 47–61, 69, 70–72, 194n25; surrender of, 193n23. *See also* Nazis

Germany Year 90 Nine Zero (*Allemagne 90 neuf zéro*, Godard), 44

Germany Year Zero (*Germania anno zero*, Rossellini), ix, xxix, 48–61, 69–76, 192n13, 193n23

Gethsemane, Garden of, 122

ghettos: as locations, 128

Ginsborg, Paul, 121

Giorni di gloria (De Santis / Serandrei / Visconti), xiv, 195n32

Giotto di Bondone, 138, 145, 148, 158, 213n41; *The Expulsion of the Devils from Arezzo*, 159

God: icons of, 165. *See also* Jesus Christ

Godard, Jean-Luc, 44, 181n30, 190n1

Goethe, Johann Wolfgang, 203n35; birthplace of, 194n24

Gora, Claudio: *Il cielo è rosso*, 44

Gospel according to Matthew, The (*Il Vangelo secondo Matteo*, Pasolini), xxxi, 118–65, 206n3, 207n10, 208n15, 209n24, 212n40; locations search for, 120–36, 154–65

Gospel of Mark, 126–27

Gospel of Matthew, 117, 122, 134, 142

Gramsci, Antonio, 81

grandeur: humility and, xvi, 105

Greco, El, 213n41

Grido, Il (Antonioni), 12, 38

group shots, 108–9

Guattari, Félix, 178n19

Guitti, Francesco, 204n42

Gulf of Hammamet: Topographical Lyricism (Molinari), 21–22

Gulf War (1991), 185n13

Guttuso, Renato, 86, 187n25

habitation. *See* housing

habits: cycles of, xxx

healing, 52

Henry V (Olivier), 118

Herculaneum (Italy), 75

hermits. *See* monasticism

heroism, xiv–xvi; Fascist, 17–18, 27–28, 30, 80; monuments to, 68, 71; rhetoric of, 26, 183n4; in Verga's work, 81

high-angle shots, 26, 35, 57, 60, 152, 154, 184n10, 190n42. *See also* angles, camera

history, xxiv, 2, 44, 46, 72, 131, 198n42

Hitler, Adolf, 17, 57, 59–60, 61, 194n25

Holland, Louise Adams, 216n1

Hollywood. *See* films: American

Holocaust, 197n41

Holy Face. *See* Jesus Christ: face of

Holy Land. *See* Palestine; *Terra Sancta, the*

Holy Sepulcher, 122, 130, 209n19

Homer, 102; *Odyssey,* 103–5

housing, vii–ix, xxx, 42, 46, 64–65; construction of, 65, 68, 69, 196n37; monuments as, 42–43, 48–49; ruinous, 43, 50–54; shortage of, 45, 62–63

Huillet, Danièle, 197n41

humanism, xxiii, 22, 37, 47, 197n39; neorealist, xiv–xv, 1–2, 83

humans, xxiv, 38, 164; absence of, 37, 53; bodies as ruins, 76, 77; nature and, xxx, 3, 105. *See also* figures: human

humility: of Christ, 164; grandeur and, vii, xvi, 105; of Holy Land, 122, 124–29, 131, 162; of Italian sites, x, 132; sacredness and, 160

iconography/icons, 138–42, 144–45, 147–48, 155–56, 158–61, 211n31,n34; De Chirico's, 188n39; narrative, 212n38, 214n48. *See also* Jesus Christ: face of; relics

identification: alienation and, 31, 184n12

identities: cinematic, 158; new, xxi, 179n19; restoration of, 45, 52–53

ideologies: Antonioni's, 4, 35; capitalist, 179n21; Fascist, xx, 29, 81–82; neorealist, 83; Pasolini's, 136; traditional, 25; vernacular, 69; Visconti's, 115–16, 204n41 image(s): Christian, 131; cinematic, xi, xx, 136–37, 210n26,n31; devotional, 138, 159, 212n38; monumental, 59, 72, 74; mythic, 89–90; narrative and, 141–42, 148; postwar, 42–43; realist, 120, 209n26. *See also* iconography / icons; landscape-images; signs

imagination: archaic, 155–56; modern, 4; national, 2; regional, 88

immediacy: effect of, 155

imperialism, 20, 21–22, 24, 28–29

Impressionism, xix, 13, 92, 145, 183n8

imprints, 211n31

INA-Casa national housing plan, 65, 68

Incarnation, the, 127, 131, 138–39, 142, 164, 165

indexicality. *See* cameras: photographic effects of; signs: indexical

India, 119–20, 127–28, 179n19, 207n5

industry, 3, 167, 168; modernization of, 12–13, 26, 176n7

insert views, 71

institutions: questioning of, xiv

intellectuals, 1, 13, 68, 106

intelligence, 5–6; capital and, 182n3

interiors, 74, 204n41; cinematic, 107, 110–11; ruinous, 50–51, 54, 71

interruption, xx, xxvii, 118

intervention: neorealism as, 45–47

Ionian Sea, 113

Israel, 121–33, 206–7n4, 215n54. *See also* Palestine

Istituto LUCE (L'Unione per la Cinematografia Educativa), 22, 28–30, 188n32,n34

Italian (language), xiv, 88–91, 106, 125

Italy: avant-garde in, xvii, 14, 20, 22; aviation in, 17, 23; cinema in, xiv, xviii, xxvii, 79–80, 182n3, 197n39, 207n7; culture of, xii, xvi, xvii, xxviii, 7, 14, 39, 179n22; economic miracle, vii, x, xxx–xxxii, 182n32; Fascism, 14–30; image of, x, 31, 37, 47; landscapes, xx, xxxi, 19, 21, 82, 198n43; as location, 119, 127, 128–29, 167; modernism in, 14, 30, 67, 176n4; modernity in, 167, 176n7, 186n19; modernization of, 80–81; neorealism in, xvii, xxiv, xxvi, 18–19, 46; northern, 103, 204n42; post-Fascist, xiii–xvi, 1; postwar, vii–xiii, xii, xxii, xxix, 45–49, 178n18; realism in, xx, 45–48; regionalism in, xi, xvi, 103, 162–63; Resistance in, 191n10, 195n29; restoration of, 57, 62, 65; ruins in, 47–49, 63; southern, 102, 103, 106, 131–34, 139, 160–62, 182n32; unification of, 25. *See also individual regions and towns*

Jacobson, David, 175n3

Jameson, Fredric, xxi–xxii, 178n19, 179n20, 191n7

Janus, 171, 216n1
Jeli il pastore (Verga), 83
Jerusalem (Israel), 122, 128, 130, 132–33, 160–61, 162, 209n19, 213n47
Jesus Christ: Baptism of, 154–55; face of, 139–41, 143, 149, 164–65, 210–11n31, 213n41; life of, 122, 124–25, 127–29, 133, 134, 137; Passion of, 162–64; values of, 210–11n31, 213n42
Jetée, La (Marker), 44
John XXIII (pope), 121
Jordan (country), 122, 126, 206–7n4
Jordan River, 121, 122, 124, 129
Joseph, Saint, 156, 164
Journey to Italy (*Viaggio in Italia*, Rossellini), xxxii, 48–49, 72–78, 198n43,n45

kibbutz, 121, 124
Koshar, Rudy, 194n24,n26, 214n25
Kracauer, Siegfried, 15, 184n12
Krauss, Rosalind, 183n8
Kumbha Mela (Antonioni), 189n42

labor/laborers, xxi, xxx, 1, 79
Laestrygonians Destroy Ships in Odysseus's Fleet, The (fresco), 104
La Martella housing project, 161–62
Lamprecht, Gerhard: *Somewhere in Berlin*, 44, 50–51
Land Reform of 1950, 182n32
landscape(s): aerial, 15, 21; altered, 28, 30–39, 170, 198n42; Antonioni's, xxix, 3, 7, 12, 38,

167–68, 189n41; archaic, 165; biblical, 126–27, 143–44, 167, 214n51; cinematic, xxviii, 13; enframed, 142; frontality of, 146–48; human looks and, 164; Italian, xx, xxxi, 19, 21, 82, 198n43; modern, xvi, xviii, 3–5, 12–14, 49, 162; mythical, xxxi, 5, 89–90, 104; natural, 28, 49, 112–13, 149, 152, 181n27,n31, 190n42; neorealist, xii, 6, 59, 102–16; 1960s, xxx–xxxi; Pasolini's, 120–36, 154–65, 167, 171–72; as photographic image, 184n12; possession of, 27, 79; postwar, vii–xi, 41–47, 57; of poverty, 126; quotidian, xvi, 46; regional, 2, 14–30, 49, 162, 187n31; Rossellini's, xxix–xxx, 47–48, 169, 193n19; ruinous, xii, xviii, xxix–xxx, 41–78, 125–26, 190n4, 191n4; rural, 12, 25, 214n51; theatrical, 104, 111–16; urban, xi, xv, xxvii, 53, 152, 187n31, 193n19; Verga's, 96; Visconti's, xvi, xxix, 104–16, 202n27, 206n47. *See also* figure-ground dichotomy; locations; *Terra Sancta*, the; topography; *and specific geographic locations*
landscape-images, xv, xxi, xxiii, 15, 35, 110–11, 189n41
language, xxi–xxii, 86, 91–92, 209n25. *See also* Italian
La Spezia, Gulf of (Italy), 21
Last Days of Pompeii, The (*Gli ultimi giorni di Pompei*), 43

Latin America: cinema in, 179n19
Lattuada, Alberto, xv, xviii
Lazio region (Italy), 128, 162
Lefebvre, Henri, 181n27, 191n7
lenses, 143–47, 159, 214n49
Leo XIII (pope), 139, 211n35
Libera, Adalberto, 20–21
liberation: cinematic culture
    of, xii–xiii, xvii; neorealist,
    xvii, xviii, xxvi; thematics of,
    192n13; war of, 47, 49
life: art and, 206n46; death juxta-
    posed with, 75, 76
lighting: cinematic, xv, 143; pho-
    tographic, 98; in Renaissance
    art, 155, 214n50
limit vision, 42, 74, 75–76, 78, 190n3
Lissitzky, El, 183n10
literature: anti-Fascist, 46; avant-
    garde, 200n7; cinema and,
    xi, xvi–xviii, 4, 6; German,
    177n14; Italian, 179n22; Judeo-
    Christian, 126–27; neorealist,
    xvii–xviii; nineteenth-century
    European, xxi–xxii; realist,
    xx, 1, 80, 93, 178n19; Russian,
    177n14. See also fiction; poetry
Littoria (Matarazzo), 26
Livorno (Italy), 114
local, the: national bound with, xi
locations, xix, 13; ancient, xxxi;
    Antonioni's, 169; cine-
    matic, xi–xiii, xx, xxiii–xxv,
    xxviii–xxix, xxxii, 13, 35; Fell-
    ini's, 169; marginal, vii–viii,
    xi, xxxi, 118–19, 161, 170–71;
    monumental, 66; mythical,
    xxxi, 5, 89–90, 104; neoreal-

ist, xviii, xxi, 42, 169, 180n25;
    Pasolini's search for, xxxi,
    120–36, 154–65, 207n5; realist,
    xxv, 4; Rossellini's, 65, 68,
    169, 193n19; shooting on, 4,
    47; as terra sancta, 120–36. See
    also landscape(s); and specific
    locations
London (England), 128
Longhi, Roberto, xix, 138, 146,
    148, 152, 213n42, 214n50
long shots, 137–38, 145, 205n45
Lorentz, Pare: The River, 5
loss, xxiv, 31, 42, 48, 68, 71–72
love, 25, 133, 137–38
Lucania (Italy), 132
Luciano Serra pilota (Alessandrini),
    17, 23–24
Lukács, Georg, 199n4
Luperini, Romano, 82, 89, 91,
    200n7

Macchiaioli, 25, 92, 201n24
Macchina ammazzacattivi, La (The
    Machine to Kill Bad People,
    Rossellini), 196–97n38
Macciocchi, Maria Antonietta,
    209n24
Madonna della Misericordia (Piero
    della Francesca), 156
magical realism, xvii, 177n14
Magnani, Anna, 177n13
Malavoglia, I (Verga), 79, 82–94,
    102–3, 116, 200n7, 201n24. See
    also Terra trema, La
Malevich, Kasimir, 183n10
Mamma Roma (Pasolini), 119, 144,
    176n6,n7, 213n42

Mandylion, the, 139, 140
Mangano, Silvana (actor), vii–viii, x, xi, 175n3
Man of Aran (Flaherty), 200n10
Manzoni, Alessandro, 79
mapping, vii, viii, xi, xvi, 33, 129–31. See also cartography
Marcello, Flavia, 196n34
Marchesini, Alberto, 213n41
March on Rome, 25
Marcus, Millicent, 203n34
marginality, xviii, 18, 69; in locations, vii–viii, xi, xxxi, 118–19, 161, 170–71
Marinetti, F. T., 17, 20, 22, 185n16, 187n25,n26
Marker, Chris: La Jetée, 44
martyrdom: narratives of, 119
Marxism, 83, 90, 105, 106, 109
Mary (mother of Jesus), 155–56
Masaccio, 138, 145, 146, 148–50, 213n41; Adoration of the Magi, 152, 153
Mascalucia (Sicily), 96, 98
Masoero, Filippo, 22, 23, 185n14; From the Airplane, 24
Massacre of the Innocents, 133
Massafra (Italy), 132
mass ornament, 15, 30, 184n12
Mastro Don Gesualdo (Verga), 83, 93
Matarazzo, Raffaello, 26
Matera (Italy), 132, 158, 160–64
material, the, 139; symbolic bound with, xi
Matthäus-Passion (Bach), 122, 125–26
Maupassant, Guy de, xviii

Mausoleum of the Fosse Ardeatine, 65–67, 195n32
Medea (Pasolini), 120, 127
media, the, power of, xxxii
Mediterranean Sea, xxx, 110, 112–13, 128, 206n46
medium shots, 155, 156
melodrama, xiv, 18, 24, 44, 75
memory, 45–46, 63, 72, 196n38. See also past, the: recalling
Mergellina Caves (Naples), 42–43
Messina (Italy), 203n35
Metamorphoses (Ovid), 103
metonymy, xxv, 71
metteurs-en-scènes, 101
Micciché, Lino, 179n19
middle class: rise of, 176n7
Milan (Italy), viii–ix, 22, 27, 65–67; Verga in, 88, 90, 102
militarism, 21, 22, 28, 185n13,n15. See also war
Miracle in Milan (Miracolo a Milano, De Sica), viii–ix
miracles, 214n50
mise-en-scène: frontal, 142–43; in Gente del Po, 32; Pasolini's, 154; Visconti's, 25, 107, 110
modernism, xii, xvi–xxxi, 80, 176n7; aerial, 23; Antonioni's, xxii, 1–39, 118; architectural, 19–20, 65; avant-garde, xxiii, 176n7; cinematic, xxii, 13, 30, 116, 120, 170; in documentaries, 29–30; Fascist, x, xxix, 4, 81; Italian, 14, 30, 67, 176n4; midcentury, xxi, xxix, xxx–xxxi; neorealist, xix–xxvi, 13, 68; Pasolini's,

138, 175n3, 181n32; political, 105, 162, 176n7; prewar, 38, 67, 71, 195n34; realist and, 179n20, 184n12; reconstructive, xxi, 47, 195–96n34; regional, xxix, 21–23, 24; Rossellini's, 43; ruins of, xxii, 41–72, 74; universal, 20, 22–23, 28; verismo and, 86; Visconti's, xix, 111. *See also* antimodernism; consciousness: modernist

modernity, 124, 176n7, 184n12; advent of, 89, 102, 104; Antonioni's, 167, 170; archaic within, ix–xi, 119–20, 126, 132–34, 160–62, 207n10; consciousness of, xviii, 14, 27; Israeli, 133; Italian, 186n19; landscapes of, xvi, xviii, 3–5, 12–14, 49, 162; late, 39, 44, 167, 168, 170, 179n20; monument's place in, 62, 68, 70; nature and, 5; neorealism and, xxi–xxiii; nineteenth century, xxx; Pasolini's, 117, 133, 167; photographic, 14, 101, 170–71, 184n10; postwar, 74, 161; regional, 19, 24–26; Visconti's, xix

modernization, x, xii, xxix–xxx, 80–81, 167, 181n32

Moholy-Nagy, László, 184n10

Molinari, Mario: *Gulf of Hammamet: Topographical Lyricism*, 21–22

monasticism, 131, 160

monumentalism / monuments: gestures of, 196n37,n38; neo-

realism and, xi, xvi–xvii, 18, 41–43, 69, 72; Pasolini's, xxxi; preservation of, 45, 194n26; reconstruction of, 52, 61–69, 194n24, 197n41; Roman, 31; Rossellini's, xxxi, 70, 78, 191n9; ruins as, 45–46, 48–49, 54–57, 61–65, 72, 74; unintentional, 194n28; urban, 22

Monument to the Dead in the German Concentration Camps (Milan), 65, 66

Morin, Edgar, 193n23

Moscati, Giuseppe, 139

Mountain of the Beatitudes, 125

movement(s), 14, 159; camera, 7, 27–28, 107–8, 110–12, 164–65; mass, xxiii; river's, 35; stasis and, 144, 145; of translation, 130–31. *See also* modernism; neorealism

Mumford, Lewis, 62

Mura di Sana'a, Le (The Walls of Sana'a, Pasolini), 215n54

Murderers Are among Us, The (*Die Mörder sind unter uns*, Staudte), 44

Mussolini, Benito, 25, 186n19, 195n31

Mussolini, Vittorio, 1, 16–18, 26, 82

Mussolinia di Sardegna (Matarazzo), 26

myths, 203n36, 208n14; ancient, 103–5; Christian, 129–30, 134, 137; Fascist, 71, 81; folk, 18, 80; Greek-Mediterranean, 128; locations of, xxxi, 5, 89–90,

104; photographic, 98–99, 102, 126, 209n26; Roman, 31

Nadar, Felix, 14, 94
Naples (Italy), xxxii, 41–42, 54, 74–75, 127, 198n44
Napoli '43 (Rossellini), 190n2
narrative(s): causality in, 80; cinematic, xxv, 155, 179n21, 192n15; in *Gente del Po*, 32, 33, 35, 38–39; iconic, 212n38, 214n48; images and, 141–42, 148; of martyrdom, 119; neorealist, xxii, xxiv, 35; postwar, 191n9; techniques of, 180n26; traditional, 30; withdrawal of, 38–39, 46. *See also* space(s): narrative
national, the, 2, 20, 22; local bound with, xi
nationalism, 197n39
naturalism, 80, 94, 109, 136, 199n4
nature, 5, 193n19, 202n27; dramaturgy of, xi, 79–116; humans and, xxx, 3, 105. *See also* landscape(s): natural
Nave bianca, La (The White Ship, Rossellini), 25, 48
Nazareth (Israel), 121, 122
Nazis, xiv, xxix, 56–57, 192n13, 194n26; complicity with, 47–48, 53–54; massacre by, xxv, 65, 66, 195n32; monumental projects, 61
Nazzari, Amadeo, 23, 177n13
neocapitalism, xxx, xxxi, 125, 162, 167
neoclassicism, 19, 20

neorealism, x–xxii, 59, 72, 102–16, 171, 178n18, 180n26, 187n31, 196n35; aesthetics of, xxii, xxiv, 47; Antonioni's, 1–7, 31–33, 35, 37–38, 168; avant-garde, 177n14; cinematic, xv, 35, 45–47, 69, 82–83, 114–16, 137–38, 179n19, 196n38; contingent, 105; culture of, 47, 114; documentary, 102; European, xvi, xvii, xxiv; French, 181n27; German, 177n14; Godard's, 190n1; historiographic, 46, 171, 176n8; humanist, xiv–xv, 1–2, 83; Italian, 18–19, 46; monumentality and, 41–42, 68, 69; New Wave and, 181n30; Pasolini's, x–xii, xxxi, 161, 175n2, 209n25, 210n29; photographic, xvii–xviii; reconstruction as, xiii–xiv, 42–43, 45–49, 57, 68, 69; rhetoric in, 183n4; Rossellini's, xvi, xxviii–xxx, 44, 47–48, 57, 69–70, 192n11, 198n43; urban, 162; Verga's, 83; verismo and, 86, 94, 101, 203n34; Visconti's, xix, 80–81, 84, 101–2, 106, 116, 178n16. *See also* landscape(s): neorealist; locations: neorealist; modernism: neorealist; pink neorealism
Neue Sachlichkeit (New Objectivity), xvii, 69–70
newsreels, 22, 44, 60, 144, 154, 188n32
New Wave, xxiv, xxvi, 46, 179n19, 181n28,n30, 199n45

New York City, 128
Nights of Cabiria (Notti di Cabiria, Fellini), ix
nostalgia, 3, 17–18, 24–25, 68; antimodernist, 178n18; for archaic, xx, 118, 124; artistic, 116, 215n54; Verga's, 88, 90, 102
Noto Mandori Vulcano Stromboli Carnevale (Antonioni), 168–70
Not Reconciled (Nicht versöhnt, Straub), 44, 197n41
Nous la liberté, À (Clair), ix
Novalucello (Sicily), 99–101
Nowell-Smith, Geoffrey, 192n11, 205n45, 210n29

objects, 27, 96, 138, 159, 215n56; abstraction of, 6, 184n12; landscapes and, 164; of veneration, 138–42, 144, 148, 159, 160
observers: in Rossellini's films, 43, 46, 75
Occhio quadrato (Squared Eye, Lattuada), xviii
Odyssey (Homer), 103–5
Oedipus Rex (Edipo Re, Pasolini), 120, 127, 175n3
Olivier, Laurence: *Henry V,* 118
120 Days of Sodom, The (Pasolini), 127
"One Minute of Cinema" (Zavattini), xxvi
Open City (Roma città aperta, Rossellini), ix, xiii, xiv, 48, 65, 71, 192n13
open city policy, 48–49
opening shots, 214n49
optical unconscious, 184n11

Ore di guerra nel cielo africano (Hours of War in the African Sky, Istituto LUCE), 29
Orpheus (Orphée, Cocteau), 44
Orte (Italy), 162, 215n54
Ossessione (Visconti), xix–xx, 25–26, 31, 82, 105, 177n9
Overbey, David, 177n10
over-the-shoulder shots, 152
Ovid: *Metamorphoses,* 103

paganism, 131, 139
Pagano, Giuseppe, xvii, 62–63, 65, 194–95n29; *Corfu,* 64
painting, 164–65; aerial, 20–23, 27, 120–23, 187n25; German, 177n14; Impressionist, xix, 13, 92, 145, 183n8; landscape, 104, 201n24; Macchiaioli, 25, 92, 201n24; nineteenth century, xxi; Renaissance, xix, 144–50, 152–53, 155, 214n50. *See also* art
Paisà (Rossellini), xxix, 48, 71, 74, 76, 192n13; locations of, ix, 31, 41–43, 54, 65, 74; neorealism in, xxiii–xxv, 50
Palazzo dei Congressi, 20
Palestine, 118, 120–36, 139, 163, 206n4, 208n17. *See also Terra Sancta,* the
panning shots, 110–11, 145, 164
Panofsky, Erwin, 43–44
Paris (France), 128
Pasinetti, Francesco, 27–28, 188n31
Pasolini, Pier Paolo, xxii, xxix, xxx–xxxi, 117–65; adaptations by, 126–28, 143, 208n14, 209n24; aesthetics, x, 117–18, 136–39,

142–43, 154, 206n2, 213n42, 215n54; archaism, 145–46, 155–56, 167, 175n3, 197n10, 206n1; camera work, xxix, 137–38, 142–49, 152–56; cinematic theory, 143, 160, 209n25, 210n29; frames of reference, 213n42; iconography, 175n4; landscapes, 120–36, 154–65, 167, 171–72; location hunts, xxxi, 120–36, 154–65, 207n5; modernism of, 138, 175n3, 181n32; modernity of, 117, 133, 167; neorealism of, x–xii, xxxi, 175n2, 209n25, 210n29; perspectival views, 144, 148, 149, 154, 155, 158; realism of, 138, 209n25; reverential attitude, 142; semiology, 209n25,n26. *See* contamination: Pasolini's notion of

Pasolini, Pier Paolo, works: *Accattone*, 119, 143, 207n10; *Appunti per un film sull' India*, 119–20, 127–28; "The Cinema of Poetry," 214n49; *Comizi d'amore*, 128, 133, 134, 135, 208n15; *Decameron*, 127, 175n3; *The Gospel according to Matthew*, xxxi, 118–65, 206n3, 207n10, 208n15, 209n24, 212n40; *Mamma Roma*, 119, 144, 176n6,n7, 213n42; *Medea*, 120, 127; *Le mura di Sana'a*, 215n54; *Oedipus Rex*, 120, 127, 175n3; *The 120 Days of Sodom*, 127, 207n10; poetry, 171–72, 175n1, 176n6, 214n49, 216n2; *La ricotta*, 121, 176n6, 207n7; *Sopralluoghi in Palestina per il Vangelo secondo Matteo*, 118–36, 162, 163, 213n47; *Teorema*, 175n3; *La terra vista dalla luna*, vi, vii–xi, xxxi, xxxii, 175n3, 179n20; "Una disperata vitalità," 175n1

past, the, xii, 72; forgetting, 52–53, 54, 65; idealized, 108, 138; modernism and, x, xxii–xxiv; present bound with, xi, xvi, xix–xx, 38, 46, 48–49, 55, 102; recalling, 43–46, 197n41, 198n42. *See also* archaic trope; memory

Pastrone, Giovanni: *Cabiria*, 43

patriotism, 17, 23

Paul (Saint), 128

peasantry, 25, 79, 161, 162

people. *See* humans

perception: aerial, xvi, 31, 38–39; Antonioni's, 167, 181n27; cinematic, xvi, 106–7, 165; human, 4; modern, 15, 22, 31; neorealist, xii, xxv, xxvi; spatial, 14, 20–21, 25

periodizing, xv, xxi

periphery: center and, xvi, 64

perpendicular shots, 190n42

persons. *See* humans

perspectival views, 7, 20–21, 49, 117, 204n42; in Pasolini's work, 144, 148, 149, 154, 155, 158

Perugia (Italy), 21

phantasmic, the: reality and, 126

photogrammetry, 183n8

photography, 70, 145, 183n7, 196n38, 201n27, 208n16; aerial, 13–30, 35, 183n8, 184n11, 185n13,n15, 188n33, 189n40, 190n42; Antonioni's, xxxii, 8–11, 35, 170, 183n6; documentary nature of, xiv, 98–99, 101–2, 106, 108–9; images of, 139–41, 183n7; modern, 14, 101, 170–71, 184n10; mythical, 98–99, 102, 126, 209n26; neorealist, xvii–xviii; objectivity of, 202n31; realist, 14–15, 80, 126, 180n24, 184n12; regional, xvii, 80, 101–2; spaces in, 183n10; still, 183n7; Verga's, 92–102, 108, 115–16, 202n29,n30, 203n32; verismo, 94–102, 110; Zola's, 202n29. See also cameras

Piccioni di Venezia, I (The Pigeons of Venice, Pasinetti), 27

Piero della Francesca, 138, 146–48, 156, 213n41

pilgrimage, 128, 130

Pilota ritorna, Un (A Pilot Returns, Rossellini), 25, 48

pink neorealism, 175n3, 176n8

Pinto, John A., 216n1

place, xxiv, 131; intelligence of, xxix, 38–39, 167, 189n41; spirit of, 2–3, 5–6, 27, 164

play: signs of, 49–51, 53–54, 71

plots, xxii, 23

poetry, 2, 71, 106; Pasolini's, 171–72, 175n1, 176n6, 214n49, 216n2; Verga's, 83, 101, 106

politics: Fascist, 16, 37; modernist, 105, 162, 176n7; neorealist, 46; Pasolini's, x; Rossellini's, 192n11, 197n39

Pompeii (Italy), 49, 72–78, 198n45

Pontelagoscuro (Italy), 12, 17

populism, viii, 1, 46, 47, 68

Po River/Valley, xix–xx, xxiv–xxv, 17; Antonioni's film on, 1–14, 26–38, 189n41

portraits, 141–43, 211n31

portrait shots, 149

Postman Always Rings Twice, The (Cain), xix–xx, 81–82

postmodernism, xxii

post-sync tradition, 155

power, xxxi, 35

predella, 213n48

present, the, xxiv, xxvii, 3–4, 72, 165, 197n41; in Pasolini's work, 161; past bound with, xi, xvi, xix–xx, 38, 46, 48–49, 55, 102. See also modernity

privilege: prohibition and, 130

Pro Civitate Christiana, 120–21

profane, sacred and, 130. See also sacred, the

profilmic world, xxiv, 2

progress, 3–4, 5, 18, 20, 26–27, 124, 134, 198n42

progressivism, xx, 80

prohibition: privilege and, 130

Project for a Symbolic Arch at E-42 (Libera), 20, 21

propaganda: documentary, 5, 22, 24, 26, 28, 30, 185n13; Fascist, 28, 71, 192n11, 197n39

Protestantism, 139

proto-modernism, xvii–xviii. *See also* modernism

proto-neorealism, 18, 25, 62, 64, 81. *See also* neorealism

proto-realism, 1. *See also* realism

proximity: distance and, xxviii

Puccini, Gianni, 81, 85

Puccini, Mario, 85

Puglia (Italy), 125, 128

Quattrocento frame of reference, 142, 144, 145, 146, 158

racism, Fascist, 17

realism, xii, 31, 200n10; artistic, xx, 91–93, 101; cinematic, xviii, xx, 86, 114, 136–37; devotional, 214n48; diverse, xi, xvi, xxi, 176n7; documentary, 82–83; in *Gente del Po,* xiv; illusionist, 61, 76; Italian, xx, 45–48; literary, xx, 1, 80, 93, 178n19; mimetic, 41; nineteenth century, 92–93, 101; ontological, xxiv–xxv; oppositional, xxi–xxii, xxviii, 69, 178n19, 179n20; Pasolini's, 138, 209n25; photographic, 14–15, 80, 126, 180n24, 184n12; postwar, 45–48, 68; regional, xix, 79–80; Renoir's, 205n45; Rossellini's, 43, 50, 74, 180n25; traditional, xxvii, 25; values of, 38–39; Verga's, 83, 90; verismo and, 113–14; Visconti's, 84–85, 104, 106–7

reality: abstract, 192n15; artistic, 92, 101; cinematic, 118, 136–37, 209n25; fractured, xxvi, xxvii, 4; images of, 120, 209n26; material, xxv, 49, 69, 120; modern, 184n12; myth and, 203n36; objective, xxiv; Pasolini's, 142; restored, 45, 116; Visconti's, 203n36, 204n41; visual and plastic, 6, 86, 91, 93, 103, 115

real time, xxiv–xxv

reconnaissance, aerial, 13, 16, 188n33

reconstruction, x, 127; cinema's role in, xvi, xxiii, xxvi, xxxi, 35, 72, 105–6; intellectual, 91, 94; modernist, 47, 195–96n34; national, xiii–xiv, xv, xxii; neorealist, 42–43, 45–49, 57, 68, 69; post-Fascist, xxx, 116; postwar, 37, 44, 52, 64, 71, 161, 191n10; Rossellini's theme of, xxix–xxx; of ruins, 47, 49, 54, 56, 61, 74, 194n24,n25. *See also* housing: construction of; restoration

Red Desert (*Il deserto rosso,* Antonioni), 176n5

redemption, x, xxix, xxxii, 51, 138–39

referentiality, 31, 171, 210n26; abstraction and, 184n12; sacred, 139

reflections, aesthetic, 6, 101–2

reframing, 7, 108. *See also* framing

refugee camps, xiii, xxiii

refugees, 133

regionalism: architectural, 65; in art, xvi, 104, 199n3; cinematic, xix–xx; culture of, xii, 3–5, 19, 208n14; Fascist, xxix, 1, 14–30, 80, 81, 82, 186n19; in *Gente del Po*, 33, 38–39; Italian, xi, xvi, 103, 161–62; in literature, xviii; modern, xxix, 19, 21–26; neorealist, 14, 46; photographic, xvii, 80, 101–2; realist, xix, 79–80; Verga's, 88–89; Visconti's, 82. *See also* landscape(s): regional

Reichlin, Bruno, 177n10

Reichstag (Berlin), 55–61, 69, 70, 72, 194n25,n26

relics, 70, 131; Nazi, 59. *See also* iconography/icons; monumentalism/monuments; ruins

religion, 143. *See also* Christianity

Renaissance, 117, 142, 144–46, 158, 176n7, 214n50

Renoir, Jean, 81, 205n45; *Day in the Country*, xviii, xix, 188n38; mentorship of Visconti, xviii, xix, 178n15, 205n45; *Toni*, xix

repetition, xxii, xxvii, 158

reportage, 106, 155, 180n26, 188n32; in cinema, xiii–xv, 128; in painting, 148–50. *See also* documentaries; newsreels

representation(s), xiii–xiv, 203n36; cinematic, xxiv–xxv, 33, 37, 115, 120, 138, 154, 170; collective, 69; interstices between, 6; landscape, xvi, 2, 13, 15; language of, xxii; modernist, xviii, 22; photographic, 13, 98; quotidian, 64; realist, 35, 39, 93. *See also* iconography/icons

reproduction, photographic, 109, 171

Resistance fighters, xxiii; communist, 48; Italian, 195n29; myth of, xii–xiii, 46–47, 49, 191n10

re-siting, 127–28; of the sacred, 130, 139

restoration: of Germany, 52–54; of Italy, 37, 62, 116; modernism's role in, xxi; neorealism's role in, xiii–xiv. *See also* reconstruction

reverse shots. *See* shot/reverse shot technique

revision, xxiii; modernism's role in, xxi

revolution: drama of, xxx; energy for, 27, 118, 167; Fascist, 186n19; filmic, x, xiii; industrial, 176n7; Marxist, 90; modern, 3, 162; tradition and, 105, 200n12

rhetoric: antimonumental, 46; dramatic, 2, 5; Fascist, xx, 6, 30, 125; heroic, 26, 183n4; iconic, 139, 160–61. *See also* antirhetoric

Rhodes, John David, 175n2

Ricotta, La (Pasolini), 121, 176n6, 207n7

Riegl, Alois, 194n28

Ringbom, Sixten, 141, 212n38

Ritorno a Lisca Bianca (Antonioni), 189n42

ritual, 129–30, 190n42

River, The (Lorentz), 5

Rivette, Jacques, 198n43
Rizzo, Pippo, 187n25
Rocco and His Brothers (*Rocco e i suoi fratelli,* Visconti), xxiii
Rodchenko, Alexander, 183n10
Rogers, Ernesto Nathan, 68
romance: values of, 25
Romanticism, 2–3
Rome (Italy), vii, 25, 31, 56, 67; amphitheaters, 205n43; housing projects, 65, 68; as location, 128; neighborhoods, 38, 119, 195n31
Roof, The (*Il tetto,* De Sica), ix
Rosi, Francesco, 79, 110
Rossellini, Roberto, 41–78; aesthetics, 43, 49, 61; camera work, 57, 59–61, 70–71; death of son, 192n13; landscapes, xxix–xxx, 47–48, 169, 193n19; locations, 65, 68, 169, 193n19; modernism of, 43; monumentalism of, xxxi, 70, 78, 191n9; neorealism of, xvi, xxvi, xxvii–xxx, 44, 47–48, 57, 69–70, 192n11, 198n43; photography, 196n38; politics of, 192n11, 197n39; realism of, 43, 50, 62, 74, 180n25; ruinous landscapes, 49–78; study of war, 41–49, 78
Rossellini, Roberto, works: *Amori di mezzo secolo,* 190n2; documentaries, 38; *Germany Year Zero,* ix, xxix, 48–61, 69–76, 192n13, 193n23; *Journey to Italy,* xxxii, 48–49, 72–78, 198n43, 198n45; *La macchina*

ammazzacattivi, 196–97n38; *Napoli '43,* 190n2; *La nave bianca,* 25, 48; *Open City,* ix, xiii, xiv, 48, 65, 71, 192n13; *Paisà,* ix, xxiii, xxv, xxix, 31, 41–43, 48, 50, 54, 65, 71, 74, 76, 192n13; *Un pilota ritorna,* 25, 48; *L'uomo dalla croce,* 48; war trilogy, 25, 48, 191n9,n11, 197n39
Rossellini, Romano, 192n13
Rouch, Jean, 181n30
ruinous trope, xxviii, 41–78, 190n4
ruins, 193n19, 194n24,n25, 197n41; ancient, 70–78; locations of, xxxi, 171; modern, xxii, 41–72, 74; preservation of, 45–49; of war, viii, x, xiv–xv, xx, xxix, 45, 61–62. *See also* Germany, ruins in; landscapes, ruinous
ruptures, xvii, xxiv, 82; continuities and, xii, xv–xvi, xix–xx, xxviii, 72, 106, 114
rural areas, xx, 5, 12, 18, 25, 26, 81–82, 241n51
Ruskin, John, 2–3
Russia. *See* Soviet Union

Sabaudia (Matarazzo), 26
sacred, the, xix, 74, 129, 139, 143, 164–65. *See also* iconography/ icons; *Terra Sancta,* the
saints, 129, 131
Salò (Italy), 31, 127
Salò, or, The 120 Days of Sodom (Pasolini), 127, 207n10
Sander, August, 202n30
Sansoni, Guglielmo, 187n26

Sartre, Jean-Paul, 134, 209n24

Sassi, 132, 161, 163

scenarios. *See* plots

Schwartz, Barth David, 207n5

Sciuscià (Shoe Shine, De Sica), xxvii

Scogli dei Ciclopi (Sicily), 104, 111

Scully, Vincent, 205n43

sculpture, 183n10, 196n35

sea, the, xxx, 110, 112–13, 204n41. *See also* Galilee, Sea of; Mediterranean Sea

Second Futurism, 1, 20

Second World War, xxii–xvii, 179n20; aftermath of, 4, 47, 70, 179n22; Antonioni's work during, 39, 116, 167–68, 170; effects on filmmaking, 31, 37; ruins of, xxix–xxx, 44, 65, 191n4. *See also* Europe: postwar; Italy: postwar; reconstruction: postwar

Sekula, Allan, 183n8, 185n13

self-consciousness, xv–xvi, xxii, 114, 117–18, 176n7

semiology, 136, 209n25,n26

Senso (Visconti), 114, 177n9

Senza pietà (Without Pity, Lattuada), xv

Serandrei, Mario, xix, 178n16, 188n31; *Giorni di gloria,* xiv, 195n32

shelter, 42, 54, 69. *See also* housing

short films, xv, xxv

short-story format, 41

shot / reverse shot technique,

xxv, 68, 71, 76, 112, 149, 156, 164, 198n45

shots, 145, 192n15, 205n45; duration of, 38, 137–38, 163–64; modernist, 26. *See also specific types of camera shots*

Shroud of Turin, 210–11n31

Sicily, xxx, 25, 116, 168–70, 203n35; photographs of, 94–102; in Verga's writings, 81, 82–83, 88–91, 93. *See also* fishermen, Sicilian

signs: cinematic, 137; indexical, xxiv, 93, 201n26, 211n34. *See* iconography / icons; image(s)

silent films, xxii

sites. *See* landscape(s); locations; re-siting

Six-Day War, 206n4

slums, vii–ix. *See also* housing

Snowden, Frank, 186n19

soldiers, xv, 28, 41

Somewhere in Berlin (Ingendwo in Berlin, Lamprecht), 44, 50–51

Sopralluoghi in Palestina per il Vangelo secondo Matteo (Locations in Palestine for *The Gospel according to Matthew,* Pasolini), 118–36, 162, 163, 213n47

soundtracks, 155, 156. *See also* voice-overs

Soviet Union, 27

space(s), 54; altered, xii, xxiii, xxv; cinematic, 44, 110, 149, 154, 171, 205n45; cleaned-up, 193n17; closed, 25, 108, 111, 114, 154; command of, 23, 27;

diverse, 107, 118; liberation of, 20–21; mapping of, vii–viii, xi, 33; narrative, xii, xiv, 4–5; negative, 159; new, xxi, 149; open, 79, 108, 111, 114; photographic, 183n10; postwar, xiii, 42, 47; private, 75, 108, 188n38, 194n25; psychic, 52; public, 75, 108, 113; regional, xviii; restoration of, xvi, 63; of ritual, 129–30; ruinous, 56, 65; theatrical, xxx, 108, 110–11, 180n25, 204n41; time and, xxiv–xxv, 38, 44, 149; underdeveloped, 133; virtual, 171. *See also* exteriors; interiors

Speer, Albert, 61

Spender, Stephen, 55–56, 61, 65, 194n25

spirit. *See* place: spirit of

splitting. *See* fracturing; ruptures

stasis: movement and, 144, 145

Staudte, Wolfgang: *The Murderers Are among Us,* 44

St. Jerome and a Devotee (Piero della Francesca), 146–48

Stokes, Adrian, 205–6n46

Story of Theophilus (Masaccio), 152

St. Peter Healing with His Shadow (Masaccio), 148–50

Stramilano (Ultra-Milan, D'Errico), 27

Straub, Jean-Marie: *Not Reconciled,* 44, 197n41

streets, 74, 75, 78

Streghe, Le (The Witches, compilation film), vii, 175n3

Stromboli (Sicily), 168–69

studio style, xxv

suicide, 51–52

surface: depth and, 101, 145–46, 184n12

surrealism, xvii

sventramenti, 63

symbolic, the: material bound with, xi

Tabor, Mount (Israel), 121, 122

Tacchella, Jean-Charles, 206n46

Tafuri, Manfredo, 41, 66, 67, 68, 196n34

Tébidi (Sicily), 95, 99

Technicolor, vii–viii, xxxii

technology, 3, 13, 25, 26, 167, 170–71

temporalities: changes in, 14, 127; cinematic, xxvi–xxviii, 39, 43–44; diverse, 118; interstices between, 6; modern, xxx, 3; mythical, 84; photographic, 28, 30; rural, xx. *See also* time

Teorema (Pasolini), 175n3

Termini train station, 195n31

Terragni, Giuseppe, 186n21

terrain. *See* landscape(s); topography

Terra madre (Mother Earth, Blasetti), 25, 199n1

terra sancta, 160, 208n17

Terra Sancta, the, 120–36, 165

Terra trema, La (Visconti), 79, 89, 99–101, 105–16, 156, 180n25, 203n32, 205n45; landscapes of, xxix, xxx, 81–85, 94–95, 206n46

Terra vista dalla luna, La (The Earth as Seen from the Moon, Pasolini), vi, vii–xi, xxxi, xxxii, 175n3, 179n20

texts, as cinematic locations, xi

theater, 41, 204n42,n43. *See also* space(s): theatrical

theology, 136–37, 142–43

Tiburtino housing project (Rome), 65, 68

time: Christian understanding of, 131; cinematic, 149, 179n21; malleability of, xxiii; proper course of, 65; sense of, 3; space and, xxiv–xxv, 38, 44, 149. *See also* temporalities

time-images, 190n3

Toni (Renoir), xix

topography, 113, 129–30, 216n1

Totò (actor), vii, viii, x

tourism/tourists, vii, 31, 59–61, 70, 90–91

tracking shots, xxv, 214n49

tradition, xx, xxviii, xxx, 30, 49, 161, 200n12

"Tradizione e invenzione" (Visconti), 102–3

transformation. *See* change

transitions, xv, xx, xxi, 4, 28, 172

translation: movement of, 130–31

traveling: filmmaking and, 118–36

traveling shots, 41, 110, 155, 189–90n42

Trecento frame of reference, 144, 145

Tribute Money (Masaccio), 152

Troilus and Cressida (Visconti), 114, 115

tropes, xi, xxv; aerial, xxviii, xxix, xxxii, 1–39, 167; archaic, xxviii, xxx–xxxi, 101–2, 113–14, 117–65, 167; choral, xxviii, 79–116; late-modern, 44; neorealist, xxi; pictorial, 101; ruinous, xxviii, 41–78, 190n4; topographical, 216n1

truth, 102, 106

Tuscany region (Italy), 31, 114

UFA (Universum Film AG), 71

Umberto D. (De Sica), xxvii

Umbria (Dottori), 23

Umbrian region (Italy), 21

"Una disperata vitalità" (Pasolini), 175n2

universalism, modernist, 20, 22–23, 28

Universal light, 214n50

Uomini sul fondo (Men on the Bottom, De Robertis), 25

Uomo dalla croce, L' (The Man with the Cross, Rossellini), 48

urban areas: anxieties in, xx; as cinematic locations, xi, xv, xxvii, 53, 152, 187n31, 193n19; Italian, xxxi, 25–27; reconstruction of, 52, 63; ruinous, xxix, 61, 74. *See also* corpse-cities; culture: urban; *individual cities*

urban planning, 15, 63, 162, 215n54

utopia: modernist, ix, 20–21, 23, 28; Verga's, 93

values: Christological, 210–11n31, 213n42; quotidian, 49; realist, 38–39; regional, 161; traditional, xix, 23–25

Vecchia guardia (Old Guard, Blasetti), 25

veneration, 131, 137–38, 154; objects of, 138–42, 144, 148, 160

Venezia minore (Minor Venice, Pasinetti), 27

Venice (Italy), 27, 114

vera icona, 139

Verga, Giovanni: adaptations, 86–89; "L'amante di Gramigna," 81, 83, 86–93; *Cavalleria rusticana,* 96; "Fantasticheria," 90; landscapes of, 96; *I Malavoglia,* 79, 82–94, 102–3, 116, 200n7, 201n24; *Mastro Don Gesualdo,* 83, 93; photography of, 92–102, 108, 115–16, 202n29,n30, 203n32; poetics of, 83, 101, 106; verismo practice, 80–95, 203n32; "I Vinti," 93

verismo, 80–102; cinematic, 115–16, 208n15; literary, 80–94, 98; neorealist, xxiv, 113–14, 203n34; photographic, 94–102, 110; Verga's, 80–95, 203n32; Visconti's, 101, 108–9, 113–14, 116

vernacular, the, 65, 74, 161

Veronica, the, 139

Vertigine (Vertigo, Antonioni), 189n40

Via delle cinque lune (Chiarini), 188n31

Via Dolorosa, 122, 130

Viale Etiopia (Rome), 65, 68

video, xxii

Vigo, Jean, ix; *L'Atalante,* 176n4, 188n38

"Vinti, I" (The Vanquished, Verga), 93

violence, xiv–xv, xxxi, 39, 44

Visconti, Luchino, viii, xviii, xxii, 38, 79–116; camera work, xxix, 25, 101, 107, 110, 113, 204n41, 205n43; landscapes, xvi, xxix, 104–16, 202n27, 206n47; modernism of, xix, 111; neorealism of, xix, 80–81, 84, 101–2, 106, 116, 178n16; ornateness of, 180n25; realism of, 84–85, 104, 106–7; reality of, 203n36, 204n41; regionalism of, 82; Renoir's mentorship of, xviii, xix, 178n15, 205n45; verismo practice, 101, 108–9, 113–14, 116

Visconti, Luchino, works: *Giorni di gloria,* xiv, 195n32; *Ossessione,* xix–xx, 25–26, 31, 82, 105, 177n9; *Rocco and his Brothers,* xxiii; *Senso,* 114, 177n9; *La terra trema,* xxix, xxx, 79, 81–85, 89, 94–95, 99–101, 105–16, 156, 180n25, 203n32, 205n45, 206n46; "Tradizione e invenzione," 102–3; *Troilus and Cressida,* 114, 115; *White Nights,* 114

Viterbo (Italy), 154

Vittorini, Elio, xvii–xviii

Vizzini (Sicily), 96, 97

voice-overs, 32, 33, 57, 60, 106, 122. *See also* soundtracks
voices, xxx, 89, 125; Verga's, 81; Visconti's, xxx

Wagner, Martin, 193n22
war, 16–17, 24, 192n13; aerial photography, 185n13,n15,n16; documentaries about, 28–29; response to, xvi, xxvi, xxviii; ruins of, viii, x, xiv–xv, xx, xxix, 45, 61–62. *See also* Cold War; First World War; Second World War
Weimar Republic: art of, xvii
Wenders, Wim: *Wings of Desire*, 44

White Nights (Visconti), 114
"White Telephone" (Cinecittà), 81
windows, glass, 204n39
Wings of Desire (Der Himmel Über Berlin, Wenders), 44
withdrawal, xxix, 38–39
Wood, Christopher, 212n38
workers, xxi, xxx, 1, 79
World's Fair (1942), 19–21, 62

Zavattini, Cesare, xxvi–xxvii, 181n30
Zola, Émile, 80, 94, 200n7; photography of, 202n29
zoom shots, 154, 214n49

Noa Steimatsky is associate professor of film studies and the history of art at Yale University.